BEYOND THE
SKILLS GAP

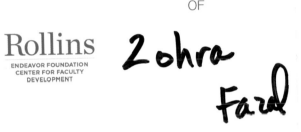

BEYOND THE SKILLS GAP

PREPARING COLLEGE STUDENTS FOR LIFE AND WORK

MATTHEW T. HORA

with ROSS J. BENBOW
and AMANDA K. OLESON

HARVARD EDUCATION PRESS
Cambridge, Massachusetts

Paperback ISBN 978-1-61250-987-7
Library Edition ISBN 978-1-61250-988-4

Library of Congress Cataloging-in-Publication Data
Names: Hora, Matthew T., 1972- author. | Benbow, Ross J., author. |
    Oleson, Amanda K., author.
Title: Beyond the skills gap : preparing college students for life and work /
    Matthew T. Hora, with Ross J. Benbow and Amanda K. Oleson.
Description: Cambridge, Massachusetts : Harvard Education Press, [2016] |
    Includes bibliographical references and index.
Identifiers: LCCN 2016025912| ISBN 9781612509877 (pbk.) |
    ISBN 9781612509884 (library edition)
Subjects: LCSH: Active learning—Wisconsin—Case studies. |
    Employability—Wisconsin—Case studies. | Vocational qualifications—
    Wisconsin—Case studies. | Education, Higher—Political aspects—
    Wisconsin—Case studies. | Curriculum planning.
Classification: LCC LB1027.23 .H68 2016 | DDC 378.1/9809775—dc23
    LC record available at https://lccn.loc.gov/2016025912

Published by Harvard Education Press,
an imprint of the Harvard Education Publishing Group

Harvard Education Press
8 Story Street
Cambridge, MA 02138

Cover Design: Wilcox Design
Cover Image: © Studio-Pro/iStock
The typefaces used in this book are Life BT, Publica Sans, and Gotham.

CONTENTS

INTRODUCTION

Why Study the Skills Gap in Wisconsin?

Soon after the effects of the Great Recession of 2008 hit the nation and waves of the unemployed (and underemployed) hit the streets, newspapers and websites were inundated with reports about something called a "skills gap." The basic idea behind these stories was that plenty of jobs existed, but skilled workers did not. At the height of the 2012 presidential campaign, even President Barack Obama and candidate Mitt Romney claimed that thousands of US employers yearned for skilled workers and that the nation should invest in more advanced vocational training. CNBC went further, claiming that this skills gap was "killing millions of jobs."[1]

Who or what was the primary culprit for the apparent paucity of sufficiently prepared job applicants? According to many proponents of the skills gap theory, it was US high schools' focus on precollege academic curriculum over vocational, hands-on training; a societal dismissal of skilled trades and the value of two-year technical and community colleges; and four-year universities' grounding in liberal arts programs that had no real worth in the labor market.[2]

But while some claimed that a skills gap was a real phenomenon plaguing companies across the country and even the world, others argued that it was a myth concocted by business interests to shift the burdens of employee training to the public sector.[3] Furthermore, outside of statistical analyses of large datasets in the field of labor economics, there were few rigorous studies of people's actual experiences in the field with these skills problems.

As an applied anthropologist originally intrigued by the complex issues implicated in people's food habits, which included the overlapping spheres of the economy, history, geography, culture, and politics, I had come to the University of Wisconsin–Madison to study a similarly complicated problem: how to improve teaching within research universities. When debates about the skills gap began to touch upon issues like the future of public higher education and which majors college students should pursue, it quickly became evident that here, too, was a "wicked" systemic problem that could whet my intellectual curiosity. As arguments about skilled workers and the role of public higher education in society became enveloped in many of the policy debates in my newly adopted home state, it also became clear that the skills gap debate was only the tip of the iceberg, and that a study on these issues could contribute some new insights and evidence to a topic that was becoming increasingly political, contentious, and influential around the United States and the world.

STUDYING EDUCATION–INDUSTRY RELATIONS IN POLITICALLY DIVIDED WISCONSIN

I didn't know much about Wisconsin growing up in southern California. There, everything east of the Colorado River was a bit of a wheat- and corn-soaked blur until you hit the Eastern Seaboard. If anything, I imagined the typical images of Wisconsin—Packer cheeseheads, Miller beer, and lots of cows. But in college I discovered something about the political history of the state: this is where the Republican Party was founded; where the Progressive movement began; where the Wisconsin Idea— about higher education's connection to public service—originated; where Aldo Leopold wrote his famous environmental works; and where the labor movement had many of its origins and first victories.

All of this history became impossible to ignore after newly elected Governor Scott Walker signed a piece of legislation called Act 10. The bill included a set of reforms to the state's collective bargaining laws, public employee benefits, and much more that ultimately led to the national media setting up camp in downtown Madison to cover the unfolding drama. Thousands of people filled the streets of Madison in protest, and neighbors and pundits alike discussed what these changes meant for the status of public employees, the future of public education, and whether the public good was being protected and advanced by these new policies. No matter whose side you were on, it was clear that these were potentially watershed moments in the history of the Badger State. Upon close inspection, it was also evident that the skills gap was a centerpiece of the reformist agenda being advanced by the government, based on the notion that public higher education needed to be restructured in order to better meet workforce needs.

It was in this context that I began to explore the underlying issues behind the skills gap idea. Unlike other researchers, I wasn't attempting to prove or disprove the existence of skills gap; instead my goal was to offer a systemic analysis of the underlying issues based on the perspectives of people in the field. I visited manufacturing and biotechnology businesses in and around the Madison area, touring cavernous warehouses and tidy research labs, interviewing human resource directors, CEOs, and supervisors who regularly interacted with the company's production staff. I selected these sectors to study because they represented something of the "old" and "new" economies in Wisconsin, and in some cases, a combination of the two as manufacturing businesses are increasingly using high-tech robotics in their facilities.

While I certainly heard about the lack of applicants in certain occupations, primarily middle-skill (and middle-pay) jobs such as welding and machining, a so-called more common complaint from business owners pertained to the lack of "soft" skills across *all* job categories. For example, a biotechnology executive spoke of the importance of communication in the firm's team-based work, observing that, "Just simple communication is an unbelievable problem." In fact, the company had some brilliant scientists on staff, but one in particular was "virtually impossible to work with in a team and that's just not conductive to the work we do."

At a company that manufactured pumps for industrial engines, in a cleanly scrubbed and well-lit warehouse that belied the common perception of manufacturing as a smoky Dickensian nightmare, a supervisor described how the changing nature of the industry had led to a shift in the competencies required in its workforce. "A diesel technician ten years ago would work on the same pump every day for years and become an expert on it," he said, but now because the work is more contract-based, the company is making new products on a more rapid schedule. In short, it now needs people "that can handle change and adapt," or what some call lifelong learners. Why the focus on this ability and willingness to learn? Given people with some basic core competencies like a strong work ethic, this employer felt he could train them on their specialized machinery and procedures to fit the company's specific needs. The more factories and labs I visited, the clearer it became that the problems (and subsequent solutions) about skills were not as straightforward as they at first seemed. It wasn't just a lack of technical training that was plaguing the business community.

Jim Morgan from Wisconsin Manufacturers and Commerce (WMC), which represents the state's manufacturing industry and is often referred to as the largest business lobby in Wisconsin, shared something he repeatedly heard in a series of focus groups he had held with manufacturing executives:

> About halfway through, one of the folks said, "You know, what we measure when we're trying to hire somebody is YOTF." And I said, "What is YOTF?" And the guy said, "Years off the farm." And if I could summarize the skill set that's missing, I think that's it. If you think of kids who grew up on a farm in terms of work ethic—I mean you're getting up at six o'clock in the morning, you're working every night, you never get a day off—they get that, and they get the problem-solving part because if something breaks down on the back forty, you've got to figure out how to fix it.

This idea—combined with what I was hearing in the field—helped to reframe the issue. Addressing the apparent challenges facing employers as they sought qualified employees was not a simple issue of making higher education more responsive to workforce needs or convincing more high school students to study welding instead of French literature. While there were certainly difficulties with educational pathways and academic programming, they were not the only factors shaping the types of skills and aptitudes that students developed and then took into the labor market as job applicants.

What Jim captured and what I was seeing in the field was a far more complicated *cultural* issue that had much to do with how (and where) someone was raised, and the beliefs, habits of mind, and values instilled in them by role models and peers in school, sports, and work. This fact implicated parents, employers, workplace trainers, soccer coaches, and the broader society itself that lay far outside the mandate or reach of post-secondary educators, who were nonetheless being singled out as the primary cause of the skills gap problem.

THE PURPOSE OF HIGHER EDUCATION

Further complicating matters was a big question: What is the purpose of higher education in today's society? Is it to prepare students to get a job (the "vocationalist" perspective) or to develop their moral character, sense of civic responsibility, and intellectual skills more generally (the "liberal arts" perspective)? Is its purpose to contribute to the public good by addressing issues and challenges that face all of society—such as climate change, income inequality, and a sluggish economy—or to provide students and other well-placed individuals with increased wealth and privilege for their own private gain? Or is the purpose of college somewhere between these polar opposites—to teach *both* the "practical arts" and classical subjects, as envisioned by the developers of the land-grant universities in the United States, support the intellectual and moral development of students, and contribute to a more democratic society and vibrant economy?

Of course, these questions are not new, and the relative value of a vocational versus a liberal arts education, as well as the ultimate mission of US higher education, have been debated since the late 1800s. But in this digitally interconnected world, these questions and the skills gap idea had become ubiquitous in the mass media and policy makers' rhetoric. As the idea expanded from a simple explanation of slow economic growth to encompass these bigger questions about the purpose of higher education, the topic demanded a more extensive analysis than my small pilot study was able to offer.

So I proposed to the National Science Foundation a larger study on education-workforce alignment issues where, in addition to business owners, I would also talk to a group of people who were largely invisible in the skills gap debate: professional educators. To me they played a crucial role in any productive and comprehensive accounting of the skills gap because they were on the front lines designing the curriculum and teaching the employees of tomorrow. Since they were apparently doing a poor job of preparing students for work, shouldn't we find out what skills they thought were important for student success and what they were doing to cultivate them? With a PhD in the learning sciences and hundreds of hours spent observing college-level classes, I thought I could bring some useful perspectives to these issues.

So I gathered a team at the Wisconsin Center for Education Research at UW-Madison to examine these issues across the entire state, from the traditional manufacturing powerhouse of Milwaukee to the less well-known industrial hub of Superior in the north, and from the flagship university in Madison to the smaller technical colleges in the state's rural midsection. I found two colleagues who would embark on this ambitious project with me. The first was Amanda Oleson, who hailed from Wisconsin Rapids, Wisconsin, and whose sharp eye, keen wit, and skills in interviewing random people were a perfect fit for the study. The second was Ross Benbow, who was born in Neenah, Wisconsin, and raised in Madison, and whose experience conducting international fieldwork, natural sense of story, and grasp of social theory rounded out the team.

A side note: As employees of UW-Madison with careers invested in the educational enterprise—whether through teaching and/or conducting research on the topic—we certainly have "a dog in the fight" of the skills gap debate. Our university, of course, is the subject of many critiques and budget cuts. But, we are professionally trained researchers who engage in empirical research with a diligent objectivity, which for us meant entering the field with no predetermined conclusions. While some social scientists adopt a more advocacy-based approach when designing their studies, we have focused all along on documenting and describing the systems implicated in the skills gap debate in as rigorous and detailed a manner as possible, and not on advancing any particular agenda. Once the evidence was in hand, however, it became clear that we had a responsibility to communicate how our findings contradicted the dominant narrative being advanced in Wisconsin and abroad about higher education's role in workforce development and society itself.[4]

From the end of 2013 through 2015 we fanned out across the state and talked with seventy educators in two- and four-year colleges and universities. We asked them about their curriculum, their goals for students, and how, if at all, they interacted with industry. We also met with seventy-five HR directors, CEOs, and shift supervisors in nearby companies, speaking with them about their experiences with the labor market, the types of skills they valued, their training programs, and how, if at all, they interacted with colleges and universities in their regions.

To better understand the complex interplay among individual behavior, cultural factors, and the educational, business, and political sectors, we utilized a theoretical framework that integrated perspectives from three different disciplinary traditions: cultural models theory from anthropology, field theory from relational sociology, and systems perspectives from engineering and organizational studies. With this framework we focused on the way in which students acquire—via education and training—new competencies and habits of mind, which they then take into the labor market as a form of "cultural currency" that ideally results in job offers and promotions. Importantly, a systemic account offered us a way to discuss the myriad interconnected factors that shape learners' identities and development, instead of the more dominant way of thinking about these issues: in linear terms where one cause (i.e., educators) leads to one effect (i.e., a skills gap).

THE CENTRALITY OF CULTURE: CULTIVATING TWENTY-FIRST-CENTURY HABITS OF MIND

Through our analysis we made some discoveries about the types of competencies that educators and employers found valuable, strategies for cultivating them in college and university classrooms, and forms of partnership that appear to bridge the gap between the two sectors so that students are prepared to succeed in life and work.

These valued competencies, what we call twenty-first-century habits of mind, include skills, knowledge, and aptitudes such as technical knowledge and abilities, critical thinking, teamwork, communication, and work ethic. These competencies are invaluable because they are necessary to perform the nonroutinized, creative tasks that are increasingly the hallmark of many workplace tasks and problems.[5] The term habit of mind conveys that we are not speaking of discrete skills or knowledge alone, but of a more comprehensive way of thinking, acting, and being in the world. For example, the habit of mind that was perhaps the most commonly discussed throughout our study was the ability to engage in the kind of complex problem-solving tasks that inevitably (and regularly) arise in the workplace. This competency is remarkably similar to the critical, open-minded, and flexible way of investigating and understanding oneself and the world that is the hallmark of a liberal education.[6]

To foster these habits of mind, however, is no small feat. Instead of being a simple matter of quickly conveying skills or abilities in a two-week bootcamp or short course, educators and trainers must design curricula and learning activities that enable students to actively cultivate new habits of mind over longer periods of time. Furthermore, to facilitate learners' abilities to transfer newly acquired skills or knowledge to the novel situations they will face in the workplace, classroom activities need to actively engage students in problems that combine rigorous disciplinary concepts with authenticity, such that other newly acquired knowledge can be mapped onto real-world settings. Such an approach is not dissimilar to traditional apprenticeship, where contextualized learning is overseen by experts who gradually "fade out" their mentoring over time as learners acquire more and more experience, which has led some to call this new approach to instruction a "cognitive apprenticeship."[7] Unfortunately, the overly didactic lecture with students sitting passively in their seats for fifty minutes remains all too common in college classrooms.

Still, while a more enlivened postsecondary classroom is certainly an important venue for cultivating students' habits of mind, it is not the only one. Employers also have a considerable amount of responsibility for supporting their employees in acquiring valued competencies throughout their careers via training and professional development opportunities. Yet here, too, there exists room for improvement. Workplace training is rarely brought up in discussions about the skills gap and, in our study, relatively few business owners provided formal training for their staff. Further complicating the skills gap narrative, in which technical skills in "high-demand" disciplines will get you a job, we often heard hiring described as an issue of "screening for cultural fit." Even with the right technical credentials, a qualified candidate still may not get the job if their personality and other intangibles do not match the organizational culture.

With these results in mind we argue that the quandary facing higher education and the workforce is a decidedly cultural issue, in that it is not simply "skills" that many educators strive to cultivate or that employers desire, but ways of thinking and acting that are acquired through a long-term immersion in a cultural milieu, whether it be a physics classroom, a biotechnology company's lab, or the family dairy farm. In this way, it is not only educators who are implicated in these issues, but also family, places of worship, and business owners, whose practices play a not inconsiderable role in who gets hired and how, if at all, employees' competencies are cultivated throughout their careers.

Based on the evidence, we also conclude that the skills gap narrative should be rejected and replaced with a more comprehensive and nuanced perspective on the relationships among higher education, the workforce, and society. While localized skills shortages do exist for certain occupations, the narrative misses the far more important fact that there is a widespread need for twenty-first-century habits of mind across all occupational groups and throughout people's entire working lives, and that the teaching profession is central in cultivating these competencies in college students. The skills gap argument also ignores discussions of classroom teaching and curriculum design, focuses on technical skills alone, assigns blame to only one party (i.e., education), overlooks multidisciplinary education (i.e., the liberal arts), ignores the cultural aspects of teaching and hiring, and most importantly, fuels an overly narrow vision of higher education and public policy that places much greater value on private gain rather than the public good. Unfortunately, in states such as Wisconsin, skills gap proponents' impatience with a purportedly out-of-touch professoriate has led to the systematic defunding of public higher education, which ironically undermines the educational sector's ability to cultivate in students the very competencies needed to address the economic and societal challenges of the twenty-first century.

However, we do not suggest that change is unnecessary in the higher education sector. The evidence suggests that the adoption of active learning teaching methods is slow and spotty at best.[8] The student debt crisis and the rising price tag of a college education also make ignoring students' future job prospects—a not uncommon practice in some nonprofessional programs in four-year institutions—an untenable stance. Instead, we conclude that the most propitious course of action for higher education in the early twenty-first century is a "new vocationalism," or a program based on the liberal arts tradition of cultivating well-rounded students via a multidisciplinary education, but with careful attention to students' career prospects and needs. UW-Madison has belatedly figured this out: in 2012 it launched a Career Initiative in the liberal arts–based

College of Letters and Sciences, designed to help students "connect the dots between the liberal arts and a career" by offering career counseling, résumé development services, and tips on internship opportunities.[9] Through integrating a more concerted focus on career counseling into a robust liberal arts education, the university is addressing key elements of what we call the *skills infrastructure*, or the policies, programs, and people that most support the development of graduates with twenty-first-century habits of mind. The other components of this skills infrastructure, which implicate noneducational entities such as government and business, include supporting teachers (and workplace trainers) who are adept at using active learning techniques, investments in company-based training, and education-workplace partnerships that create the conditions for collaborations between educators and employers.

Ultimately, our analysis revealed that no "silver bullet" solution exists to the challenges facing higher education and the labor market. Instead, each aspect of the skills infrastructure must be engaged and leveraged in order to truly prepare college students for life and work. Unfortunately, the exclusively vocational conception of higher education that is sweeping the globe, transforming the ways colleges and universities are funded and operated leaves no room for such nuance, such as the notion that the liberal arts model has a viable role to play in the twenty-first-century college or that the business sector itself shares responsibility for skills-related problems. This approach, which was being promulgated in Wisconsin during our study, is a tragic error, particularly when translated to fiscal policy. Coupled with the elimination of government revenue through tax cuts and a refusal to generate additional funds, the neoliberal vision has led to massive budget cuts in public higher education throughout the United States in order to "balance" budgets—a draconian response to a self-imposed problem.

Our conclusion is that this market-first vision of higher education is leading the state, nation, and world down the wrong path, and our data clearly indicate that such an approach actively harms educators' ability to cultivate the creative, rigorous thinkers that the business community needs and that have made the US higher education system the envy of the world. The focus on education as workforce development above all else also undermines the notion of collective responsibility and public service encapsulated by the Wisconsin Idea, raising questions about who precisely will be looking out for the interests of the public and advancing knowledge for the benefit of the many and not the few. The neoliberal view that the logic and goals of the market should be inseparable from public education is doing real, lasting damage—whether through the layoff of 10 percent of the county extension workforce that has provided technical assistance to Wisconsin farmers for over a century, or through arguments that art history departments have no role to play in today's public institutions. Ultimately, the ideology, whether adopted by policy makers from the left or right of the political spectrum, impairs postsecondary educators' ability to prepare students to deal with the pressing social, environmental, and economic issues affecting the world today, tomorrow, and for generations to come.[10]

ORGANIZATION OF THE BOOK

The purpose of this book is to recount our experiences studying higher education-workforce systems amidst the political drama that took place between 2011 and 2015 in Wisconsin, while also advancing a vision for a different way to think about higher education–workforce relations, for what postsecondary teaching can and should look like, and for reframing the debate about the future of higher education in society. This vision includes a systems-oriented roadmap for cultivating students' twenty-first-century habits of mind based on the expertise and insights of practitioners and scholars in the field, all of which point to the necessity of having a highly skilled and institutionally supported instructor in every college and university classroom.

As we interviewed teachers in both university and technical college classrooms, the way in which several of our study respondents approached teaching struck us as particularly promising. They talked about their classrooms as venues for cultivating technical skills as well as other competencies such as teamwork and communication. Their perspectives on the purposes of education, the role of formal schooling *and* industry in addressing workforce issues, the relationships they shared with the community (including local businesses), and above all, the way they structured their classrooms around best practices from current learning theory led us to closely examine their lives, perspectives, and approaches to the profession of teaching.

We were familiar with these theories based on our experience in the learning sciences and the growing movement in STEM (science, technology, engineering, and mathematics) education to encourage faculty to adopt interactive, hands-on approaches to teaching. After our initial interviews, we followed up with several individuals and returned to their colleges, speaking more extensively about how they approached their courses. We also sat in on some classes to observe their teaching practice firsthand.

These educators acted as our guides through the educational system of Wisconsin, where students are being prepared for careers in manufacturing and biotechnology:

- Tim Wright, a composites instructor at the Wisconsin Indianhead Technical College in Superior;
- Lisa Seidman and Mary Ellen Kraus, instructors in a biotechnology program at Madison College;
- Peter Dettmer, an instructor of automated manufacturing at Madison College;
- Tom Heraly, an electronics instructor at the Milwaukee Area Technical College;
- Ron Petersen, an electronics systems and maintenance instructor at Western Technical College in La Crosse;
- Scott Cooper, a professor of cellular and molecular biology at the University of Wisconsin–La Crosse; and
- Janet Batzli, the associate director of the University of Wisconsin–Madison's Biology Core Curriculum (Biocore) program.

In each region of Wisconsin they walked us through the nuances of labor market dynamics and educational issues in their particular industry and locale. We heard about their colleges' challenges and successes and were given a front-row seat to the skills gap issue as it unfolded in the state's classrooms. Their insights brought to life the often-abstract debate about the skills gap, and we were fortunate to have been granted an insider's perspective that complemented our own findings and that of other academic researchers.

We have organized the book to tell the unfolding story of the political developments surrounding public higher education in Wisconsin as a backdrop to our discussions of the skills gap debate, the importance of twenty-first-century habits of mind, strategies for improving teaching and student support services, and ultimately, our vision for the future of higher education.

First, we review the context of our study, including the political environment of Wisconsin and the historical debates about the purpose of higher education in the United States (chapter 1). Then, we introduce the primary aspects of the skills gap argument that is motivating a considerable amount of public policy on higher education (chapter 2), followed by alternative accounts of the relationships among education, the labor market, and society (chapter 3). We then discuss the theoretical framework used in our study and the centrality of cognition, culture, and context to these debates about higher education and the workforce (chapter 4). Next, we take a close look at the types of competencies that employers and educators in our study and the research literature argue are essential for students if they wish to succeed in school, life, and work (chapter 5). Then we shift gears and focus on the classroom and strategies for change. Based on our fieldwork and the research literature, we describe some of the teaching strategies we observed in the field that target communication, teamwork, self-regulated learning, and critical thinking (chapter 6). Then we introduce our systems-oriented analysis of the factors that most support (and impede) progress toward enacting these teaching practices in every college classroom (chapter 7). These include a well-trained teaching workforce that is adequately compensated and supported by organizational and political leadership (chapter 8), career and academic support services for students (chapter 9), and education-industry partnerships that facilitate the development of new programs, school-to-work pathways, and high-quality curricula for both academic courses and training programs (chapter 10). Finally, in our conclusion we offer a new way of thinking about the tension between liberal arts and professional preparation, and ways that policy makers can make this vision a reality.[11]

Individual stories show us, in stark relief, that no one is a caricature—neither of the ivory tower liberal nor the community college technician. As debates rage in Wisconsin and across the nation over the best way to invest taxpayer resources in higher education and economic revitalization, educators like Tom Heraly are quietly but deliberately thinking about how best to give those they teach the opportunity to improve themselves and their lives.

"That's what you have to wrestle with," Tom told us, as we sat in an empty, nondescript classroom in the old downtown Milwaukee building that houses his electronics program. Programs at the technical college where he teaches are a last chance, in many ways, for nontraditional students in the Milwaukee area to get an education and a better job. Tom had spent many years in industry, but asked himself one question constantly: "Am I training or am I educating?" After a thoughtful pause, he said, "A manufacturer wants training, and they want them to know it now—they need it immediately." But was that best for the student? Society? Industry? "If I train you how to use this [specific] software, that's training, the short term," he observed, concluding that despite pressures from industry, this was not his ultimate goal. Instead, Tom's vision extended beyond that first job to students' entire working lives, where they likely would change jobs and even careers multiple times. Ultimately, he decided, "I want the educational part of it."

Business, Education, and the Role of Government

The Great Education Debate in the Badger State

> *What greater gift can we offer the republic*
> *than to teach and instruct our youth?*
>
> —MARCUS CICERO

FIRST SIGNS OF CHANGES TO PUBLIC EDUCATION IN WISCONSIN

Elected in the 2010 midterms that swept multitudes of Republican politicians into office throughout the United States, Scott Walker took Wisconsin politics by storm. A little-known county executive from Milwaukee, Walker had campaigned on a jobs-first platform as well as promises to cut corporate taxes, reduce state spending, and refuse federal funds for Medicaid expansion and high-speed rail. "Our plan is largely about getting government out of the way," he told the *Oshkosh Northwestern*, echoing the small-government position of many in the GOP.[1]

Shortly after Walker took office, however, as the state announced a huge deficit, his spokesperson warned that "bill collectors are waiting at the door of the State Capitol," and that aggressive reforms and legislation would be necessary.[2] To fill this budget gap Walker proposed a set of reforms that included effectively ending collective bargaining rights for teachers and other state employees, requiring public employees to contribute 50 percent toward annual pension payments, and separating UW-Madison from the UW System to grant it more "flexibilities" in exchange for a $250 million budget cut.[3]

These proposals, which were enshrined in Wisconsin Act 10 (also known as the "budget repair bill"), surprised many observers of Wisconsin politics on both sides of the aisle because reforms to collective bargaining and the restructuring of the state's education system had not been a major part of Walker's campaign platform. But some weren't surprised. Julie Mead and Julie Underwood, education professors at UW-Madison, later observed that lawmakers in Indiana and Ohio had considered remarkably similar legislation based on "model" legislation drawn up by the American Legislative Exchange Council (ALEC), a nonprofit organization based in Washington, DC, whose members are state legislators "dedicated to the principles of limited government, free markets, and federalism."[4]

The public response to Act 10 was swift and dramatic. Polls at the time indicated a 50-50 split in public support for the legislation, and many in the half who disagreed with the bill flooded the streets of Madison in protest.[5] Hundreds camped inside the historic capitol building, while many marched outside carrying signs that read "Support public schoolteachers" and "Firefighters for labor." As fourteen Democratic state senators raced to the Wisconsin-Illinois border to prevent the quorum necessary to allow the legislation to pass, the resulting midwinter firestorm not only drew tens of thousands of protestors and the national media's attention to Madison, but also significantly heated up a debate in which educators had become front and center.

In the blink of an eye, the partisan maneuvering between factions on the left and right—in a state long renowned for its midwestern politeness and political civility—hardened into battle lines: on the left were the public sector unions representing teachers, firefighters, and state employees who decried the dramatic cuts to their wages and removal of collective bargaining rights, while on the right were Walker, the Republican legislature, and advocates of the broader conservative resurgence across the country. But the spectacle took a darker tone when the Wisconsin Republican Party filed an open record request to obtain the e-mail records of William Cronon, an internationally recognized UW-Madison professor

of geography and history.[6] Cronon had recently written a blog post pointing out that the source of Act 10 was in fact ALEC, arguing that the public needed to pay closer attention to the group's role in legislation rolling
back environmental protections and collective bargaining rights across
the country.[7] Many saw the Republicans' request as an abuse of power and
an attack on academic freedom—so much so that the *New York Times*
editorial page stated that "These demands not only abuse academic freedom, but make the instigators look like petty and medieval inquisitors."[8]

Eventually, the Democratic state senators returned, and in June 2011
Governor Walker signed the changes into law, including an $800 million
cut to public schools, the $250 million cut to the state's university system
(without splitting the flagship UW-Madison from the rest of the UW System), and a 30 percent cut—to the tune of $35.8 million annually—to the
Wisconsin Technical College System.[9] These cuts were said to be necessary sacrifices to balance the state budget that would be "evened out" by
savings, as districts and institutions would now be free to shop around for
health care and avoid costly negotiations with unions.[10]

As the stream of dollars slowed to higher education—especially the
university system—further seeds of doubt were sown regarding whether
the state's postsecondary system was really doing its job. In a hugely influential 2012 report, former manufacturing CEO Tim Sullivan castigated
the state's higher education system for delaying "entry into the job market and not educating students for the workforce," both of which, he con-
tended, led to a pronounced skills gap in the state.[11] Further inhibiting
progress was a K–12 system that had eliminated shop classes in favor
of more "academic" coursework focused on getting John or Sally into a
four-year college—a problematic agenda, Sullivan argued, because after
college, John may end up as a parking lot attendant and Sally a coffee
shop barista, both with debilitating student loan debt accompanying their
art history or English degrees.

Amid growing concerns about college affordability and equitable
access, these arguments hit home, particularly with a business community reporting shortages of workers in certain trades, such as information technology, nursing, and welding, where many jobs did not require a
four-year degree. On the surface, it looked like a yawning gap did indeed
exist between the skills employers were demanding and those being cultivated by the state's educators. Fueling all of this money shifting and finger

pointing were important questions: What was really going on inside the walls of the ivory tower? Were educators at four-year colleges indoctrinating students into left-wing ideology, as was sometimes suggested by conservative commentators, or were they teaching job-ready skills? Or both? Did these educators deserve the target on their foreheads?

CULTIVATING TRANSFERABLE SKILL SETS IN A LIBERAL ARTS PROGRAM

Noland Hall, located on the sprawling University of Wisconsin–Madison campus, is a blocky, gray building erected in 1970 and named after the prominent zoology researcher and professor Dr. Lowell Evan Noland, known for his interdisciplinary contributions to his classes and the Integrated Liberal Studies program during the mid-twentieth century.[12] The building now operates as a hub for the intensive honors program Biocore, short for Biology Core Curriculum. Biocore, a four-semester-long biology course sequence started in 1967 as an intercollege honors program, aims to provide a broad, in-depth, and integrated background for college sophomores and juniors interested in biology. The formal description of the courses underscores the application of biological concepts "through the process of science—how we know what we know."

Dr. Janet Batzli, the program's associate director, grew up in the western suburbs of Chicago, and her love of plants took her first to UW-Platteville and then to UW-Madison. After a stint at the National Arboretum, she established herself in a teaching career back in Madison.

Janet, who has been part of Biocore since 2002, described the program goals as aligned with the general learning outcomes of the university, which include knowledge of human cultures and the natural world, intellectual and practical skills, personal and social responsibility, and integrative learning.[13] The program is taught by faculty and staff from across campus through a combination of lectures, field trips, lab-based projects, and discussion sections. Among other opportunities, students can become Biocore "Outreach Ambassadors" who run science nights at local middle and high schools.

In a climate where the employability of graduates is of utmost concern, and as the parent of a college student herself, Janet understands the wider debate, especially on issues of affordability—where technical colleges are seen as a cheaper, more job-centered career pathway. But, she said, "we're not just trying to churn out more workers here." The current administration, she intimated, seems myopically focused on "skills, skills that are technical skills." While Biocore can (and does) train students in lab techniques, Janet observed that politicians don't seem to understand that the goals of a bachelor's degree in general, and programs like Biocore in particular, are to develop students' competencies in critical thinking, reasoning, collaboration, communication, and the scientific process.

Janet also highlighted the importance of time in accomplishing these goals, and specifically how a four-year program is necessary for students to iteratively practice and develop new skills, habits of mind, and complicated scientific knowledge. "It's really difficult to develop certain reasoning and communication skills in one semester, two semesters, or even two years," she said, because students need a long time to figure out how to "craft" these skills and translate them to career- and industry-specific applications. The length of the Biocore program helps Janet and her colleagues feel equipped to develop students from learners of biology into working biologists, and to supply them with the technical expertise as well as the thinking, communication, and collaboration skills "you would actually need to become a biologist out in the field."

Asked if and how she was connected with local industry—whether to gain insights about hot new jobs or to tailor her curriculum to meet the needs of employers—Janet said she isn't; neither are other instructors in Biocore. With the exception of recruiting lunches with companies inquiring about interns, she really has no direct contact with industry. However, since Biocore students are getting jobs after graduating, Janet feels that the program is doing its job despite the program's lack of industry contacts.

Janet also spoke about the value of liberal arts training and research opportunities that are available at a university like UW-Madison. Essentially, she feels that a liberal arts program teaches students "about being a person, a mature adult in our society," and "an informed citizen" who can critically reflect on their own philosophies and ideology. Those skills, she believes, are transferable to many jobs, fields, and life situations. Of course, these observations belie the common perception that disciplines such as biology are not part of the liberal arts, which are often considered the domain of the arts and humanities. Instead, science and mathematics have long been a central feature of the multidisciplinary liberal arts tradition, and this is no different at UW-Madison.

The insistence on a more reflective, comprehensive scientific education as described by Janet, however, is becoming decidedly unfashionable, especially when it comes to the kinds of technical, skills-oriented approaches that were heavily favored during the early years of the Walker administration. Despite her disconnection from industry, however, and her praise for the supposedly outmoded liberal arts style of education, Janet and her Biocore colleagues are cultivating in their students precisely the types of competencies that employers are looking for. Their approach is also firmly grounded in UW-Madison's history and intellectual traditions that go back more than a century.

WISCONSIN LEGACIES OF HIGHER EDUCATION: THE WISCONSIN IDEA

Charles Van Hise was raised on a family farm in the flat, corn- and soybean-rich part of southern Wisconsin. After Charles graduated from UW-Madison in 1881, he became a faculty member in geology at his alma mater, making a name for himself as a teacher and researcher before being elected president of the university by the institution's Board of Regents in 1903. His 1904 inaugural address, in which he established his vision of a state university, is often cited as an influential model for the American university: "A university which is to serve the state must see to it that scholarship and research of all kinds, whether or not a possible practical value can be pointed out, must be sustained," he said. "A university supported by the state for all its people, for all its sons and daughters, with their tastes and aptitudes as varied as mankind, can place no bounds upon the lines of its endeavor, else the state is the irreparable loser."[14] He further underlined the point in a 1905 press briefing, telling reporters he would "never be content until the beneficent influence of the University reaches every family in the state," a notion that has been the basis of the Wisconsin Idea for more than a hundred years.[15]

Though the Wisconsin that Van Hise cared so much for was nearing its sixtieth year of statehood around this time, the character of the Badger State itself had been long in the making. The native tribes that met the first French explorers in the territory's wilderness in the 1600s were numerous and diverse—from descendants of the area's first settlers, the Paleo-Indians, who arrived around 10,000 BC and built thousands of conical and animal-shaped mounds throughout the area, particularly on the isthmus between two large lakes where the UW-Madison campus now lies; to the Ho-Chunk (previously known as the Winnebago), who had been hunting, fishing, and developing a rich culture in the region for centuries; to more recent migrants from the eastern Iroquois wars, such as the Sauk and Fox peoples.[16] Through the late seventeenth and eighteenth century, an obsession with warm and waterproof beaver-pelt hats in Europe fueled a booming fur-trade industry in the region, which brought the first white settlements and ensured continued British interest until they lost control of the region with the onset of the War of 1812. Soon after, enough settlers were living in the territory to allow it statehood, which it received in 1848.

While overhunting would mark the end of the fur trade, work in logging, farming, mining, and eventually manufacturing would soon replace it as waves of new immigrants—many from the eastern United States as well as a large number from Germany, Britain, and Scandinavia— came to Wisconsin through the nineteenth century to find work, scores of whom established the farms that came to characterize much of the state's identity and economy.

Many of the early examples of the Wisconsin Idea, in fact, were linked to the agricultural nature of the state, with researchers and outreach specialists dedicated to helping farmers with pest control, crop management, and other aspects of the growing dairy, corn, and soybean industries. One of these researchers was Professor Steven Babcock, a chemist studying the chemical properties of milk in the 1890s. Hearing from Wisconsin dairymen that an inexpensive test was needed to identify the butterfat content of milk so that it could be accurately priced in the marketplace, a colleague encouraged Babcock to shift from his more theoretical research to focus on the butterfat test. Using a centrifuge to spin a solution of milk with sulfuric acid (which dissolved the casein—a protein—in the milk) enabled the fat to rise and separate from the milk. With a simple measurement, the percentage of butterfat could be read, and in an instant the dairy industry in the United States was revolutionized.[17]

Instead of patenting the test, however, which would have undoubtedly brought Babcock fame and fortune, he elected to give it away for free in order to address what he saw as inequities in the dairy industry, writing that "in the hope that it may benefit some who are striving to improve their stock and enable creameries to avoid the evils of the present system, the test is given to the public."[18] Some estimated that because the test allowed creameries to make more accurate assessments of fat content they were able to save $800,000 a year, which in 1904 dollars was more than double the budget for the entire university.

As the state's population grew, cities such as Milwaukee and Madison, with the poverty and political corruption that accompanied rapidly growing urban centers in the late nineteenth century, eventually sparked the burgeoning Progressive movement in the 1890s. "Fighting Bob" La Follette was one of the early leaders of the Progressives, and he worked feverishly to transform public policy, education, and working conditions in the state first as a public advocate and then as governor starting in 1900.

Based on the notion that the government should serve the interests of the common people, Progressives in Wisconsin and across the country instituted a wave of reforms, increasing taxes on the wealthy and regulations on businesses, changing election laws to allow voters to directly choose candidates, and conserving state and federal lands. In Wisconsin, Progressives established the nation's first state-based community college system in 1911, requiring towns of five thousand people or more to launch vocational schools for adult learners, apprentices, and those who had left school early. Wisconsin Progressives also began to work in tandem with scholars and experts from the University of Wisconsin to shape a wide range of policies, including those advancing the cause of workers through safety protections, child labor laws, and worker compensation rules, among others. The Wisconsin Idea, which closely linked effective governance with scholarship, eventually became a cherished part of postsecondary culture in the state, shaping how students, faculty, and staff thought about the role of research and education in addressing the real problems and needs of citizens throughout Wisconsin.

Still, that did not mean that "basic" research, or scholarship undertaken primarily to generate knowledge and explore new ideas, played no role in Charles Van Hise's view of higher education. Indeed, he argued that faculty should be encouraged to "advance knowledge without respect to immediate practical value" much like the German universities upon which many American institutions modeled themselves.[19] This perspective, however, was not universally shared in 1910, and it certainly is not today. In fact, the American conversation about the purposes of higher education that Van Hise and the Progressives blew open in the early twentieth century had been going on since at least the 1700s, often shifting between vocational and intellectual emphases with the social and economic winds of the times.

FROM JEFFERSONIAN IDEALS
TO MIDDLE-CLASS DREAMS

Institutions of higher education in the early years of the American republic were effectively professional schools for the clergy, such as the College of William and Mary, which was founded in 1693 to train Anglican priests. The character of postsecondary education began to change, however, with the active reforms of Thomas Jefferson, who believed religious vocational training should be separated from a more comprehensive education in the sciences, arts, philosophy, and literature, primarily for the elite ruling class of the young republic. For Jefferson, college was an opportunity for young people to achieve intellectual and moral enlightenment not only through scientific insight, but also by grappling with complex questions of ethics and morality. This vision of higher education informed his plans for the establishment of the University of Virginia, an accomplishment of which he was so proud that it was inscribed on his gravestone. Universities and colleges through the mid-nineteenth century generally followed Jefferson's lead, offering a multidisciplinary "liberal arts" education that many believed would give students the kind of preparation they needed for a productive, enlightened, and civically engaged life.

Higher education institutions, however, were continually changing in response to labor market demands, local constituencies, and public pressure. Thus, as the economy and demographics of the United States changed in the mid- to late-nineteenth century, colleges began to shift their emphases to an education that prepared students for more highly skilled urban jobs.[20] The Morrill Act of 1862, which granted federal lands to state colleges willing to emphasize agriculture and the mechanical arts, was a full-throated endorsement of this view, and is often seen as the first formal acknowledgment of vocational training as a function of higher education in the United States.

The beginning of the twentieth century brought new forms of organization to higher education across the country.[21] A combination of the vocational education movement, creation of normal colleges for teacher training, growing demands for skilled labor, and Progressive era reforms advocating for universal education ultimately led to the creation of technical colleges intended to provide vocationally centered training upon the completion of high school. The Smith-Hughes Act of 1917, which was modeled after early technical colleges in Wisconsin, required that all states develop a board for vocational education and set in motion the development of a multitiered higher education system that persists to this day.

A growing industrial sector hired chemists and physicists in droves between 1900 and 1940, which led many universities to expand their science programming and further tailor their offerings—and their research—to the labor market.[22] By the 1950s, as the US higher education system was booming with student enrollments via the GI Bill, Cold War research needs, and substantial increases in public funding for infrastructure and research, universities and colleges were competing for students in a marketplace pushed more by labor force and applied research demands than ever before.[23] With the tightening of state requirements for practice in the medical, law, and engineering fields, spurred on in part by zealous professional organizations, universities and colleges also began to form professional schools that drew increasing numbers of students for vocation-specific training.[24]

Two-year technical and community colleges expanded as well, developing after World War II into state-based systems of publicly supported colleges offering affordable access to higher education for nontraditional students living nearby. Wisconsin's system expanded with further state and federal support, and local demand for vocational training essentially doubled enrollments from the late 1960s to the early 1980s.[25] Designed to boost the state economy by offering vocationally oriented, technical education to adults seeking specific workforce opportunities, their missions differed substantially from those of the established state universities, whose goals in many ways still spoke to Jeffersonian ideals regarding a mutually reinforcing, comprehensive education for life and work in a democratic society.[26]

In response to continuing shifts in the labor market and corresponding public demands, higher education became more and more differentiated—with state-based, two-year community college systems and transfer institutions growing alongside four-year colleges and universities from the 1960s onward. This has led to the development of a variety of pathways between the postsecondary education system and the workforce, which feed into and sometimes intertwine with one another as adults seek additional education throughout their working lives (see figure 1.1).

Growing enrollments and the diversity of postsecondary offerings would only continue. In Wisconsin, as in the rest of the country, enrollment in both two-year and four-year programs increased dramatically between 1965 and 2005—by nearly 400 percent across the United States, in fact—largely because higher education was often being billed as *the way* to attain middle-class success in American society.[27]

CREATING A BIOTECHNOLOGY PROGRAM AT MADISON COLLEGE

About five miles away from UW-Madison and across the isthmus between Lake Monona and Lake Mendota sits one of eight Madison College locations that collectively serve approximately forty thousand students. Started in 1987, the Madison College Associate Degree Biotechnology

FIGURE 1.1 Pathways between education and the workforce

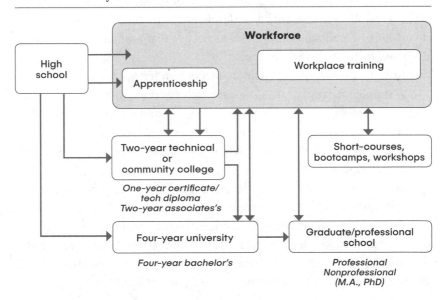

Laboratory Technician Department was created as a fledgling biotechnology industry began to spring up around Dane County, due in large part to spin-off companies created by UW-Madison faculty. The two-year program, which had been meeting a growing demand for technicians in these companies who typically earn $15 to $17 an hour, has added various certificates and post-baccalaureate courses over the years.[28]

Dr. Lisa Seidman, a faculty member of the Biotechnology Department since its inception, discussed how job placement is the primary mission of the college (which boasts an 89 percent placement rate within six months of graduation) and of the biotechnology program. "So our goal is that most of our students will get jobs when they get out, and that's how we are judged," she explained. "That's how we judge ourselves."

In order to achieve that goal, the program needs to build strong ties with local employers. In fact, the development of new technical college programs sets in motion just these kinds of partnerships, as state statute mandates that industry representatives serve on advisory boards to help design such programs and give direct feedback about existing ones. The creation of the biotechnology program was no different, according to Lisa: "Our entire curriculum is actually based on what employers want." Another valuable source of information is program alumni, who periodically come back for a course called Careers, where they describe their experience with the program and how it has translated into the workplace. Overall, the program has multiple ties with industry through which it constantly recalibrates its courses to ensure that graduates can meet the evolving demands of the workplace.

Still, Lisa emphasized, business owners understand that the program is not simply an external training program for their companies. Instead, employers want students with a variety of skills and knowledge, or as Lisa noted, "all the kinds of things that you would want students to be working on in college." Similarly, Mary Ellen Kraus, the director of and instructor in the program, observed how the course she was teaching—Making Biotechnology Products—clearly addressed workforce needs but also incorporated other skills, like communication and critical thinking, that were also taught throughout the general education curriculum. In focusing on oral communication, for example, Mary Ellen strives to prepare her students for the moment when "your boss comes up and asks what you're doing [and you need to] communicate that in a concise way."

These nontechnical competencies are considered so valuable that the college recently formalized them as "Core Workforce Skills." Critical thinking, teamwork, and active listening skills (to name but a few) now must be taught in all programs. But the focus on these skills is not due solely to a programmatic requirement. Instead, Lisa observed, "As educators we want to go beyond training into true education, because we think that our students' future success and options depends on their ability to think, solve problems, respond to change, and take on new challenges." Put another way, the education provided at Madison College is not solely targeted at getting students a job upon graduation, but as Lisa said, "educating them for a future career that no one can imagine or predict."

So at Madison College, the design of the curriculum is informed by a combination of the institution's primary mission to prepare students for the workforce through technical training, as well as the conviction that nontechnical competencies are part of that very same goal. With two-year technical college programs like this one that are likely to land a student a job, albeit one that may or may not command a pariticularly high salary, why do many students feel compelled to attend a four-year college with a much higher sticker price?

"COLLEGE FOR ALL," LIBERAL ARTS, AND DISILLUSIONMENT

One of the defining characteristics of the postsecondary landscape in the late twentieth century was the "college for all" movement, which can be distilled to one basic notion: that the golden ticket to the middle class is a four-year college degree.

While the movement began as a reaction against what many saw as a culture of low expectations and discrimination in the country's K–12 schools, the growing emphasis on college was also a result of a steady stream of findings showing that some form of higher education— whether a one-year technical, two-year associate's, or four-year bachelor's degree—would be required to work in the coming century.[29] Economists at the Georgetown Center on Education and the Workforce, for instance, projected that by the year 2020, 65 percent of all jobs in the US economy would demand postsecondary education and training beyond high school.[30] The push toward four-year colleges was also fueled by evidence that the lifetime earnings of those holding a bachelor's degree was $2.2 million, versus those with associate's degrees ($1.7 million), some college ($1.5 million), or a high school diploma ($1.3 million).[31]

The influence of the "college for all" ethos was especially apparent in high schools, where the curriculum shifted from a broad-based selection of academic and vocationally oriented coursework (i.e., hands-on, technical training) to a narrower focus on college preparatory classes meant to prepare students for a four-year college. As time went on, however, many began to question the need for *all* students to go to a four-year college, particularly since a considerable number of students simply were not interested in pursuing a bachelor's degree.[32]

Additionally, skepticism about college for all began to extend to educational programs that included subjects that had no immediate, obvious, or "in-demand" counterpart in the occupations, such as English, art history, or ethnic studies. Since most institutions that follow the multidisciplinary liberal arts tradition have general education requirements for associate's or bachelor's degrees featuring such courses, the term *liberal arts* has mistakenly become synonymous for many pundits and policy makers with supposedly non-workforce-related disciplines and majors, largely in the arts and humanities. This misreading of what liberal arts really means overlooks its origins in classical European training and the Jeffersonian vision of a multidisciplinary education that would lead to a healthy democracy, a skilled workforce, and enlightened and free-thinking citizens. In the latter half of the twentieth century, this was the idea behind general education requirements that students in all majors—engineering, for example—had to complete to acquire their degrees.[33]

The idea that students should be exposed to a variety of disciplines and perspectives also became enshrined in numerous small residential colleges, like Amherst College in Massachusetts, Lawrence University in Wisconsin, as well as within the core curriculum of many public two- and four-year colleges and universities.[34] Such ideals are often a central feature in many public universities' missions, as they are in UW-Madison's, which seeks to "offer broad and balanced academic programs that are mutually reinforcing" as well as help students "develop an understanding and appreciation for the complex cultural and physical worlds in which they live."[35] The liberal arts model proved so powerful in the early years of American higher education that it came to be viewed as synonymous with American creativity and industrial innovation, and is often viewed with envy by nations such as China that aspire to develop a similar higher education system.[36]

Critiques of the liberal arts tradition in general, and of arts and humanities in particular, however, have become increasingly common in the wake of the 2008 recession, as people began to wonder if such programs would ever lead to a decent paycheck. These concerns are not merely hypothetical as students are beginning to vote with their feet. Majors in professional schools, for instance, increased over 50 percent between 1969 and 1975 as more students chose to pursue more career-oriented programs, while majors in the social sciences and humanities took a hit of equal proportion.[37] At UW-Madison the percentage of juniors and seniors majoring in the STEM fields rose from 32 percent in 2000 to 41 percent in 2014, while enrollment in previously popular courses, such as Introduction to American Politics and Government, declined.[38]

In the face of such trends, a number of voices have lamented the loss of a national focus on intellectual and moral development, as well as the broadmindedness that Jefferson believed so important for higher education and a democratic society. Dr. Michael Roth, president of Wesleyan University, is one of those people. A reporter asked him what America would look like without a liberal education and he stated: "Without an education that cultivates an ability to learn from the past while stimulating a resistance to authority, without an education that empowers students for lifelong learning and inquiry, we would become a cultural and economic backwater, competing with various regions for the privilege of operationalizing somebody else's new ideas. In an effort at manic monetization without critical thinking, we would become adept at producing conformity rather than innovation."[39] With the exception of a small but vocal minority of liberal arts advocates such as Roth, however, the rhetoric of moral and intellectual enlightenment has all but disappeared in conversations about higher education. Much of the discourse has now turned to how institutions of higher education can better meet new, twenty-first-century workplace needs—which begs the questions of what exactly employers are looking for and how students should be prepared for the new global economy.

HOW TO GET A JOB AT YOUR LOCAL BIOTECHNOLOGY COMPANY

Situated across the street from the local Culvers in Middleton, Wisconsin, sits an unassuming building with little indication of the activities unfolding inside. A plain white sign perched near the road advertises "Lucigen" with the byline "Simplifying Genomics," which explains the basic functions of the company: to develop research products, technologies, and diagnostic tests for the life sciences, with a focus on genetic cloning. Founded in 1998, Lucigen has become a jewel in the Madison-area crown of growing biotechnology companies, especially since it has taken a lead role in pursuing a cure for Ebola and other infectious diseases.

When asked about the types of skills needed to get a job at Lucigen, and to thrive in the industry over the long term, David Mead, the founder and then-CEO of the company, answered: "Deep knowledge from books and articles and teaching as well as lab training on how to operate equipment and design experiments and interpret results." This description succinctly captures the types of diverse skill sets that Janet Batzli is trying to cultivate in the Biocore program at UW-Madison.

However, Jeff Williams, Lucigen's COO, discussed the relative pros and cons of hiring from the big research universities. UW-Madison students tend to have strong training in the theoretical aspects of biology, he said, but they also tend to lack practical bench skills like running experiments or taking good lab notes. Students from the local technical college, on the other hand, tend to have strong training in bench skills, though they may hit an advancement ceiling due to a lack of book knowledge. David said that "without going back to school to achieve the level of understanding to do molecular biology experiments, it would be very hard for them to try and move into a more senior level R&D position." This is largely due to a lack of "depth of knowledge and problem solving" skills in these graduates. Holding only an associate's degree, then, stymies those workers' opportunities in the company, though David was quick to observe that bachelor's-trained employees would hit a ceiling as well, as a PhD is required for most senior research positions.

Given all of this, is one college program preferable for preparing the future biotechnology workforce to the other? Jeff feels that while they would prefer to have applicants with both "bench experience" and "book knowledge," the two types of programs essentially feed into two different types of positions at the company: a lab technician and a research associate, respectively. The former pays an average of $32,000 a year, while the latter pays about $51,770.[40] Arrival at these different jobs necessarily requires students to pursue distinct educational pathways to get there. The UW-Madison Biocore program likely directs students into mid-wage research associate positions, whereas the Madison College biotechnology program fulfills the need for lab technicians with practical bench skills—two different pathways in two different colleges with different costs in time and tuition, but with differential rewards in the labor market in terms of pay and advancement.

These are important considerations for Lucigen, because hiring and retaining a skilled workforce is essential in order to beat their competitors and be able to quickly ramp up production. While hiring the upper-level scientists who would run projects could draw on a worldwide network of PhD-level scientists, cultivating the entry-level workforce who could run the experiments, manufacture the products, and ideally stay with the company for years relies heavily on home-grown students—the high school and college graduates in southern Wisconsin willing to stick around the Badger State for a while.

Given the historical trajectory of higher education in Wisconsin and the United States, with foci on professional preparation and broad liberal arts education waxing and waning over time and with the political winds, the case of Lucigen indicates that there is a need for both types of educational programs. In Wisconsin at the time of our data collection, however, vocationalists dominated the discourse, trumpeting the benefits of two-year technical degrees while questioning the merits of bachelor's degrees in general, and the liberal arts model in particular. Consequently, Governor Walker and the Republican-dominated legislature were actively reshaping the state's budget, and the governance of Wisconsin's public colleges and universities, to reflect this perspective. And at the heart of the matter was a little something called the skills gap.

The Skills Gap Narrative

A Critique of Higher Education

I've said this before and I'll say it again: we don't have a jobs crisis in Milwaukee, we have an education crisis.

—TIM SULLIVAN[1]

WMC FOCUS GROUPS AND THE RELEASE OF THE "ROAD AHEAD" REPORT

In Wisconsin, the state's chamber of commerce and largest business trade association, Wisconsin Manufacturers and Commerce (WMC), has taken a particular interest in advancing the idea of a skills gap. WMC's Jim Morgan organized public meetings across the state to discuss "Wisconsin's Workforce Paradox." In more than fifty focus groups with over three hundred manufacturing executives and supervisors, he heard employers describing their difficulty in finding employees with particular skills, the importance of "years off the farm," and most of all, their challenges with finding employees with a strong work ethic.

But perhaps the biggest lesson from these focus groups, at least for Jim, was the need to redefine the meaning of "success." Jim recounted the decline of vocational and technical education in K–12 schools, and

33

how his generation was told that, "if you get a four-year degree, you're a success," which meant that technical colleges became a last resort, the second-class citizen of the postsecondary world. Similarly, while plush office jobs or work in law or medicine were considered markers of success, skilled labor occupations such as carpentry, farming, and welding were looked down upon as the low-status and low-pay jobs of yesterday. Instead, Jim argues, the message sent to young people should be that there are multiple pathways to success, and that students and families should be provided with balanced and up-to-date information about various jobs and careers so that they can make informed decisions. This is especially important, he said, given that parents and students are "going to drop forty, fifty, sixty, eighty thousand dollars" on a college degree, but often without a game plan or informed career planning. In a 2012 op-ed describing the listening sessions, Jim hinted at the shift in emphasis. "As we focus on 'college and career readiness,'" he wrote, "we might want to put 'career' first."[2] These were not idle observations, as WMC is the state's largest and most influential business lobby and has the ear of Governor Walker and many Republican legislators in the Wisconsin government.

WMC is not alone in its work on advocating the skills gap to state policy makers. The issue has long consumed Tim Sullivan, the former CEO of Bucyrus International, Inc., which manufactured heavy machinery used in mining operations around the world.[3] Once singled out by the mayor of Milwaukee for "believing and investing in our city," by 2011 Sullivan was reportedly struggling to find qualified welders to work at his company, leading him to contact officials in Texas about a possible relocation. Officials from the town of Kilgore promised eighty factory-grade welders would be waiting when the company arrived, which was a far cry from what Tim felt Milwaukee could offer. Sullivan claimed that Milwaukee Area Technical College (MATC) was unable to provide skilled workers, which he believed was due to a systemic failure in the educational system, where there existed "a complete disconnect between jobs and education and training." It didn't help, Sullivan said, that "many Milwaukee-trained welders simply are not mentally prepared" by the area's K–12 schools.[4]

In response, a welding instructor at MATC, Larry Gross, wrote an op-ed in the *Milwaukee Journal-Sentinel*, stating that Sullivan's claims were "untrue." MATC had created a customized curriculum for Bucyrus, but "MATC welding graduates have more attractive options than Bucyrus's, which are among the most arduous, hot, and dirty in the marketplace," he wrote.[5] (In fact, one MATC class toured the facilities at Bucyrus and another large manufacturer, and every single student elected to work at the other company.) Gross argued that instead of blaming educators and MATC, there should be "outrage" directed at Governor Walker's budget, which "decimates" funding for Milwaukee schools and cut funding to MATC and other technical colleges by 30 percent. Sue Silverstein, another welding instructor at MATC, noted that the school's advisory board members, many of whom are local business owners, have long informed its programs, thus ensuring that its curricula are well aligned with industry needs, but that not all welders want to do the type of welding that companies like Bucyrus require. She pointedly added that "we teach it all, but they are adults and they pick and choose where they want to go."[6] Regardless of this hullabaloo, however, Sullivan was tapped by Governor Walker to prepare a study on the skills gap in Wisconsin, which led to a hugely influential report that was released in 2012 called "The Road Ahead: Restoring Wisconsin's Workforce Development."

Though there are a variety of recommendations in the report, including reforming the tax code and overhauling unemployment insurance, Sullivan's concentration on education is apparent from the start, as he identifies the primary source of the skills gap as being "an education system that has not been able to keep pace with evolving workforce needs."[7] In his analysis, Sullivan chides the postsecondary sector for problems with completion rates in technical and community colleges as well as rising debt loads among four-year graduates, and offers a variety of solutions, including stackable credentials, an online flexible option for the UW System, and career counseling for K–12 students. Notably, Sullivan does not raise the issue of classroom teaching nor of businesses' role in their own employees' professional development.[8] As he introduced Sullivan at the release of "The Road Ahead," Governor Walker touted Sullivan's report as a key force in helping to "develop and drive" the state's workforce development policies.[9]

Around the same time, a coalition called Competitive Wisconsin, Inc., was also actively releasing reports on the topic. Billed as a nonpartisan group bringing higher education, business, labor, and agriculture to the table, Competitive Wisconsin, Inc., released "Be Bold 2: Growing Wisconsin's Talent Pool" a few months after "The Road Ahead" came out. The crux of the report was communicated in a warning only four pages into the document: "Aging, retiring and departing workers, fewer young people entering the workforce, and net outmigration of highly educated and skilled workers clearly foreshadow serious worker shortages in Wisconsin's not so distant future."[10] With the table set, the authors went on to identify the key "skills clusters" most in demand in the state, including software development, health-related work and nursing, mechanical engineering, and metal manufacturing—all clusters the authors predicted would see shortfalls in the near future. (Interestingly, the report equates skills with occupations, and not the specific skills, knowledge, and abilities utilized in those jobs.) "Be Bold 2" ended with recommendations for more education-industry alignment, real-time labor market information being made available, and the general promotion of what they called "rightly skilled" workers (i.e., those in one of their occupational clusters) in Wisconsin.[11]

Though there are hundreds of such reports, with accompanying press releases, circulated by advocacy organizations every year across the country, these were decidedly atypical. They were not just released by cloistered think tanks hoping upon hope that a reporter or legislator *somewhere* might pay attention. In point of fact, by way of the social and political contacts the authors had with policy makers—and the elections of 2010 that swept into office politicians who were focused on a combination of shrinking government and job creation—these reports made things happen.

For instance, "Be Bold 1," the first report published by Competitive Wisconsin, set in motion the formation of the Wisconsin Economic Development Corporation, a public-private organization meant to drive business development in Wisconsin. "The Road Ahead" is another prominent example, as it became the blueprint for a piece of legislation called Wisconsin Act 9, popularly known as Wisconsin Fast Forward (WFF), which the governor signed into law in March 2013. The aforementioned "Be Bold 2," Competitive Wisconsin's second report, also played an important role in shaping WFF. In fact, Scott VanderSanden, president of Competitive Wisconsin and CEO of AT&T Wisconsin, said, "We are pleased the work of 'Be Bold 2' is appreciated and has been incorporated into Governor Walker's thinking on workforce development."[12]

WHAT IS THE SKILLS GAP?

Despite the increased attention it has garnered in Wisconsin (and beyond) in recent years, the idea of a skills gap, when we encountered it, certainly was not new. The view that the decline of skills in certain age cohorts is due to a failed educational system has its roots in Cold War–era fears about the scientific accomplishments of the Soviet Union. A series of national reports, including the 1983 report *A Nation at Risk* and the influential 1991 report from the Secretary's Commission on Achieving Necessary Skills (SCANS), further reinforced the idea that the US workforce severely lacked the skills and education that were needed to fuel the national economy.[13] Employers have long echoed these fears as well. Indeed, when a board member of the Manufacturers' Alliance for Productivity and Innovation was asked in the late 1980s how long his industry had struggled to find well-trained mechanics, his answer was "since World War II."[14]

By 2015, over 3,200 newspaper articles and 2,200 journal articles mentioned the "skills gap," with the Ex Libris database showing a sharp uptick in academic and media attention around 2010 (see figure 2.1).

The increase in references to the skills gap was likely caused, not surprisingly, by the Great Recession of 2008, which at its worst saw the economy shed an average of 712,000 jobs *a month* from October 2008 through March 2009.[15] As the economy began to recover, albeit haltingly,

FIGURE 2.1 Number of news and journal articles citing a "skills gap"

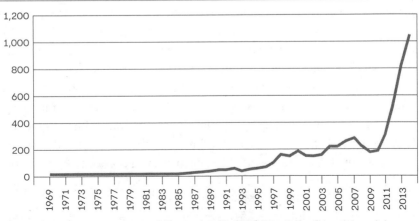

Source: Article search on "skills gap" (September 15, 2015), http://www.library.wisc.edu/#articles.

the news media began to feature numerous stories about how companies could not find skilled workers to fill job openings, despite persistently high unemployment. Because of this lack of skilled workers, many companies reportedly were unable to take on new accounts or hire new workers. Larry Willer, an operations manager for a company making stainless steel tanks for the food and beverage industry in central Wisconsin, put it simply. "We lost a lot of business," he said, "because we do not have enough people (especially welders) to staff our shop."[16]

Even the leader of the free world got on board with the idea. During the 2014 State of the Union address, President Barack Obama emphasized the need in "this rapidly changing economy" to make sure that Americans could fill available jobs before relaying to the audience his request that Vice President Joe Biden "lead an across-the-board reform of America's training programs." The reform, Obama said, had one goal: to "train Americans with the skills employers need, and match them to good jobs that need to be filled right now."[17] Politicians of all stripes, at the federal and state level, sounded similar notes. As we have seen, Wisconsin's Governor Walker, not exactly President Obama's ideological brother-in-arms, also publicly worried about the issue, saying, "The skills gap is a very real concern in Wisconsin and around the country."[18]

But what exactly is a skills gap? It's always worth scrutinizing jargon and phrases that people (particularly politicians, advocates, and academics) repeatedly use without offering any clear definitions. *Skills gap* is such a phrase, and indeed, it has become something of a *meme*—a vehicle for spreading cultural ideas, assumptions, behaviors, and styles from person to person. Often thought of in terms of viral Internet phenomena such as Grumpy Cat or the Honey Badger, *meme* can also refer to academic ideas that take on a life of their own in the culture and mass media. In other words, a meme can become so large a part of popular culture that it is often repeated without knowledge of its roots, nuances, or accuracy. Anytime there is such an influential meme, particularly one with the potential to drive the global discourse surrounding the future of public higher education, it is worth digging a little deeper to see what propels the narrative.

Key Ideas Driving the Skills Gap Meme

First of all, it is useful to understand that the notion of a skills gap is but one of a handful of ideas referring to skills-related problems. Dr. Peter

Cappelli, a professor of management at the University of Pennsylvania's renowned Wharton School, distinguishes among three different types of skills issues that labor economists are accustomed to studying.[19] The first is a *skills mismatch*, which refers to the notion that the general supply and demand for certain skills could be out of whack, with either an oversupply or undersupply of skilled workers. The second is a *skills shortage*, which is a more particular type of skills mismatch where people with specific skills are unavailable despite employer demand, such as information technology workers in Silicon Valley. Finally, a *skills gap* is a far more expansive argument that builds on the idea of a skills shortage but adds a culprit (i.e., education) to the equation while also claiming dire impacts on the economy such as lost orders, company relocation, and so on.[20] In other words, the skills gap idea is not limited to specific shortages of workers in a given occupation, but goes much further by claiming a causal relationship among higher education, skills shortages, and economic outcomes. In examining the arguments underlying this idea, we discerned no fewer than six distinct yet interrelated assumptions that undergird the skills gap argument.

Employers are having a difficult time finding skilled workers

Perhaps the most basic premise behind the skills gap is that employers are having a hard time finding the employees they need, and there is some data supporting this point. In its 2015 annual "Talent Shortage Survey," for instance, the consulting firm ManpowerGroup surveyed 41,700 hiring managers across several dozen countries, finding that 38 percent of respondents reported difficulties filling jobs. Interestingly, this percentage is remarkably close to the 40 percent of employers making the same complaint in 2006, which of course was at least a year before the start of the Great Recession. In any case, hiring challenges vary considerably country by country, with Japanese businesses having the biggest issues (where 83 percent indicated problems), followed by Peru (68 percent) and Hong Kong (65 percent). Challenges also appear to be concentrated in a few occupations such as skilled trade workers (e.g., mechanics, electricians, and bakers), sales representatives, engineers, and drivers.[21]

In analyses of the situation in Wisconsin, WMC found that 70 percent of manufacturing executives in the state experienced difficulties with finding qualified employees, with just over half reporting that their problems stemmed from a predominance of applicants with inadequate or inappropriate qualifications for position openings.[22] Ultimately, the key point here is that a considerable proportion of employers report that the applicant pool in certain occupational areas is sorely lacking.

Technical or "hard" skills utilized in specific occupations are what industry needs

However, the specific types of skills or competencies desired by employers are often left unstated by policy makers and analysts. Instead, it is assumed that these expectations pertain primarily, if not solely, to technical expertise needed in specific occupations. For example, in advocating for more students to attend technical colleges, WMC's Jim Morgan argued that "technical skills" are the primary skill set an applicant needs to get a middle-skill job in manufacturing.[23] When specific skills are described in greater detail, the popular but highly ambiguous categories of "hard" (i.e., technical) and "soft" (i.e., nontechnical) skills are sometimes used. More commonly, discussions center on industries writ large (e.g., health care or manufacturing), specific jobs (e.g., nursing or welding), or occupational categories (e.g., middle-skill) that are then used as stand-ins for the types of skills and competencies needed in the labor market. For example, the "Be Bold 2" report talks about the "skills clusters" of mechanical engineering and software development. Thus, a key aspect of the skills gap narrative—the notion of "skills"—is often ill defined and generally assumed to be the technical knowledge linked to an occupation, if not the occupation itself.

The focus should be on middle-skill jobs that don't require a four-year degree

A central argument of skills gap proponents is that by removing vocational education from high schools and defining success solely in terms of going to a four-year college, the educational system has short-circuited the production of workers for "middle-skill" jobs, or those occupations that require some postsecondary training (e.g., associate's degree or a certificate) but not a bachelor's degree. These include many of the jobs that are reported to be in high demand in states like Wisconsin, such as registered nurses, welders, lab technicians, and machinists.

TABLE 2.1 Job projections by educational attainment in Wisconsin: 2008–2018

	2008	2018	% Change
High school dropouts	231,000	241,000	4%
High school graduates	984,000	1,026,000	4%
Some college	664,000	704,000	6%
Associate's	338,000	366,000	8%
Bachelor's	554,000	600,000	8%
Graduate	231,000	255,000	10%

Source: Anthony P. Carnevale and Nicole Smith, *The Midwest Challenge: Matching Jobs with Education in the Post-Recession Economy* (Washington, DC: Georgetown University Center on Education and the Workforce, 2014).

There is evidence that many current and future jobs fit into this category. Estimates from Georgetown's Center on Education and the Workforce (CEW), a research center that is widely quoted as an authority on skills-related issues, indicate that of the 164 million total jobs projected to be available in the United States through 2020, only 35 percent will require a bachelor's degree or higher.[24] Fueling this argument in Wisconsin is the estimate that 73 percent of the projected 3.1 million jobs in the state will not require a four-year degree by 2018.[25]

In the Chicago area alone, which is just south of the Wisconsin border, some estimate that two of the region's growth industries, health care and transportation, will generate twenty thousand job openings a year until 2019, with positions such as radiologic technicians enjoying a $28-an-hour median wage, and bus mechanics earning $22 an hour.[26] Importantly, occupations such as these would provide a family of two adults (with only one working) and one child with a wage above the regional living wage of $21.49.[27] As Sullivan argued in "The Road Ahead," advertising and promoting these careers is not meant to discourage people from obtaining bachelor's degrees, but "it is inefficient to have students earning four-year degrees when what they really need for work is a two-year degree."[28] This argument is often bolstered with reports that many graduates with bachelor's degrees remain un- or underemployed, such that some graduates even have to return to two-year technical colleges to obtain marketable skill sets. Additionally, the price of a four-year degree and rising student debt loads are also held up as reasons why students should consider the less expensive option of a two-year college.

However, not all analysts think that categorizing jobs into low-, medium-, and high-skill clusters by educational attainment is a valid approach, given that the types of skills acquired in different educational programs vary considerably by field and institution. Alternative approaches will be described in the next chapter, but the takeaway here is that the skills gap narrative generally emphasizes occupations that do not require a bachelor's degree, and that, given demographic (e.g., retirement of the Baby Boomers) and economic trends, Wisconsin appears to be at a particular risk for not attracting enough workers in the coming years.

Postsecondary curricula and the liberal arts are the primary causes of the skills gap

One of the defining characteristics of the skills gap argument, in contrast to the notions of a skills mismatch or a skills shortage, is that the educational sector is the primary source of the problem. In the quote opening this chapter, Sullivan told a reporter for the *Milwaukee Journal-Sentinel* in no uncertain terms that Milwaukee's dour economic circumstances were not caused by industry trends, the quality or availability of jobs, or other such factors, but instead were solely due to "an education crisis."[29] But it is not the educational sector writ large that is the problem according to the skills gap narrative. Instead, it is the liberal arts tradition and general education courses that are often singled out as inadequately suited for preparing students for the world of work.

The curricular issue begins in high school, where technical and vocational education has declined in favor of overly theoretical coursework meant to prepare students for college. Then, the proliferation of four-year college majors that are not directly tied to specific, high-demand occupations makes matters even worse for the labor market. For example, at the inaugural Future Wisconsin Project summit in Milwaukee, which was hosted by WMC, Ken Gronbach, a demographer and futurist, confidently said, "the age of liberal arts education is about to give way to measurable training because business and industry is saying to colleges 'please don't send us any more art history majors.'"[30] The director of the Georgetown CEW, labor economist Anthony Carnevale, went even further, raising questions about whether public universities should be supporting disciplines that demonstrably lead to lower wages than others. "We don't want to take away Shakespeare," Carnevale said, "we're just talking about helping people make good decisions" by providing them better career counseling in high school and college.[31]

The skills gap is a technical problem best addressed through programmatic solutions

Policy makers and skills gap proponents have largely argued that supporting vocationally oriented training programs is the best solution to the nation's workforce challenges. This could translate into adding new associate's degree programs in welding or nursing, or expanding capacity in high-demand fields like computer science that are leading to wait lists at UW-Madison and UW-Superior. Thus, the skills gap is primarily a technical problem grounded in the availability (or lack thereof) of certain academic programs and courses in the nation's colleges and universities.

One of the issues with the reliance on programmatic solutions, of course, is the time lag that inevitably occurs between when an industry recognizes a need and when traditional institutions can produce graduates with those skills. An instructor at a technical college described the situation in colorful terms: "We can go buy a gun, and we can put a bullet in the gun, and we can pull the trigger, but it's a year before the bullet comes out," he said. In other words, businesses do not have time to wait for a regular college or university to get a program up and running. Indeed, fields such as software development or biotechnology are sometimes evolving so rapidly that techniques or skills learned in school become obsolete rather quickly.

In response, many advocate for new, short-term training programs to be created or expanded in two-year institutions, or even "bootcamps" that could quickly train a cohort of un- or underemployed workers for jobs experiencing shortages. The growth in short-term programs is also related to the alternative credentialing movement in higher education, which argues that badges or certificates should be awarded upon completion to signal to employers that an applicant has certain skill sets or competencies.

The focus of change should be on one sector: education

This assumption is rather simple: though the notion of a skills gap implicates a variety of parties including employers, government, society at large, and educators, change should be taking place in only one of these venues. As Sullivan wrote in "The Road Ahead": "Wisconsin should focus on what it can change: education."[32] In particular, the idea of "alignment" is repeatedly cited by skills gap advocates as a necessary condition required to shift the emphasis of postsecondary curriculum and programming from the liberal arts toward employer needs. For instance, the Business Higher Education Forum, a national advocacy organization made up of business leaders and university presidents, made this oft-cited observation in a 2011 report: "Critical disjunctions exist between what is taught and learned in postsecondary education and the skills that are in high demand in the workplace."[33] The appropriate response, it argued, was to more closely "align" education and business to "ensure that students graduating from high school are college-ready and can progress more easily through the system and into jobs and careers."[34] The subtext of this argument is clear: educators and employers should form partnerships, but only with the goal to change practice and curriculum in schools, colleges, and universities. Basically, educators must respond to the "signals" of industry, not the other way around.

These are the six primary assumptions powering the skills gap narrative, and part of our interest as scholars was to examine these ideas and to see what people in the field had to say about them, because, unlike other viral Internet memes, the conversation was shaping policy discussions and determining how public monies were being spent nationwide.

HOW THE SKILLS GAP IS DRIVING PUBLIC POLICY IN WISCONSIN

In March 2013, seated at a wooden desk with a bold, blue-and-white sign reading "Investing in Our Workforce" displayed in front of him, Governor Walker signed Act 9 into law at Jay Manufacturing in Oshkosh, a city of almost seventy thousand on the western shore of Lake Winnebago.[35] Reggie Newson, Secretary of the Wisconsin Department of Workforce Development (DWD), looked on behind him, as did a dozen or so Jay Manufacturing employees.

Act 9 included a host of new initiatives that were intended to spur economic growth, primarily by boosting the state's capacity to develop a skilled workforce. The legislation included funding for a new labor market information system and a new Office of Skills Development (OSD) at the DWD, increased funding for the Wisconsin Technical College System, and provided $15 million for new workforce training grants—a combination of initiatives that built on the recommendations of Tim Sullivan's and Competitive Wisconsin's reports.[36] According to observers, the legislation marked the first time general-purpose funds from the state had been allocated to support workforce development programs.[37]

Newly appointed OSD Director Scott Jansen said the initiative's goal was nothing short of "reinventing the workforce," which it would accomplish by "articulating" employers' skills demands, and then building education and training collaborations (called *supply-side* programs) around those needs.[38] Jansen, formerly a vice president at AT&T, said a distinctive feature of the workforce development grants was that "businesses will drive what the curriculum will be."[39] This sentiment left no room for interpretation regarding whose interests would set the agenda.

DWD began distributing grant money in 2013 to Wisconsin businesses that could show, first, that they had training needs for employees in high-need skill areas and, second, that they could match fifty cents on the dollar that the training would cost. While some employers had already partnered with local technical schools to develop training programs, the OSD also worked with qualifying businesses to develop in-house training curricula that would meet their particular needs. Examples included a $206,500 award to RockTenn, LLC, to provide training for 165 employees on new equipment that would "transform" the company's facilities where it manufactured packaging materials, and a $123,523 award to the biotechnology firm Exact Sciences to create a training curriculum on specimen processing that would be used to train 110 new employees.[40]

While Wisconsin Fast Forward addressed key parts of the complex higher education–workforce system in Wisconsin, it is also evident that the initiative focused on a relatively small portion of that system. Approximately 53 percent of the workplace training grants were awarded to the manufacturing sector, and of 145 awards made between 2013 and 2015 worth over $12 million, only 22 (or about 15 percent) targeted nontechnical skill training. The program clearly favored one type of competency over another—that of technical or "hard" skills over "soft" skills—in one sector of the state's diverse economy.[41]

Upon closer inspection, it also became clear that the program was tailored to only one segment of the labor market: low-wage jobs. This was evident in the fact that the average post-training wage after the first round of grants was $17.19 an hour, and $12.17 after the second round. If at first glance this does not seem like the kind of "family supporting wage" often talked about in workforce policy circles, that's because it isn't. According to the MIT Living Wage calculator, a living wage for a family of four in Green Bay, Wisconsin, is $21.95 an hour. The average hourly wage for employees of Fast Forward grantees was barely above the hourly poverty wage of $11.00 an hour.[42] Despite the numbers, the program continued its expansion with additional dollars awarded as part of Governor Walker's Blueprint for Prosperity, a program initiated in 2014.[43]

Obviously, policies such as Act 9 that aim to jump-start the economy did not appear out of thin air. Importantly, the programs and the reports that led to their enactment emerged from a particular perspective regarding the ultimate purpose of higher education, one that did not view the role of public colleges and universities as advancing knowledge, serving the public good, and producing well-rounded graduates with training in the arts, sciences, and humanities in the tradition of Thomas Jefferson or Charles Van Hise. Instead, the worldview that inspired Act 9 and the educational philosophy of the Republican Party in Wisconsin was that the primary (if not the sole) purpose of higher education was to meet the needs of the business community, which would thereafter reward Wisconsin with a more competitive economy. To do so required reforms that made public colleges and universities act more like privately held corporations, focusing on meeting customer needs (i.e., primarily the business community, secondarily students in search of career prospects) and operating with a top-down managerial ethos that prioritized efficiency and accountability above all else.

THE NEOLIBERAL APPROACH COMES TO WISCONSIN HIGHER EDUCATION

Many trace the ascendance of vocationalism and the depreciation of liberal arts to the heightened focus on a market- and economic-driven ethos ushered in by conservative political movements in the United States, Germany, and Britain in the late 1970s and 1980s often referred to as *neoliberalism*.[44] As a political philosophy, a discourse, and a set of policies all rooted in deregulation, privatization, and free-market solutions to public problems, the trend would eventually set the terms of debate in the United States on a host of fronts, especially when it came to higher education. No longer would taxpayers be "subsidizing intellectual curiosity," as Ronald Reagan famously put it in reference to the University of California system; instead, colleges and universities receiving government support would be expected to better prepare students for the workforce, not intellectual navel gazing.[45]

With this focus on market-driven efficiency, institutions, programs, and even faculty members came to be seen primarily in terms of productivity, accountability, and profit. According to this view, higher education should operate like a business, with academics acting like "state-subsidized entrepreneurs" who are expected to secure external grants and create spin-off companies.[46]

In Wisconsin these ideas were being actively promoted by the Wisconsin Policy Research Institute (WPRI), a think tank with the tagline "free market paths for better lives."[47] According to the WPRI, the solution to the skills gap was to reorganize the UW System to operate more like a private company where administrators adopt an "entrepreneurial management" approach to running their campuses in order to spur economic development.[48] Because the bureaucracy of the UW System and the strong tradition of faculty governance were seen as a hindrance to realizing such a goal, the WPRI recommended reforms including giving administrators the power to eliminate academic programs, oversee faculty personnel decisions, reform tenure policies, and create new accountability metrics for higher education.

One of the primary flexibilities needed was the authority to cut programs deemed irrelevant to the labor market. Which ones would those be? (Hint: a familiarity with the works of Sandro Botticelli may not help you run a CNC machine.) In a diagnosis of the situation, the WPRI rhetorically asked, then answered, its own question: "Is the education system not adequately preparing the workforce? The consensus is yes. Too many colleges are graduating students with liberal arts degrees in limited-job specialties such as Renaissance art."[49]

The sentiment neatly encapsulated the national mood among politicians on the right, who found ever more colorful ways to rail against the irrelevance and waste they saw in the liberal arts. In October 2011, for instance, the Republican governor of Florida said if he were to take money from citizens for higher education, he would want it to be used to create jobs.[50] He added, "Is it a vital interest of the state to have more anthropologists? I don't think so." Marco Rubio, a 2016 presidential contender, made his feelings on these subjects clear. "For the life of me I don't know why we have stigmatized vocational education," he said during one Republican debate in November 2015.[51] "Welders make more money than philosophers. We need more welders and less philosophers." Later in the year, as he outlined his ideas on how to make higher education more attuned to the work world, he took the rhetoric a step further, calling liberal arts colleges "indoctrination camps."[52]

These ideas and policies have been embraced by many policy makers and pundits not only in Wisconsin but around the country and even the world. While WMC and the WPRI were discouraging Renaissance art majors, Prime Minister Shinzo Abe was successfully pushing nationwide reforms to Japan's university system to become more focused on vocational training. In fact, the Abe administration threatened to withhold federal funds for higher education if institutions did not restructure the curriculum to deemphasize the arts and humanities in favor of workforce-ready disciplines such as science and engineering.[53] In response, by September 2015 at least fifty universities had cut or downsized many courses and even programs in fields such as art history, economics, and foreign languages, sending shockwaves around the global higher education community.[54]

But is this really the best approach for the world's students, economies, and countries? Were Thomas Jefferson and Charles Van Hise really that wrong about the type of education that best prepares students for success in school, life, and work? Is the liberal arts model, once considered the cornerstone of American ingenuity, really harming students' career prospects and the economy itself?

Perhaps unsurprisingly, the notion of a skills gap—with its underlying assumptions and attendant solutions for a sluggish economy—was not universally supported, neither across the country nor among the respondents in our study. Curiously, the voices of skepticism and outright dissent did not come only from within the rarefied ivory tower of large research universities like UW-Madison, but also from technical college classrooms. Most troubling for skills gap proponents, however, is that it was business owners, plant supervisors, and HR directors who raised the most pointed questions about an approach that ultimately hinders the educational system's ability to cultivate in students the types of broad-based skills they truly need to succeed in today's challenging and globalized economy.

Complicating the Narrative

A Critique of the Skills Gap

Everyone knows nowadays that people "have complexes."
What is not so well known, though far more important
theoretically, is that complexes can have us.

—CARL GUSTAV JUNG[1]

EDUCATING THE FUNDAMENTALS

Offering a broader perspective that runs counter to the prevailing skills gap narrative, Ron Petersen, an instructor in the Electronic Systems and Installation Maintenance program at Western Technical College (WTC) in La Crosse, Wisconsin, talked about the skills that were essential for success in the field of manufacturing. "Having been on the other side of the desk (as a hiring manager in a company), I always looked at hiring as, 'Give me somebody with some fundamental skills and a work ethic, and I can teach them what they need.'" Technical skills, Ron suggested, could only get one so far, and he observed that "when you're dealing with employers, they want someone that's teachable, someone willing to learn." Work ethic, in particular, was something Ron repeatedly brought up, speaking to the importance of a trait that is rarely discussed in policy-oriented debates about the skills gap. "When we have advisory committee meetings," he explained, "employers say, 'Give me somebody that'll show up for work, regularly, on time, and care about what they're doing.'"

Ron is a proud father of two boys currently in high school; their pictures adorn all four walls of his office and are displayed on his computer desktop. He spoke about how many skills and work-related traits come from parents and from one's broader community—not just work ethic, but basic knowledge and ways of approaching problems important in Ron's field of electrical controls, like how to handle tools. "Even the kids that come off of farms now, they're not like when I came off the farm thirty years ago, when we actually had to physically do something," he said. Ron grew up working on his father's farm just across the border in Minnesota. "Now everything is automated and all the equipment is under service contract, so they don't get to tear anything apart like we had to and fix something [themselves] in order to get going."[2]

Ron's response points toward the limits of what the educational sector can do in dealing with skill deficiencies. He argues that how and where you are raised, not to mention changes in culture, lifestyle, and technology, may have more to do with the skills an individual develops than anything that can be legislated or addressed through a new educational or training program.

But then again, Ron is a dedicated educator, and the idea that a student could be beyond redemption seems antithetical to his very nature. He touched upon something that highlighted his role as a classroom teacher, which, surprisingly, is discussed rarely (if ever) in the skills gap debate. While talk about which technical skills and majors will lead to a family-supporting wage has dominated the policy discussions in Wisconsin and elsewhere, Ron elaborated on how his goal is not to train students on specific machinery from particular employers, but rather on the core principles underlying the field of electrical repair. Since programmable logic controllers (PLCs) have become so central to manufacturing and robotics, Ron focuses on "the fundamentals of troubleshooting motors, drives, and PLCs" that students can then adapt to whichever job they end up taking. His interest is in cultivating not just a skill, but a habit of mind that allows students—when faced with a faulty system or repair job—to "visualize the whole system." In many ways, Ron was speaking about critical thinking as applied to complex mechanical problems, a competency that is a fundamental concern to many educators and employers we interviewed for our research.

Like most educators in Wisconsin, Ron is aware of the political climate and the notion of a skills gap, which he addressed by recounting a visit to WTC by the governor. "I heard (Governor Scott Walker) say, 'Well, manufacturing jobs are coming back from overseas,'" he explained. "That was kind of the sound bite—it sounds good." Ron was unimpressed, though. After Walker finished his speech and began to leave the room, Ron was able to position himself such that he met Walker face-to-face on his way out, where the two had a short exchange. "You realize you're missing a big part of that discussion, don't you?" he asked the governor. "The jobs that are coming back are not the $25–30 an hour union . . . put-square-peg-in-a-round-hole jobs. The jobs that are coming back are for our graduates to install the equipment that replaces five or ten of those [union jobs]." While the governor seemed to agree with Ron's point, he made no move to correct his statement, saying that it is hard to provide those types of details in a short speech. Ron, though, believes the sound bite rhetoric does something of a disservice to students' and the general public's understanding of these complex issues. "We cannot compete in the global world with that type of labor," he said, "when people overseas will do it for almost nothing."

Ultimately, Ron wonders whether the skills gap narrative—he referred to the whole debate as a "political process" and the skills gap as the "buzzword" of the year—really gets at the important issues. On the issue of wages, he asked, "Is it a skills gap, or is it a wage gap?" Once, he had a company owner come into class to talk up career opportunities, telling the students, "We'll start you at about $12 an hour," and Ron said that just about blew his mind. "I said, 'Excuse me? These students are coming here to learn a skill and you're going to pay them $12 when they can go to Menards and do that?'"[3] As the employer replied that $12 was the going rate locally, Ron thought to himself that something had to change. For some companies, he thought, the reason there's a skills gap is that they don't want to pay for the skills.

Ron's story is but one example of a counterargument to the skills gap narrative. To him and other critics (not only liberal arts advocates but also labor economists, instructors at technical colleges, and business owners), the situation is really not as simple as Wisconsin Manufacturers and Commerce (WMC), the Wisconsin Policy Research Institute (WPRI), and Governor Walker have made it out to be. Let's take a closer look at criticisms of the skills gap narrative, starting with what other research has shown and then subjecting each assumption outlined in chapter 2 to closer scrutiny.

THE SKILLS GAP AS A "ZOMBIE IDEA" AND A MYTH

One of the more outspoken critics of the skills gap, Peter Cappelli has written books, articles, and op-eds about the idea, often dismantling the narrative with a combination of data and logic. After reviewing a large body of labor market and educational data, Cappelli identified several flaws in the notion that poorly trained graduates were causing hiring problems and stifling economic growth.

First, employers were not necessarily troubled with applicants' technical skills. It was other skill sets that concerned them. He had seen it in the data since at least 1995, when he wrote how "surveys suggest that employers see the most important consideration in hiring and the biggest deficit among new workforce entrants as being the *attitudes concerning work* that they bring with them to their jobs."[4] If anything, this pointed to the "soft skills" of students, as well as the potential role of parenting, personality, and the broader culture, rather than to educational failures as the primary cause of hiring problems. Second, Cappelli saw structural unemployment as neither a supply nor a demand issue, but rather an over-education issue. He concluded, as have many others in the ensuing twenty years, that too many job applicants were simply *overqualified* for available jobs, which suggests that continued investments in education and skills (without attention to other features of the labor market) is simply not good policy. The problem is exacerbated when employers have a rapid uptick in job applicants, as they do during and after recessions. With so many applicants, employers can engage in what is known as "upskilling," or increasing educational requirements even while the job duties remain the same. Think of a bachelor's degree being required for a lab technician job where several years ago an associate's degree would have sufficed.

Ultimately, in Cappelli's view, the skills gap narrative is highly problematic because traditional academic research has been almost completely absent from the debate. For instance, many skills surveys, usually distributed by advocacy groups, are based on vaguely worded questions that make it difficult to ascertain which "skills" are really being investigated. Psychometric problems aside, perhaps most worrying is the fact that much of the information available on the skills gap is being disseminated by organizations with skin in the game. In Wisconsin, two illustrations of this concern are "The Road Ahead," authored by the former CEO of a manufacturing company, and "Be Bold 2," prepared by an industry-education collaborative, both of which strongly shaped higher education-related legislation in the state. These organizations, of course, are not neutral observers.

Other examples of questionable research—and logic—go back as far as the idea of the skills gap itself. Gordon Lafer, for instance, wrote about the Reagan administration's claims during the recession of 1981 and 1982 that jobs were available "for those with the talent and tenacity to work their way up," ignoring the minor detail that in many cities and regions well-paying jobs were nearly extinct.[5] Though anecdotal evidence and claims of skills gaps have usually outweighed traditional academic study in the debate, there are other scholars besides Cappelli who have taken on these topics.

Some critics, for example, disapprove of the aforementioned practice of equating educational attainment with skills, largely because most surveys fail to capture the actual competencies required on the job. In other words, we're really not sure how to measure "skills" since it's unclear, in scientifically precise terms, what they really are. James Bessen, an economist at Boston University School of Law, argues that as new technologies are introduced into the workplace, some skills become more in demand than others, and schools often are not able to teach these novel and emergent competencies. Consequently, survey developers are unable to rapidly, and with adequate validity and reliability, develop appropriate instruments.[6] With this phenomenon in mind, Bessen (like Cappelli) suggests that the actual disjuncture between employer needs and educational programming is due to the simple fact that many of the technological skills used in the workplace are too new to be integrated into formal educational curricula, and instead are often best learned on the job.

Besides Cappelli and Bessen, perhaps the most prominent skills gap skeptic is the economist and Nobel Prize winner Dr. Paul Krugman, who famously argued that, "It's a prime example of a zombie idea—an idea that should have been killed by evidence, but refuses to die."[7] Krugman observed that if the skills gap were in fact real, employers should be willing to pay more to attract skilled applicants to fill those positions. Rising wages, however, are not evident in the fields linked to the gap. In fact, the wages of highly educated Americans have not budged since the 1990s. For Krugman, the skills gap narrative persists in part because of shoddy research instruments, such as a phone survey where employers were asked, "Which of the following do you feel best describes the 'gap' in the US workforce skills gap?"[8] Ultimately, Krugman concludes that the story of a skills gap is deflecting attention away from income inequality and wage stagnation, and toward the deficiencies of workers and public education.

Professor Marc Levine of UW-Milwaukee arrived at a similar conclusion after extensive analyses of Milwaukee-area labor market data, ultimately stating that the skills gap was "a myth."[9] Levine specifically refuted the notion that there were more job openings than there were workers able to fill them, showing instead that workers were overqualified and subsequently underemployed in many supposedly high-demand occupations. Proving that Wisconsin wages in many of these positions had stagnated or even decreased, Levine identified the problem as "a sputtering job creation machine, in both the quantity and quality of jobs created."[10] Further drawing the ire of skills gap proponents, Levine took the fight directly to Tim Sullivan, using the former CEO's decision to move his company's facility to Texas in 2008 as a case study. Though Sullivan claimed his decision was forced by the lack of "qualified, factory-grade" welders in Wisconsin, Levine revealed that welders in Kilgore had a much lower educational attainment. Not only that, but they made substantially less than Milwaukee welders. "There's a skill disparity separating Kilgore and Milwaukee, all right," Levine wrote. "But it is decidedly in favor of Milwaukee."[11]

Of course, this is not to argue that all elements of the narrative are untrue—there appear to be shortages in specific occupations, certain competencies valued by employers (e.g., the ability to be a close and active listener) tend to be overlooked in many college classrooms, and as we will discuss later in this book, some recommendations made by skills gap advocates, such as improving career counseling, are consistent with our own conclusions. However, as is the case with many things in life, upon closer scrutiny, there is more to these truisms than initially meets the eye.

Key Ideas Negating the Skills Gap Meme

It is clear that implicated in this debate about jobs and education are also issues of wages and benefits, cultural norms, parenting, politics, and many other factors that collectively paint a rather complicated picture, and one that is far messier and more realistic than the skills gap narrative suggests. To further examine the claims made by skills gap proponents, we briefly revisit the key ideas driving the narrative from chapter 2, but this time with a more skeptical perspective based both on issues raised by our study respondents as well as data from other researchers.

Employers are having a difficult time finding skilled workers— but for many reasons beyond educational preparation

The biggest problem with the claim of hiring difficulties is the fact that the evidence clearly indicates that many factors contribute to this state of affairs—not just an applicant's educational preparation. In our own analysis of the WMC "listening session" data, we found that when asked about what other factors might be impeding hiring, nearly half of the respondents said the poor image of their industry was a problem in attracting qualified applicants. One-quarter said drugs and alcohol were another issue, while almost one-fifth said their company's location and low wages kept people away.[12] Thus, while this group of Wisconsin manufacturers felt that unqualified applicants were a problem in their efforts to develop a skilled workforce, they are among the first to admit that education is not the only issue.

Cappelli offers further insight into the issue of insufficient wages. "There is a difference between saying, 'We can't find anyone to hire,' and saying, 'We can't or don't want to pay the wages needed to hire,'" he observed. "Not being able or willing to pay the market price for talent does not constitute a shortage . . . at this point, it may be necessary to remind these employers how markets work."[13] Recall the frustration that Ron Petersen at Western Technical College had with the local employer talking up jobs paying only $12 an hour to his students. Based on such examples, Cappelli argues that the skills gap is in fact a human resources failure on the part of employers such that "the real culprits are the employers themselves."[14]

Cappelli also points out that many business owners deploy absurd hiring practices to vet applicants, such as running applications through screening software that looks for specific keywords, which results in self-created difficulties with hiring. One company apparently could not find a qualified engineer in an applicant pool of twenty-five thousand.[15] This phenomenon is what ManpowerGroup calls "looking for a 'purple squirrel'"; that is, companies are looking for a perfect candidate who simply doesn't exist.[16] Or, as Cappelli argues, they are viewing employees as though they are simply a part in a machine that needs replacing, which is a flawed way to think about hiring. Unlike machine parts, there is rarely a perfect one-to-one match between the specific requirements of a job and any one candidate.

Technical or "hard" skills aren't solely what industry needs and wants

While the next assumption underlying the skills gap is that technical training or "hard skills" are the primary issue, as we will review in chapter 5, it is clear that many employers are looking for much more than that. They want a combination of basic technical understanding, critical thinking and problem-solving abilities, and other competencies like a strong work ethic. As an HR professional at a large manufacturing company in Wausau, Wisconsin, put it: "What's funny is that when we talk to our development board or [the local technical college] and they talk about the skills gap, they're talking about teaching people to weld—the gap we see is that people can't hold a job and can't solve a problem."

The importance of nontechnical competencies is underscored by the fact that the skills most highly valued in high-wage, high-growth, high-demand occupations include active listening, speaking, reading comprehension, critical thinking, and writing. Economists from Georgetown's Center on Education and the Workforce (CEW) report that "96 percent of all occupations rank critical thinking as either very important or extremely important to that job," thereby underscoring the value of a competency that is almost completely overlooked in discussions about skills gaps and employer needs.[17]

Additionally, as previously noted, when skills are mentioned there is a lack of clarity regarding the specific type of skill being discussed. More commonly, skills are viewed as synonymous with occupations such as the skilled trades or truck driving. But occupations cannot be reduced to a single skill, particularly a technical competency or physical task. Thus, to become a welder it's not enough to learn just the technical aspects of how to weld; students also need to know about design and mathematics, develop critical thinking and monitoring skills, engage in complex problem solving, and understand scientific software. With the development of systems such as the Department of Labor's O*NET, an online occupational classification system, it is clear that multiple competencies are required for every occupation, and that it is misleading to make assumptions about the "skills" required for a particular job.[18] Indeed, in their projections about the types of skills, knowledge, and abilities required for the jobs of the future, Georgetown CEW analysts utilize O*NET data instead of assuming that skills and educational attainment are synonymous. The O*NET system, in capturing the competencies required for specific jobs in a much more finely grained manner, provides a far more nuanced account of "skills" than what is apparent through a credential (i.e., an associate's relative to a bachelor's degree), and belies the common notion that technical skills are the primary issue confronting the US educational system and economy.

The focus should be on a diversity of career pathways, not just middle-skill jobs

The data are consistent in pointing out that many jobs of the future will not require a four-year degree. Indeed, 29 million "middle-skill" jobs exist that don't require a four-year degree and pay middle-class wages (defined in this case as between $35,000 and $95,000 per year).[19] As Jeff Strohl, one of the lead researchers at the Georgetown CEW, said, "I would not suggest anyone look down their nose at the associate's degree."[20]

Yet what is often left unstated is that many of the jobs created are low-wage, low-skill positions that require a high school diploma or less. Indeed, the jobs with the largest projected growth in Wisconsin between 2012 and 2022 are retail salespersons (with an average hourly wage of $11.79), food preparation ($8.84), and cashiers ($9.32).[21] Furthermore, having a four-year degree or higher has an obvious and positive impact on earnings and employment status (see figure 3.1).

The evidence is clear that a four-year degree, on average, does pay off over the long term. Of the 6.6 million jobs created since 2010, only 2.9 million can be considered "good" jobs that pay over $53,000 and include

FIGURE 3.1   Earnings and unemployment rates by educational attainment

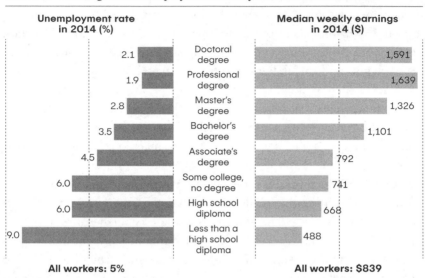

Source: US Department of Labor, Bureau of Labor Statistics, http://www.bls.gov/emp/ep_chart_001.htm.

Note: Data are for persons age 25 and over. Earnings are for full-time wage and salary workers.

benefits. Amazingly, only 100,000 of these "good" jobs were filled by individuals without a bachelor's degree.[22] Given these realities, as well as the fact that many companies admit that challenges in finding skilled labor are due to issues outside of the educational sector's control (like low wages, unattractive locations, and applicant drug problems), one questions Wisconsin policy makers' single-minded focus on "fixing" the skills gap by slashing funds to institutions providing four-year degrees and funneling high school students into the skilled trades. Even industries such as manufacturing require engineers with bachelor's or doctoral degrees, and biotechnology would likely not exist if it did not have a steady stream of bachelor's trained graduates working in the industry's labs.

Of course, this is not to say that students should be dissuaded from pursuing apprenticeships, certificates, or associate's degrees, nor that the only marker of success in the society is a four-year degree. Instead, we are advocates of the view that students should be provided with information about a diversity of career pathways including apprenticeships, professional credentials, and associate's and bachelor's degrees.

Educators' failure to prepare students for the workforce
is not the only cause of skills-related problems

Given the aforementioned unrealistic hiring practices, low wages, and other factors that contribute to employers' difficulty finding skilled workers, the notion that educators are the sole cause of hiring problems does not hold water. The idea that educators' failure to adequately prepare the workforce is causing slow jobs growth, advanced by Governor Scott Walker in late 2015 as a rationale for higher education reform, also does not pass muster with even casual economic observers, not to mention professional labor economists.[23] This is due to the simple fact that a panoply of factors, such as business cycles, demographic shifts, tax policies, government spending, and international trade and competition interact to shape global, national, and regional economies.

Still, educators should not be completely let off the hook. Critics of both K–12 and postsecondary education have long argued that school-based learning models need to shift from conveying decontextualized procedures and facts to grounding lessons in real-world problems, situations, and activities. This is because traditional modes of instruction that rely on a model of learning as the simple transmission of facts do not adequately cultivate students' abilities to transfer school-based learning into the real world.[24] This point lies at the heart of this book. In some ways, the fact that too many teachers still rely on these traditional views of learning lends credence to skills gap proponents' critiques of the educational sector. These criticisms, however, are not based on evidence from the learning sciences, and instead are grounded in the notion that the liberal arts and other non-STEM disciplines are inadequately attuned to the world of business. Such a contention not only lacks any basis in real evidence but, as we will discuss throughout this book, is also counterproductive to these very same business interests, not to mention students themselves and the society at large.

The solution is to support more programs—
both short- and long-term—in high-demand fields

It is undeniable that in some situations, real or perceived employer demands are so high that students swarm programs in both two- and four-year institutions, creating intense competition for seats and long waiting lists for entry. This is precisely what happened in the computer science department at UW-Madison, where enrollment increased 94 percent from 2010 to 2015 (from 2,400 to 4,650 students). This led to a wait list of over 900 students, which resulted in department administrators scrambling to create new sections of popular courses. Why the demand? Morgan Kemp, a sophomore majoring in biomedical engineering, said, "coding is pretty much a requirement for any job or internship," and department chair Mark Hill said that "any educated person in the twenty-first century should probably have done a little coding," a sentiment echoed by many students.[25]

In such cases where student demand is high, which is also evident in nursing programs across the country, it seems an obvious course of action to create new programs or expand existing ones. Yet the demand is clearly not only at the two-year college level, but also at four-year institutions like UW-Madison. Unfortunately, Wisconsin policy makers are primarily advocating for new programs in technical colleges, or even shorter-term programs operated by businesses themselves; they've ignored those in the UW System, where budget cuts at UW-Madison initially led the computer science department to enact a hiring freeze, ameliorated only by a $7 million gift from Milwaukee philanthropists.[26]

Besides this odd preferential treatment, however, is the fact that the longer a program, the more time a student has to acquire new technical skills, nontechnical competencies such as critical thinking, and certain habits of mind that are associated with a craft or a trade, not unlike traditional apprenticeships. Certainly, downsides of four-year programs include costs to the student and the fact that a graduate isn't available to the labor market for four years. The difference between an education obtained in a two- or four-year degree program and the knowledge gained from a six-week training program, however, can be substantial, impacting the long-term success of students in their careers.

The focus of change should be on multiple parties, not just educators

While the notion that educators should be responsible for "fixing" the skills gap is a fundamental idea among skills gap advocates, it takes but a moment of reflection to recognize that multiple parties are involved in raising, educating, and training students. But public education is often singled out as a cause for many of society's ills, and serves as an easy scapegoat upon which to hang the many challenges facing the labor market. Some of this can be attributed to what political scientist Kathy Cramer calls "the politics of resentment," which manifested in Wisconsin through rural voters' support of Governor Walker, a political figure who harnessed a widespread view that public employees were overpaid, underworked elitists to advance his agenda.[27] Given these views among segments of the electorate, public higher education is easily tagged as *the* culprit for sluggish job growth, lower-than-expected GDP, and more.

Regardless of its origins, one often-overlooked aspect of the contention that only education must change is that it implies a "transfer of responsibility," in both fiscal and conceptual terms, from the business sector to public higher education for workforce development, which Cappelli argues "would be profound in its implications."[28] Such a shift, Cappelli warns, could result in public monies being invested in workplace training that has traditionally been the responsibility of employers. Additionally, states could get involved in the career counseling game by steering students toward disciplines that are workforce-ready (e.g., STEM) and away from those that are not (e.g., arts and humanities). Encouraged to invest in "hot" occupations with no guarantee that those jobs will be available five years hence, this state of affairs would place considerable burdens on students and their families.

That said, Jim Morgan of WMC acknowledges that such a shift of responsibilities is not entirely desirable:

> I think everybody is starting to come to the realization that the world is just too complicated [for such a shift]. I can't expect any technical college or university to produce this perfect person who's going to walk into our office, know our system and data, and so on. I think the debate now becomes, do you [the employer] expect 80 percent? 60 percent? 50 percent [to be prepared by educators]? I mean, how much obligation do you [the educator] have? And employers, the very successful manufacturers, are the ones who figured out the job training stuff thirty years ago. And so we've got to have a continuous learning environment around here to figure this out.

Unfortunately, this kind of nuanced perspective is uncommon in many arguments supporting the skills gap and analyses about what is wrong with public higher education.

Indeed, ManpowerGroup concludes that employers are simply not holding up their end of the bargain. Only one out of five employers is taking active steps to deal with worker shortages such as cultivating existing human resources via training and professional development. In our own study, we found that only 12 percent of the companies we visited offered their employees any sort of formal training or professional development, whether tuition reimbursement for night school or a weekend course on the latest technology. Far more common were the 41 percent who instituted what one business owner called the "follow George" model, which entailed new hires shadowing more experienced employees for several weeks or even months to learn the ropes. While this time-honored approach has its merits, without companies offering employees formal learning opportunities throughout their tenure, it is hard to imagine Jim Morgan's "continuous learning environment" being cultivated anytime soon.[29] In other words, industry needs to be more proactive in dealing with the problem of skills development.

But beyond lack of training, something else was going on within the businesses that we visited that raised questions about the skills gap narrative, especially the idea that hiring challenges are solely due to applicants' poor skills and educational preparation. As Peter Cappelli noticed, it had a lot to do with how HR directors and CEOs were thinking about the hiring process itself.

PROBLEMATIZING THE HIRING PROCESS: SEEKING APPLICANTS WHO "FIT" THE WORKPLACE CULTURE

One of the major findings of our study was that business owners and HR managers were using a hiring process that was not a simple evaluation of an applicant's technical skills or academic credentials. According to the skills gap narrative, where the solution is merely to align educational programming to meet employer needs, hiring is a rarely discussed but implicitly unproblematic matter of simply producing graduates in high-demand fields. The assumption is that once these graduates are produced, companies will snap them up. But this is a fiction that obscures far more complicated and potentially problematic truths.

Researchers in management and administrative science have long known that employers hire not only on the basis of technical skills as represented by a degree or credential, but also on the degree of "person-organization fit," where the applicant's values and personality ideally align with what employers identify as their organization's values and characteristics.[30] Supporting this appraoch, the evidence indicates that a close fit is desirable because it leads to a higher likelihood of accepted job offers, increased job satisfaction, and higher retention rates.[31]

Indeed, in our study we found employers' subjective attempts to find employees who fit the so-called culture of their organizations to be alive and well. For example, the senior recruitment specialist at a large biotechnology firm outside of Madison described the hiring process as follows: "We have a very long, intentional interview process" to find people who will "be a great fit in the culture," she explained. This means assessing whether the applicant has certain nontechnical aptitudes such as the "ability to . . . operate in the grey" and "the ability to have great communication skills and great customer service," and personal values constituting "team fit," "attitude fit," "hardworking," and "passion for the work we do."

Overall, more than three-quarters of the employers in our study said that seeking a cultural fit between job applicants and their companies factored into their hiring process. Many clearly stated that even if applicants are "absolutely perfect on paper," those who lack certain aptitudes or personality traits that "match" the company will not be offered a job. One manufacturing company, as their representative told us, even has "a list of behaviors and values that we feel make up our culture, and we interview for those," using personality tests and cultural questions (e.g. "mechanical" hobbies, love of motorcycles and guns, and so on). In these situations, hiring can be more about fitting into a particular crowd and less about technical skills.

The idea of cultural fit as a hiring criterion is being increasingly recognized in the sociological literature on hiring, but ours is the first study to examine this issue in the context of the skills gap argument.[32] This is important because in requiring applicants to meet a host of technical *and* nontechnical requirements for a position, a company can develop unrealistic screening criteria that very few people can meet as they hunt for the proverbial "purple squirrel."[33] The question then becomes, in the face of hiring problems, are companies willing to relax their exacting criteria in finding that one candidate with ideal technical skills who also fits the local culture?

More problematically, it is entirely possible that the process of screening for fit is not simply a matter of seeking a good match for the company, but instead a systematic way to exclude certain individuals and groups of individuals from the workplace. Whether or not someone on a hiring committee *explicitly* states preferences for applicants of a certain gender, race, sexual orientation, or lifestyle may matter very little, as research indicates that subtle, implicit biases for or against individuals who identify in certain ways can be equally influential.[34] By definition, when one is seeking members of one's own "culture," that means excluding those who are considered outsiders.

Of course, seeking a good match between job applicants and a company on the basis of "intangibles" is not new, nor is it problematic if companies are not introducing racial, gendered, or identity-related biases into the process. Recall the comments from manufacturing executives to WMC's Jim Morgan about seeking employees who had a short YOTF quotient (years off the farm) because being raised on a farm often indicated that a person had certain qualities, a certain character. Who could fault an employer, whether a diesel pump manufacturer or a dairy farmer, for seeking out potential employees who clearly understand the rigors of manual labor and are adept at solving problems on the fly? What makes this observation about YOTF so fascinating is the suggestion that simply growing up in a particular environment, and being exposed to certain values and beliefs, can imprint upon a person an identity and ethos regarding work that remains with them throughout adulthood. This idea, of course, is readily accepted by many, but its implications for the skills gap narrative and postsecondary policy and practice are considerable and underappreciated.

MILWAUKEE AREA TECHNICAL COLLEGE: ROLE MODELS, SOCIETY, AND SKILLS

Born and raised in Wisconsin, Tom Heraly (pronounced "Hurly") is an electronics instructor at Milwaukee Area Technical College (MATC). Set in the heart of the state's largest city, Tom's classroom is a hop, skip, and a jump from the city's urban center, a place where poverty, unemployment, and crime have taken their toll over the past few decades. It is a social and economic reality with which MATC instructors and leaders must constantly contend. It isn't just a matter of the wage stagnation that has plagued Wisconsin for years, but also an issue of whether young people have strong role models and opportunities when it comes to work itself.

When asked about the importance of people's personal background and upbringing, Tom thought for a moment: "It's tough to teach [people how to be] on time, it's tough to teach a student how important your appearance is," he said. "There is a big disconnect between our students that may be city-centered students, and the world of work where they're going to be—which might be out in the suburbs, it might be in manufacturing plants that still have the old-guard employees." He added, "To bridge that gap, it's very difficult." Asked about this culture gap, Tom spoke to the kinds of work-related dispositions he believed colleges might be too late to help instill. "A lot of my students may not have had parents or guardians who are working in manufacturing," he explained, and so "they never got that transfer of knowledge" related to how to act in a blue-collar industrial environment.

A similar sentiment was echoed by a colleague of Tom's who spends much of her time interacting with local business leaders and community groups in her job at MATC. The challenges of linking the mostly African American kids who grew up in inner-city Milwaukee with local businesses underscore for her the explicit role that race and class play in the skills gap debate: "The difference is, farm kids have seen their parents, and may have seen more than one generation, get up and go to work every day and demonstrate that work ethic. Our inner-city children may or may not have had fathers or grandfathers or uncles or brothers that for whatever reason don't get up every day and have a job to go to, or have had a terrible time in school." Besides highlighting the fact some kids may simply not have strong examples of 9–5 working parents as part of their "frame of reference," this respondent raises an important issue— that young African Americans often have a difficult time in school—as another element in young people's experiences that should be considered along with familial background and role models.

Despite widespread assumptions that these difficulties are due primarily (if not solely) to poverty or family conditions, evidence indicates that structural racism and inequitable school-based practices also explain the relatively lower graduation and higher suspension rates of African American students.[35] The ways that educators and other authority figures may differentially punish African American students, particularly males in urban schools, compared to their white counterparts cannot help but influence how young people construct their identities and sense of self.[36] This point is also being increasingly made in regard to the "readiness" movement, or the push for a "growth mind-set" and "grit" among minority youth as a way to improve their career and college readiness—"as if," educator Andre Perry notes, "teaching proper eye contact solves health disparities, police violence, and the unemployment crisis in inner cities."[37] A myopic focus on the soft skills of young people shifts attention away from the systemic problems facing many inner-city schools—such as poorly paid and trained teachers, underresourced programming, and crumbling school buildings—and squarely onto the value or worth of these children's characters.

While the experiences of young African American students should not be solely attributed to the presence or absence of role models, it is nevertheless true that one's familial context plays an important role in shaping one's identity and beliefs about what is possible, feasible, and desirable. The important point to be gleaned from the observations of Tom and his colleague at MATC is that through their life experiences—in school, work, family, place of worship—students will acquire certain dispositions or habits of mind that shape how they think about and address new challenges. In addition, the factors that contribute to these habits of mind are not only familial or community-based, but also extend to the broader context of politics, race, class, and power that shape the structure of the society in which we live, whether or not we care to admit it.

It quickly became clear to us in the course of our research that to unpack the complicated issues raised by the skills gap narrative, we would need to figure out how to talk about these complex and multifaceted influences on students' belief systems and habits. And, like generations of anthropologists and sociologists before us, we found a productive entry point into the discussion was through the concept of culture.

Culture Theory and Habits of Mind

Where Schooling Meets the World of Work

Man is an animal suspended in webs of significance he himself has spun, I take culture to be those webs, and the analysis of it to be therefore not an experimental science in search of law but an interpretive one in search of meaning.

—CLIFFORD GEERTZ[1]

THE CULTURAL UNDERPINNINGS OF THOUGHT AND WORK

In talking about culture, Tom Heraly of Milwaukee Area Technical College (MATC) told the story of Horicon's famed company John Deere, a longtime manufacturer of lawn care and agricultural equipment and a source of considerable Wisconsin Pride. "There is a John Deere ethic," Tom said. "The John Deere ethic is that if you come to a meeting on time, you are fifteen minutes late . . . so you arrive to that meeting fifteen minutes *early*."

As Tom described it, his students would continually need to show colleagues and superiors in new contexts that they had the determination, reliability, and wherewithal to pick up on local values and adjust their thinking and actions accordingly. "Understanding the old guard, and understanding what their ethic is . . . and being able to apply that," he said, was essential for his students, and a key to many of the issues facing business owners as they strove to find skilled, reliable employees.

Whether it is called an ethic or a frame of reference, the basic idea is that as people go through life, attending school, going to work, and hanging out with friends and family, they acquire habits along the way. We use the term *habits of mind* in this book to refer to the mental propensities that people have for solving problems, talking to people of other racial groups, or dressing for work—essentially, their ingrained modes of thinking and decision making. With repetition over the years, these habits of mind become second nature, part of the fabric of a person's identity and how they interact with the world. With sufficient repetition they even become ingrained in the body itself, as repeatedly activated patterns of interconnected events, beliefs, and actions become well-traveled neural networks in the brain. As the saying goes, "neurons that fire together, wire together."

When these ways of looking at and interacting in the world are shared by a group, such as professional mathematicians, Japanese fishermen, or Grateful Dead fans, the word *culture* is often used to describe their beliefs, values, and practices. The idea of culture has proven so powerful that it has become part of our popular vocabulary, and in academic circles, it has long fled the confines of its original discipline—cultural anthropology—to be adopted by business, sociology, education, and even medicine as a way to talk about the shared patterns of behavior and thinking that develop within groups of people.

But culture is a very complicated idea, with dozens of competing theories about its composition and role in society, and not a few problems associated with its use in scientific inquiry. As a result, before we advocate its adoption in discussing an already obtuse idea—the skills gap—it is worth exploring in greater depth precisely what culture is, and which of the various interpretations available is the most appropriate for talking about the John Deere ethic or the work-related values children in inner-city Milwaukee or rural Wisconsin dairy farms develop throughout their childhood and adolescence.

WHAT IS CULTURE?

The notion of culture originated in the field of cultural anthropology, where early researchers studied the diffusion of traits across different societies, such as kinship patterns, the presence of "cultural areas" where these traits could be linked to geographic boundaries, and the idea of cultural evolution. Interestingly, despite the history of early anthropologists' association (and in some cases, complicity) with colonialism and the subjugation of native populations, some anthropologists argued that the field's role was one of debunking stereotypes and enlightening society about the diversity of humankind. For example, Franz Boas, who is widely considered the father of US anthropology, spearheaded efforts in the early twentieth century to discredit the claims of some European anthropologists that Africans were an intellectually deficient race due to innate physiological characteristics.[2]

Another goal of early anthropologists was to derive comprehensive accounts of a cultural group. For example, British anthropologist Edward Tylor defined culture as "that whole which includes knowledge, beliefs, art, law, morals, customs, and any other capabilities and habits acquired by man as a member of society."[3] While some critiqued this widely cited view of culture for being too diffuse—a kitchen sink of cultural forms, if you will—many others saw this multifaceted account as essential for capturing the complexity of social life.

As the discipline evolved, a variety of theories emerged that claimed to explain different aspects of culture and its role in society. One of the more influential perspectives of the late twentieth century was symbolic anthropology, which focused on the study of cultural symbols and how groups interpret them, and whose champion was US anthropologist Clifford Geertz. Defining culture as "webs of significance" that humans have spun, Geertz argued we are enmeshed in these webs in our daily lives such that we barely notice them.[4] While Geertz famously rejected the cognitive interpretation of culture that began to emerge in the 1960s, he did elaborate a theory of mind that extended his cultural analysis to the individual. For Geertz, the mind was a "class of skills, propensities, capacities and tendencies" that acted as a "background which lies in wait and engages whatever comes its way."[5] A similar idea was expressed by Gregory Bateson, who considered these habits of thought to be "epistemological premises" that shaped our lives and identities.[6]

The relationship between individuals and the broader society has been a classic problem in the social sciences, evident in the long-standing division—formalized in the delineation of academic departments—between psychology on the one hand, and sociology on the other. Anthropologists generally aim for the middle ground between the focus on individuals that is the hallmark of psychological inquiry and the study of structural aspects of society writ large, which has traditionally been the province of sociology. In recent decades, the disciplines have cross-fertilizèd and influenced one another such that many scholars operate in the intersections between and among them. For instance, one topic that both anthropologists and sociologists address is *positionality*, or from whose perspective accounts of social life should be derived. As an object of study, culture can be viewed as "a thing" to identify and empirically study from a researcher's perspective (i.e., what I think your group is all about), or as a phenomena that is socially constructed and understandable only through an insider's view and experiences (i.e., what you and your friends report about the group). The former, *etic* view has come under particular fire in recent decades for limiting cultural accounts to the insights of a few privileged outsiders, who historically were white males doing ethnographic research among preindustrial tribal groups.[7]

Two additional critiques of culture theory are salient to our discussion about the skills gap narrative. The first is the criticism leveled at notions of culture that assume groups have a homogenous set of beliefs and practices that are uniformly shared among all group members. Applying such generalizations about culture to entire organizations is popular in the higher education literature, where entire universities can be viewed as having a "managerial" or a "collegial" culture.[8] The problem with these accounts is that complex organizations like John Deere or UW-Madison— much like any group of human beings—comprise smaller units, such as disciplines and departments, where unique habits, practices, and beliefs develop within subcultures.[9]

The second critique pertains to ideas about cultural change and evolution. As culture theory was adopted by the business world, many became enamored with the prospect of studying and then harnessing rapidly changing corporate cultures to become more efficient, effective, and profitable. However, it quickly became apparent that the field had overstated the abilities of management to change culture, as the deeply ingrained values and routines of companies large and small proved to be more resistant to change than previously thought. Additionally, questions were raised about whether management, regardless of their ability to unilaterally effect culture change, always has the best interests of organizational members in mind.[10]

More nuanced perspectives on cultural change are available from anthropologists such as Melville Herskovits, who posited that change can be externally foisted upon a group where new cultural forms (language, artifacts, ritual) can be assimilated into older forms. Alternatively, culture can evolve through a subtler process of internal change that he called the "absorption of intangibles," which could unfold with the passage of time, changes in technology, or an environment that leads to subtle alterations of existing forms.[11] Alfred Kroeber built on this idea, suggesting that older cultural phenomena gradually and continually evolve into new forms, particularly when there is resonance between elements of the old and new.[12]

So given the history of culture theory and the debates that have characterized its evolution in the twentieth century, what is the best way to think about culture in terms of the skills gap narrative?

A Focus on Socially Distributed Habits of Mind

Geertz's view that the mind is a classifying entity that "lies in wait and engages whatever comes its way" was remarkably prescient, as advances in cognitive science confirmed that the brain acts as a network of mental structures that shape how new stimuli are encoded, interpreted, and then acted upon. These structures, called *schemata*, act as selection devices that filter out new information, specify relationships among discrete elements, and translate "abstract worlds of social interaction and discourse" into meaningful information.[13] These schemata are acquired through repeated participation in our social and physical worlds, such that over time it becomes second nature to take your shoes off when entering a Japanese home or to look for traffic signals while driving on a busy urban interchange.

Individual schema for Japanese etiquette or driving are then connected to other schema, which in turn form larger models of the world such that they "represent objects or events and provide default assumptions about their characteristics (and) relationships."[14] Further, when individuals are faced with particular stimuli, a sequence of schemata and models will be triggered in what cognitive scientists call "connectionist" networks of neural activation. Depending on the nature of the initial stimuli or trigger, the subsequent models that are activated will vary. For instance, entering a Western home versus a Japanese home will trigger different behaviors for shoe removal, though this largely depends on whether or not the individual recognizes the situation.

While each of us is a unique individual, we share many of these schemata and models with others. When schemata are distributed among individuals in a group they are sometimes called *cultural models*.[15] For cognitive anthropologists, cultural models should not be thought of as fixed rules for behavior; in fact, often they are inconsistently applied, conflict with one another, and vary depending on the situations in which they are invoked. They also can change. Evidence about the changeability of the brain's neural networks, known as neuroplasticity, indicates that schemata can be modified to assimilate new information. The mental propensities we call *habits of mind* are similar to the idea of cultural models, in that they are ways of perceiving the world and acting within it that are shared among members of a group.

Consequently, we argue that culture isn't located in a single place, object, event, or mind. Seeking a specific location or vehicle for culture that can be isolated and frozen in time—whether it be a system of symbols or an elaborate ritual that allows one to declare, "Here it is, I found the company's culture!"—is a tempting but ultimately unsatisfying endeavor. Instead, shared meanings and values are evident in the dynamic interactions among people, places, groups, and things. While anthropology provides a rich conceptual language for exploring these relationships, it is to another field—relational sociology—that we turn for a fuller explication of these phenomena.

Field Theory and the Interplay of Agency, Culture, and Larger Social Structures

One common theme in the accounts of the educators and employers we spoke with was that people's beliefs and values are strongly linked to different social contexts—whether a dairy farm in La Crosse or a steel foundry in Oshkosh—and that context matters when it comes to success in the workforce. That is, individuals' success in their careers may ultimately be shaped not only by their educational credentials, but also the quality of their workplace mentoring, the economic and political context in which they work, the global business cycle, and so on. In other words, no single factor determines someone's fate, how they think or act, or even whether a company succeeds or fails.

Because human behavior can be shaped by an almost endless number of motivations and factors, bringing clarity to this kind of complexity has been a project of social scientists for quite some time. French sociologist Pierre Bourdieu was one of the most influential social theorists of the latter half of the twentieth century, and he developed a set of concepts with precisely these problems in mind. His three interrelated concepts—field, capital, and habitus—provide a nuanced way to talk about the dynamics among context, culture, and cognition. Bourdieu sometimes used his European readers' familiarity with soccer as a metaphorical tool to elucidate the kinds of "games," or the individual preferences and styles, subconscious actions, and competition, that social life involves. With sports as a metaphor for social action in mind, let's walk through the core concepts of Bourdieu's field theory, but using the Wisconsin-based example of Milwaukee Brewers baseball instead of soccer.

Field

The first concept in Bourdieu's theory is the field, or a bounded social space within which individuals and groups share common goals and purposes, and in which they are drawn toward one another in the pursuit of similar resources such as money or social connections.[16] Bourdieu saw social life as demarcated by an almost infinite number of such spheres— from the family to the French higher education system—in which individuals, groups, and even institutions might simultaneously be involved. The most important point to recognize about the field is that it is not an objective space where anything is possible, but instead is highly structured by those who hold power and prestige within it.

Baseball also takes place in a specific kind of field. Here, the players enter a physical field (i.e., the ball park), take part in agreed-upon actions, and compete with one another. For the Brewers, the field is Miller Park, named after the stadium's main sponsor, Miller Brewing Company, a Milwaukee institution dating back to the mid-1800s. But for the team, the field is not only a physical but also a social and cultural space, alive with traditions and particular ways of doing things. Furthermore, each field is itself connected closely to other fields, as Miller Park is closely linked in spirit and in fact with rival St. Louis Cardinals' Busch Stadium and Pittsburgh Pirates' PNC Park.[17] Regardless of the ball park, however, there are always three white bases, a home plate, and the foul and base lines marking the game's boundaries. These characteristics of the space orient the physical actions and interactions of players in similar ways.

This state of affairs has two implications for our broader discussion about skills and education. First is that changes in one or more fields in the system will likely affect many of the others, particularly if those changes emanate from the field with the most power (i.e., Major League Baseball's central office or the Wisconsin state government). Second, some of the subfields in the system are more connected or less connected to one another; for example, the MLB central office likely has close and frequent communications with the front offices of Major League teams, whereas it probably has much less contact with Miller Park's ground crew. Thus, changes enacted by power brokers within a tightly connected set of fields will have a ripple effect on the entire system, such as central-office changes to rules governing how players may slide into second base while breaking up a double play.

Capital

The next concept in Bourdieu's theoretical framework is capital, which can refer to money (i.e., economic capital), social connections (i.e., social capital), or skills and credentials that people in the field find particularly valuable or prestigious (i.e., cultural capital). Bourdieu, who argued that the unequal distribution of and competition over resources was a foundational part of social life, suggested that these three types of resources determine where someone is positioned within a given field.[18] Among the three forms of capital just outlined, the most important for our current discussion is cultural capital—or the types of skills, knowledge, and habits of mind that college graduates can use to gain rewards, recognition, and new positions.[19]

What exactly are these cultural resources? They can come in institutionally sanctioned forms, such as a degree or a credential, which can be used to impress someone at a dinner party or get an interview for a new job, or they can be skills, mannerisms, and aptitudes that one acquires from a boarding school, place of worship, or the family dairy farm. Bourdieu called this particular type of cultural capital an "embodied" form because over time it becomes a normal, habituated part of the way people think and act.

However, what one group deems valuable cultural capital, another group may find useless. The kind of capital that is highly valued on the baseball field, for instance, like being able to turn a double play from the second base position, is not as highly valued (or useful) in the boardroom of a *Fortune* 500 company. Similarly, being recruited by the world-famous New York Yankees would likely impress a young college pitcher more than getting a call from the manager of the Milwaukee Brewers.

Cultural capital is an important concept in our analysis because it replaces the term *skills*, which is stripped of context and brings to mind a singular aptitude like pitching a curveball or debugging computer code. Instead, Bourdieu's concept captures a more complex array of abilities and habits of mind that are acquired through participation in various groups and places, and differentially valued depending on the field of activity in which people find themselves.

Habitus

The final concept of Bourdieu's field theory is habitus, or what he considered "a matrix of lasting, transposable dispositions" that include one's knowledge, tastes, and perceptions.[20] In baseball, what players brings to the field is their habitus, as their current play is the product of deeply ingrained habits and skill sets that they have acquired through playing the game over the course of years with different coaches and teammates.

In Bourdieu's studies, the kinds of music, food, or art one appreciates, as well as the way one uses language, are all the result of socialization experiences that one carries from field to field in the form of the habitus. This mostly unconscious set of dispositions is acquired from years of experiences with different groups such as the family, one's elementary school, or online gaming communities. In particular, it is through various forms of instruction that individuals acquire many of their habits of mind, which are heard, practiced, and eventually internalized in the form of a person's cognitive schemata. This process also involves what sociologist Omar Lizardo calls the "intersection between the field and internalized dispositions," such that two structuring entities—the field of education and the cognitive structures of the student's schemata—intersect with each other.[21] What this essentially means is that our behaviors and actions are not due completely to "free will" or to the external, dominant influences of society, but rather a combination of how our mind works and the ways that the social world is structured around us.

PUTTING IT ALL TOGETHER: FIELD THEORY, HABITS OF MIND, AND THE SKILLS GAP

With this theoretical framework in mind, one begins to gain a more complex and nuanced perspective on the issues implicated in the skills gap narrative. Integrating field theory and the notion of habits of mind into a systems-oriented accounting of the relations among cognition, culture, and context provides a perspective that stands in stark contrast to the simplistic narrative that "the liberal arts causes employer hiring problems that lead to sluggish job growth."

Ultimately, we are advancing an account not of a world that operates in terms of linear, cause-and-effect relations between a small number of variables, but one that involves a large number of factors that are constantly interacting, sometimes in unpredictable ways. Think of a complex model tracking a tropical storm over the Atlantic Ocean that accounts for prevailing winds, air and ocean temperature, land topography, vegetation, and barometric pressure versus a model that looks only at the direction the wind is blowing. One will likely lead to more accurate accounts of the current situation and provide better projections than the other.

The first stage of our approach accounts for the fact that activity (e.g., teaching or hiring) is taking place on multiple levels—not at a single, monolithic level of "higher education" and "industry." At the broadest level we have multiple fields that are influencing these activities, including the global economy, the US higher education system comprising several thousand colleges and universities, and the Wisconsin state government. Then, at the middle or meso level there are subfields that operate within these larger fields, including the governor's office, state legislature, specific industrial sectors (e.g., manufacturing and biotechnology), business groups like Wisconsin Manufacturers and Commerce, and specific types of postsecondary institutions like technical colleges and research universities. Finally, at the micro level we have specific institutions like UW-Madison and MATC, companies such as Promega and John Deere, and even individual departments and units within these organizations. Each of these fields, in turn, can be connected to another, to a greater or lesser degree, by programs, policies, and social networks, all of which may influence relationships in particular fields.

Another critical insight offered by field theory is that none of these spaces are neutral, meaning that specific regulations, power dynamics, norms for acceptable behavior or prestige, and self-interested actors shape the "rules of the game" within a given sector, company, or state. For our current analysis of the skills gap, a particularly important aspect of this point is that within each field different forms of cultural capital are considered more valuable than others. For instance, within a biology classroom a teacher may highly value the technical ability to document experimental results in a lab book, whereas in an electrical repair classroom problem solving may be a valued competency. Similarly, management of one manufacturing company may consider computer programming, welding, and teamwork to be essential skill sets, whereas management in another may find that welding skills alone are enough to get a job. This perspective exposes the oversimplicity of a one-size-fits-all approach to understanding the relationship between education and the labor market. It also helps explain why workplace training is essential for companies hoping to ensure that their own local forms of valued cultural capital are cultivated in their employees over the long term.

The viewpoint tells us something about higher education as well. Students, who bring their own preexisting habitus to their college or university, are taught a certain set of skills, knowledge, and abilities—ideally including the habits of mind that will enable them to join a broader community of practice upon graduation (e.g., a democratic society or a biotechnology company). For instance, Janet Batzli, the Biocore director at the UW-Madison, taught her students skills that she knew professional biologists would value, such as technical communication and understanding of genetics. This process of internalization involves a commingling of school-based competencies with dispositions acquired from other fields and other experiences, ideally resulting in individuals who have changed in important ways by the time they walk across the stage and receive their diploma.

Ultimately, one of the most important insights that our approach provides for discussions of skills-related issues is that the competencies students acquire in the field of education will be "transported" by job seekers into another field—the labor market—where they hope that someone will value their newly acquired skill sets and offer them a job. The question is, will the habits of mind that they have acquired in school (the skills and aptitudes educators in their academic program consider important) be equally valued by HR directors and hiring committees? As we have discussed, in addition to screening applicants for the appropriate educational credentials or technical chops, many employers also carefully vet job candidates to determine whether they will fit the company's organizational culture. This practice, in all its subjectivity, introduces a profoundly cultural element into the hiring equation that brings applicants' habitus and related intangibles into play.

While these dynamics were apparent in many of the regions that we visited, they were perhaps most noticeable in the situation of Tim Wright, who helped create a new program in aerospace composites at Wisconsin Indianhead Technical College in response to an apparent demand in the labor market for students trained in this field.

The Aerospace Composites Program at WITC

The economic history of northwestern Wisconsin is fraught with ups and downs. Attracted by the idea of shipping on the Great Lakes and enticed by iron ore deposits in the north, mining businessmen built new settlements in the nineteenth century on land that would later become the city of Superior. After its founding in 1854, lumber mills, fur trading posts, flour mills, and grain elevators sprang up, and products were loaded onto barges that traveled to Detroit, Chicago, and even to the Atlantic Ocean via the St. Lawrence Seaway. But when the iron ore ran out and the steel industry collapsed, the region began a slow decline in terms of jobs and economic growth.

That is one reason why the growth of a new industry—aerospace —has been met with such excitement and optimism. While the area may not come to mind immediately as an aerospace hotbed like Seattle (where many Boeing aircraft are designed and built), many small cities like Topeka, Kansas, and Grand Forks, North Dakota, have become centers of small plane manufacturing. And so the first field we'll introduce, in terms of Bourdieu's field theory, is that of the aerospace industry.

One of the companies that was a major player in this field was Cirrus Aircraft Corporation. Founded in 1984 in the basement of a barn in rural Baraboo, Wisconsin, by brothers Alan and Dale Klapmeier, the company later moved to Duluth, Minnesota where it grew rapidly when its five-seat plane, the SR22, became the world's best-selling single-engine aircraft in 2004.[22] However, as part of an industry that was particularly susceptible to the vagaries of the business cycle, Cirrus laid off 8 percent of its workforce (one hundred workers) and switched to a three-day workweek in the aftermath of the 2008 recession.[23] The company never fully recovered and, after subsequent rounds of layoffs, was eventually sold to the Chinese government in 2011.[24]

But before Cirrus became the property of the People's Republic, Alan Klapmeier had left to start a new company called Kestrel Aircraft, and this is where the aerospace industry meets another field—Wisconsin politics. When Kestrel was faced with the decision about where to locate its manufacturing headquarters, Maine or Wisconsin, the Wisconsin government stepped in with a $4 million grant and the city of Superior contributed another $2.4 million in January 2012. The state money was provided through the newly created Wisconsin Economic Development Corporation—the public-private agency created by Governor Walker that replaced the state Department of Commerce per the recommendations of the first "Be Bold" report.[25] In return, Kestrel promised to create over six hundred new jobs, which would have been the single largest increase in jobs in the area since World War II.

However, a troubling fact emerged—there was a lack of workers in the area familiar with *composites*, industry shorthand for a type of material with high-strength fibers commonly used to build airplanes, surfboards, and other sports equipment. For an aerospace company like Kestrel, skills in composites are essential for workers who will design, build, and repair the bodies and wings of aircrafts such as the Kestrel 350. Thus, one form of cultural capital—technical skills with composite technologies—appeared to suddenly be in great demand, with six hundred positions requiring expertise in this area on the horizon. Wisconsin Indianhead Technical College (WITC) in Superior began working with Kestrel to create a new program when the plan to relocate to Superior was announced, and soon a partnership was born.

Soon thereafter, WITC and Kestrel sought and won a $602,400 grant from the Wisconsin Covenant Foundation to create an associate's degree program in composite technology from scratch—the first of its kind in the state. These grants are designed to support investment in new equipment, facilities, and curricula with strong input from industry. In fact, a press release proclaiming the award pointed out that the initiative's primary goal was job creation via educational programming: "Through real-world training, students will earn a meaningful degree, diploma, or certificate, leading to job placement in family-sustaining occupations."[26]

So now there are at least four fields involved in this unfolding drama: the aerospace industry with Kestrel as its primary (if not only) representative, the Wisconsin state government, higher education in the form of a two-year technical college, and a philanthropic foundation. And the rationale for these fields to interact was the perceived need for a specific type of cultural capital—technical expertise with composites. Those involved in the development of the new program scoured the nation for similar efforts, finding one at the Wichita Technical Institute in Wichita, Kansas. Taking that curriculum as a model, WITC administrators ran it past Kestrel's leadership and gained approval. Then, WITC went shopping for an instructor.

That instructor was Tim Wright, who took the grant funds and built a program from the ground up, designing a classroom that was modeled after the shop floor of an aerospace company so that students could learn in an authentic, real-world setting. Tim knew what these facilities looked like from his fourteen-plus years of experience working at Northwest Airlines and Cirrus as a composites technician, workplace trainer, and union representative, as well as his experience teaching in high school and community colleges. Tim brought a very unique perspective—the various habits of mind that he had acquired throughout his life and internalized into his habitus—to this new program.

Given considerable freedom in developing the program, Tim built it around an essential idea—that to properly prepare students for the working world he would not only train them in the technical aspects of composites, but also teach them to view the work as a craft where one's entire approach was marked by care, respect, and attention to detail. In other words, Tim's notion of valued cultural capital extends beyond technical skills to include key tenets of craftsmanship. This philosophy is enshrined in a simple sheet of paper given to his students on their first day of class, *Tim's Composite Commandments*, which Tim sees as a blueprint for success in the industry and his class. The commandments include the need to maintain a clean workspace, to not steal, and to exercise craftsmanship at all times. The leaflet is a guiding force of the course that speaks as much to moral and character development as it does to learning how to be a good composites technician. Actually, Tim thinks they're one and the same.

Although his course is not explicitly intended as a training program for Kestrel, regardless of the company's close involvement in the program from the start, Tim expressed reservations about the perception that he grooms his students for a single company and even a particular industry. He noted that: "While the focus is aerospace composites, primarily because our region is becoming quite a hotbed of the aerospace industry, I believe that I would be remiss if I did not try and show as many other applications for those skill sets as possible, because that word *composites* is an awful lot bigger than aerospace." In other words, Tim feels that students should leave his program with a variety of habits of mind—technical composites expertise, craftsmanship, and awareness of other industries—that collectively will serve them well in the long term, regardless of the vagaries of the business cycle. Specifically, Tim spoke of preparing students for jobs at other companies like Cirrus or even in other industries that rely on composite technologies, like sporting goods, especially given the cyclical nature of the aerospace industry and subsequent uncertainty about long-term employment.

The story of Tim and the WITC aerospace composites program brings field theory to life in several ways. First, the pressures and influence of certain fields, namely the aerospace industry and the state government, convinced people in the field of higher education to start a new program that would enroll hundreds of students who upon graduation would be able to acquire middle-class jobs in the Superior area. The resources provided by another field, philanthropy, really set things in motion, ostensibly giving educators a venue to cultivate a form of cultural capital in students valued by members of the aerospace field.

But a funny thing happened along the way. As the instructor brought his own unique habits of mind to bear on the program, he decided to cultivate not only his students' technical expertise in composites but also another set of skills and behaviors that he knew from experience were equally important. In focusing his teaching on technical expertise, craftsmanship, as well as character development, Tim has become aligned with yet another field that was mostly invisible to this point—the liberal arts tradition. But the near-silence of this field, which is much more vocal in four-year universities and in college towns like Madison, is not surprising. Indeed, by the time the aerospace program began, the economic field had achieved such a dominant status in Wisconsin that it virtually drowned out all other voices.

Clearly, the considerable issues surrounding education and jobs should not be viewed primarily (if not solely) in technical terms—problems to solve with more programs that cultivate technical competencies in high-demand fields. Instead, policy makers and pundits alike also need to be thinking about these topics in cultural terms, as habits of mind cultivated in classrooms and taken into the often-unpredictable labor market. In particular, given the cultural nature of teaching and hiring, an unanswered yet critical question is: What types of skills, knowledge, and abilities do educators and employers really value? Is there really such a disconnection between the two fields, as skills gap advocates repeatedly suggest?

Converging Views

Comparing What Employers and Educators Want

The illiterate of the 21st century will not be those who cannot read and write, but those who cannot learn, unlearn, and relearn.

—HERBERT GERJUOY[1]

CHANGES TO THE UW SYSTEM CHARTER AND WISCONSIN IDEA

In Wisconsin, the skills gap narrative has permeated the governor's office and both houses of the state legislature to the extent that the state government's higher education and workforce development policies are firmly grounded in it. That is, policy makers in the field of Wisconsin's government, which controls postsecondary policy in the state, have been staunch devotees of the simplistic version of a skills gap where higher education, particularly the liberal arts tradition, is fully and solely to blame for the state's economic problems. A central feature of Wisconsin's version of the skills gap narrative is the view that colleges and universities need to be operated more like private companies, freed from the bureaucratic stranglehold of rules like faculty tenure, so that administrators can retool their institutions to better meet workforce needs and spur economic development.

85

For instance, in the midst of his short-lived campaign for the 2016 Republican nomination for the presidency, Governor Scott Walker submitted a budget proposal for the 2015–2017 biennium that included a proposal to spin off the UW System as a separate entity from the state while also cutting $300 million from the system's budget. In response to grumblings from faculty and staff throughout the system, the governor said: "Maybe it's time for faculty and staff to start thinking about teaching more classes and doing more work, and this authority frees up the administration to make those sorts of requests."[2] While this response ruffled some feathers, it was nothing compared to the public firestorm that was about to be ignited. In the midst of the ongoing national debate about the purpose of higher education—job training or broad-based education— Governor Walker attempted to change the one-hundred-year-old mission statement of the UW System itself by replacing the words signifying the institution's objective—namely, "to search for truth" and "improve the human condition"—with the phrase "meet the state's workforce needs" (see figure 5.1).

Almost immediately, furious letters to the editor were published throughout the state, and elected officials' phones began ringing off the hook. "I'm nearly speechless," the chairman of the UW-Milwaukee

FIGURE 5.1   Excerpt from Governor Scott Walker's 2015–2017 budget revisions to the University of Wisconsin's mission

Section 1111. 36.01 (2) of the statutes is amended to read:

36.01 (2) The mission of the system is to develop human resources to meet the state's workforce needs, to discover and disseminate knowledge, to extend knowledge and its application beyond the boundaries of its campuses and to serve and stimulate society by developing develop in students heightened intellectual, cultural, and humane sensitivities, scientific, professional and technological expertise, and a sense of purpose. Inherent in this broad mission are methods of instruction, research, extended training and public service designed to educate people and improve the human condition. Basic to every purpose of the system is the search for truth.

Source: Tom Kertscher, "Despite Deliberate Actions, Scott Walker Calls Change to University Mission a 'Drafting Error,'" PolitiFact Wisconsin, http://www.politifact.com/wisconsin/statements/2015/feb/06/scott-walker/despite-deliberate-actions-scott-walker-calls-chan/.

faculty university committee said. "The budget cuts are one thing. This aims at the heart of the Wisconsin Idea and smashes it."[3]

Why the backlash? Because the mission statement was seen as synonymous with the Wisconsin Idea, one of the defining traditions of the state's higher education system. Put another way, it was a cultural model regarding the purpose of higher education as a public good that was widely shared among the state's residents—the notion that students, staff, and faculty in the UW System would be thinking not just about themselves but also about the general welfare of their neighbors and fellow citizens.

And now Governor Walker was altering the Wisconsin Idea without any consultation. When confronted by a journalist, he attributed the change to a "drafting error."[4] Unfortunately for the governor, it quickly became apparent that it most certainly was not a drafting error, and after an investigation this claim was given a "pants on fire" rating by PolitiFact Wisconsin.[5] Instead, the changes had been deliberately inserted by the governor's budget office, and UW System officials had expressed strong concerns about the language five days before the budget was introduced. In response, university officials were told in no uncertain terms that the changes would remain in the budget.

Though the backlash eventually forced a hasty retreat with regards to changing the UW System's mission statement, what might these actions tell us about the policy makers' real views on the purpose of higher education? Dr. David Vanness, an associate economics professor at the UW-Madison School of Medicine and Public Health, interpreted state actions as a philosophical statement "that universities should primarily exist to train the workforce, not to educate people; that research should have immediate practical implications for business; and that the university should be nimble and flexible to go where current workforce needs are and not necessarily invest in the long-term education of whole people."[6] If this was, regrettably, the sole guiding principle shaping the future of higher education in Wisconsin, it raised questions. What precisely were these workforce needs? That is, what forms of cultural capital did those in the business sector actually value, and were postsecondary educators really missing the mark? Luckily, having just come back from a field study where we'd interviewed almost 150 business owners and educators about these very issues, we were in a good position to answer these questions.

The Skills Valued by Employers

The first thing that we asked the CEOs and HR managers in our study was a free-list question. Originally developed for use in psychology, the free-list technique involves presenting a topic to people and asking them what comes to their mind first; respondents articulate those thoughts using single words or short phrases. In describing the exercise to interviewees, we used the example prompt of "Wisconsin," which could inspire responses such as "long winters," "Packers," "cheese," "Laverne & Shirley," or "Bo Ryan." For our question, we asked people to list the words that came to mind when they thought of the skills required for entry-level workers to succeed in their industry—biotechnology or manufacturing.

In our results, the salience statistic is the average percentage for how frequently a term was mentioned across respondents, while also accounting for the order of the term in each list. Thus, the higher the salience, the more frequently and quickly a term was mentioned by respondents (see table 5.1).[7]

Our findings were clear. When asked to imagine an "ideal" employee, employers envisioned a hardworking individual with technical training (knowledge as well as the capacity to apply it), solid problem-solving skills, and the ability to communicate well, work in a team, and continually learn new things. These are the habits of mind that many in Wisconsin's business community hope students are acquiring in college.

When presented with these findings in early talks about this study, some audience members' immediate reaction was essentially "Oh, they want 'hard' *and* 'soft' skills." This way of thinking about skill sets is extremely common in the media, among policy makers, and in the general public. But rarely, if ever, will these terms be used in academic research, and for good reason: not only are they are simply too ambiguous to be useful, but they also convey judgments about what competencies are important and what competencies are not. While it is difficult to know exactly what "soft" means when referring to skills, we can guess it means something lighter and less rigorous than "hard." (Indeed, an educator in a Paper Science and Engineering program at a four-year college said, "I don't refer to them as 'soft skills' because it implies that they're not as important.") An increasing amount of research even suggests that these so-called soft skills may be as important, if not more so, as technical training to one's success over the long run.[8]

TABLE 5.1 Most salient terms mentioned by employers regarding success in their field

		PARTICIPANT GROUP					
Total sample (n=115)		**All employers (n=66)**		**Manufacturing employers (n=59)**		**Biotechnology employers (n=7)**	
Term	*Salience*	*Term*	*Salience*	*Term*	*Salience*	*Term*	*Salience*
Technical ability	0.348	Work ethic	0.350	Work ethic	0.388	Experience	0.345
Work ethic	0.310	Technical ability	0.322	Technical ability	0.342	Lifelong learning	0.301
Technical knowledge	0.259	Technical knowledge	0.275	Technical knowledge	0.302	Technical ability	0.227
Problem solving	0.180	Lifelong learning	0.171	Lifelong learning	0.144	Communication	0.226
Communication	0.153	Problem solving	0.141	Problem solving	0.132	Problem solving	0.182
Teamwork	0.149	Communication	0.130	Adaptable	0.132	Work ethic	0.163
Lifelong learning	0.142	Adaptable	0.125	Interpersonal	0.112	Detail-oriented	0.153
Innovative	0.105	Self-motivated	0.115	Attitude	0.112	Self-motivated	0.150
Detail-oriented	0.101	Interpersonal	0.109	Teamwork	0.112	Background	0.149
Self-motivated	0.099	Teamwork	0.107	Communication	0.111	Technical knowledge	0.141
Adaptable	0.098	Experience	0.107	Self-motivated	0.108	Educational background	0.114

That said, we highlight two surprising things about our data. First, many employers emphasized the importance of people wanting to continually learn new things as their career progressed. Some called it "lifelong learning," while others talked about the "aptitude to learn." Manufacturers, for whom technology and production processes were rapidly changing, especially valued this trait in their staff. One company that took short-term contract work, for example, had to change machinery, personnel, and procedures every few months, which meant employees had to learn new processes for making different automotive parts on a regular basis. Back in 1990 Anthony Carnevale and colleagues had considered this ability—learning how to learn—to be absolutely "foundational," and our data and evidence from the learning sciences support that view.[9] Unfortunately, in the ensuing twenty-five years, workforce and skills gap discussions have overlooked this critical competency.

Second, we were told repeatedly about the importance of work ethic, which turned out to be a slippery term at best. Just as Jim Morgan of Wisconsin Manufacturers and Commerce heard in his listening sessions, we, too, heard employers talk about the *necessity* of having workers who were ready and willing to put in the hours to get the job done. Dependability was often key; one manufacturer, for instance, talked about it in terms of "the attitude of being to work on time, ready to work."

Sometimes work ethic was linked to generational norms, particularly the seeming inability of "young people" (which often translated to the so-called millennial generation) to understand that the working world demanded consistency, reliability, and continual effort. Again, a manufacturer spoke to this point. "It seems to be a work ethic issue," he said. "It may be a generational issue. I'm not sure, but we don't find the [nose to the] grindstone type out of the younger generation that we find out of the older generation." Some of these qualities are related to ideas of "persistence" or "grit" that are increasingly being used in character education in K–12 schools. Ultimately, their importance to workplace success is undeniable. As we mentioned while recounting the stories of Tom Heraly of Milwaukee Area Technical College and Tim Wright of Wisconsin Indianhead Technical College, what was fascinating to us was that work ethic also implicated a variety of forces beyond formal education, such as parenting, peer influences, community values and norms, and the mass media. Pierre Bourdieu would have agreed, noting that the habitus is shaped by the innumerable fields in which one grows up.

Still, what employers want and value is only half of the equation when it comes to skills. So we asked these same questions of the educators who were working in the public two- and four-year colleges and universities throughout Wisconsin, who were cultivating in their students the competencies that *they* felt were essential.

The Skills Valued by Postsecondary Educators

When asked about the competencies people need to succeed in their industry, an instructor of Industrial Maintenance Technology at a technical college unhesitatingly replied: "Hands-on, technical knowledge, sequencing, staying focused, communication, tools, timeliness, willingness, and a sense of achievement." Results from other educators' free-lists echoed this perspective, revealing that while some differences exist between employers and educators, they both generally agree upon the competencies that a person will need to succeed in the workplace (see table 5.2).

This might seem like a strange finding. After all, employers and educators inhabit fields that have their own unique rules and expectations—the former group is focused on the health and profitability of the company, while the latter prioritizes student learning and success. Thus, it would not be unreasonable to expect their free-list results to be dramatically different, much like one may expect an abstract painter from Manhattan and a rancher from rural Wyoming to have wildly divergent worldviews.

Still, if we look more closely, we notice some subtle differences in how employers and educators think about the competencies required for long-term success in their fields. For example, critical thinking was not as high on the list of employers' top skill sets as it was for educators, who placed it near the top. Critical thinking, remember, is often cited as the calling card of the liberal arts, where the ability of students to critically assess information, reason through a process of rational argumentation, and generally be sophisticated and original thinkers is often held up as a central goal. Thus, it was no surprise that the educators in our study listed critical thinking near the top, though it is worth noting that employers listed a close cousin of critical thinking—problem solving—high in their lists. In the next chapter we will explore the similarities among critical

TABLE 5.2 Most salient terms mentioned by educators regarding success in their field

	PARTICIPANT GROUP						
Total sample (n=115)		**All educators (n=49)**		**Two-year educators (n=26)**		**Four-year educators (n=23)**	
Term	*Salience*	*Term*	*Salience*	*Term*	*Salience*	*Term*	*Salience*
Technical ability	0.348	Technical ability	0.381	Technical ability	0.365	Technical ability	0.398
Work ethic	0.310	Work ethic	0.257	Problem solving	0.285	Technical knowledge	0.258
Technical knowledge	0.259	Technical knowledge	0.238	Work ethic	0.257	Work ethic	0.256
Problem solving	0.180	Problem solving	0.232	Teamwork	0.254	Innovative	0.199
Communication	0.153	Teamwork	0.204	Technical knowledge	0.221	Detail-oriented	0.179
Teamwork	0.149	Communication	0.183	Communication	0.221	Teamwork	0.148
Lifelong learning	0.142	Critical thinking	0.156	Critical thinking	0.181	Communication	0.141
Innovative	0.105	Innovative	0.154	Lifelong learning	0.118	Hands-on	0.130
Detail-oriented	0.101	Detail-oriented	0.145	Troubleshoot	0.117	Critical thinking	0.126
Self-motivated	0.099	Lifelong learning	0.103	Detail-oriented	0.115	Adaptable	0.098
Adaptable	0.098	Troubleshoot	0.099	Innovative	0.114	Self-motivated	0.088

thinking, problem solving, and troubleshooting, and how they all refer to a similar habit of mind that is highly valued in both fields.

Recall, too, that some skills gap proponents argue that educators are out of touch with the real needs of the working world, and that many programs offered by colleges and universities inadequately prepare students to get a job. While these assertions may have a grain of truth to them— elements of the educational system certainly can be improved to help students better prepare for life after graduation—the argument that educators in Wisconsin's colleges and universities do not understand what it takes to be successful in the workplace is inaccurate.

Furthermore, and perhaps most importantly, the dominant framing of the skills gap in Wisconsin—with its focus on technical expertise and corresponding assumption that the skills gap can be "corrected" simply through the creation of more vocationally oriented programs—is misleading. While technical ability and knowledge are certainly high on most of the free lists we analyzed, they are by no means the only skills considered valuable. In fact, both employers and educators often discussed the need for a variety of skills such as technical knowledge, habits of mind like problem solving, and social competencies like teamwork and communication as part of an integrated whole.

Jim Morgan, the WMC representative whose own focus group respondents told him about the value of a rural upbringing, came to much the same conclusion: Wisconsin needs college graduates who demonstrate technical expertise *and* a variety of other competencies. Manufacturing employers, in particular, believed that a strong work ethic, problem-solving abilities, technical skills, and competencies aquired from experiences like working on a farm, significantly increases a potential employee's value.

Still, despite these findings, WMC continues to advance the notion, popular among skills gap proponents, that liberal arts education is the primary cause of the state's economic and workforce-related ailments. The solution, they conclude, is a renewed focus on vocational training centered on technical aptitudes in STEM fields and the skilled trades. As our data show, this notion, unfortunately, ignores a more complex reality. Without courses and instructional techniques that also focus on critical thinking, collaboration, communication, and work ethic, the myopic focus on technical STEM training advocated by WMC and supported by the Wisconsin government will fall far short of meeting the long-term needs of employers in Wisconsin, not to mention the long-term needs of students and the general public.

While an avalanche of research, popular books, and policy analyses have trumpeted the importance of focusing on technical expertise as a "silver bullet" solution for the skills gap and economic growth over the last several years, the narrative has been debunked by years of research. Indeed, scholars across a number of disciplines have been examining how a more diverse range of knowledge, abilities, and aptitudes are required for success in school and work since the 1950s.

THE CONSENSUS GROWS: TWENTY-FIRST-CENTURY HABITS OF MIND ARE CRUCIAL

One of the earliest and most influential skills frameworks was advanced by economists Frank Levy and Richard Murnane in their 2005 book *The New Division of Labor: How Computers Are Creating the Next Job Market*. The book addresses concerns that technology is affecting the nature of work and skills needs across the entire labor market, but especially in sectors that can be easily replaced by automation, or robots. It is the potential of the "rise of the robots" to render current workers and educational programs obsolete that has fueled many concerns about twenty-first-century skills, and no accounting of skills-related issues would be complete without considering their findings and warnings for the future.[10]

Levy and Murnane discuss two primary competencies that will be necessary for human workers to compete with advanced technologies: *expert thinking*, or the cognitive ability to develop knowledge and use it to identify patterns and solve new kinds of problems, and *complex communication*, or the social skill to work with diverse colleagues, exchange and understand large amounts of complicated information, and cultivate trust and understanding. Both of these aptitudes, of course, were also considered by our study respondents to be essential for student success in the workplace.

Their argument was based in part on research they had conducted with economist David Autor in an effort to answer "what it is that computers do—or what it is that people do with computers—that causes educated workers to be relatively more in demand."[11] They found that computers substitute workers performing rule-based ("routine") tasks and complemented workers performing more analytical or creative ("nonroutine") tasks. Combined with the lower cost of computing hardware, these developments have resulted in an increased demand for those who are proficient at performing nonroutine tasks (see figure 5.2).

Another prominent voice in this line of inquiry is James Heckman, who has been conducting research on the development of skills, or what he refers to as *human flourishing*, at the University of Chicago. This research program involves scholars from economics, developmental psychology, and neuroscience who are collectively investigating educational

FIGURE 5.2   Trends in routine and nonroutine task input

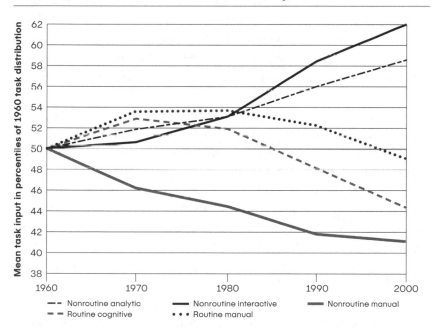

Source: David H. Autor, Frank Levy, and Richard J. Murnane, "The Skill Content of Recent Technological Change: An Empirical Exploration" (working paper no. 8337, National Bureau of Economic Research, 2001).

Note: Figure is constructed using Dictionary of Occupational Titles 1977 task measures by gender and occupation paired to employment data for 1960 and 1970 Census and 1980, 1990, and 1998 Current Population Survey (CPS) samples. Data are aggregated to 1,120 industry-gender-education cells by year and each cell is assigned a value corresponding to its rank in the 1960 distribution of task input (calculated across the 1,120, 1960 task cells). Plotted values depict the employment-weighted mean of each assigned percentile in the indicated year.

programs that best lead to greater health, earnings, and academic success over a person's lifetime. Essentially, Heckman and his colleagues study the very foundations of the skills gap, though his scholarship is rarely (if ever) cited by Wisconsin policy makers or other advocates of the skills gap narrative.[12]

In his research Heckman focuses on what many labor economists call *noncognitive* skills, or personal inter- and intrapersonal attributes such as perseverance, self-esteem, or empathy that are not typically measured by IQ and other achievement tests.[13] These tests instead measure *cognitive* abilities that center on what psychologists call *crystallized intelligence*, or specific, acquired knowledge.[14] While standardized tests are designed to capture this more general knowledge—long thought to predict important outcomes, such as success in school and the labor market—Heckman and colleagues found that although GED graduates scored similarly to high school graduates on the Armed Forces Qualifying Test (an exam focused on general knowledge, taking into account their measured ability and the years they spent in school), they earned lower wages than high school dropouts.

So, even though they were just as "smart" as their high school graduate counterparts, GED graduates suffered worse labor market outcomes than high school noncompleters. The main conclusion from Heckman and colleagues' work on GED students was that the credential sends a "mixed signal"—that the obtainer is smart, but is a "wiseguy" who lacks noncognitive skills. In a 2012 study summarizing much of the research on the topic, Heckman and Tim Kautz unequivocally stated that noncognitive skills "predict success in life; they causally produce that success," and that programs that focus on these competencies "have an important place in an effective portfolio of public policies."[15]

In 2012 the National Research Council (NRC) built on much of these efforts and published a report on skills-related issues called *Education for Life and Work*.[16] The report was the product of several years work by the Committee on Defining Deeper Learning and 21st Century Skills, led by James Pellegrino and Margaret Hilton, which was charged with no less than the following tasks:

- to define the key skills meant by terms such as "college and career readiness," "the new basic skills," and "twenty-first-century skills";

- to summarize the research findings regarding the importance of these skills for success in academic and workplace settings; and
- to identify how these skills can be taught and learned.

In a nutshell, the report describes how literature in cognitive psychology, education, and economics is all converging on two key ideas. First, a combination of skills, knowledge, and abilities is required for what the authors call *deeper learning*, or the internalization of not just the facts associated with biology or welding, but also their more complex principles and ways of solving problems. Second, the issue of *transfer* is critical. Transfer is a long-standing problem in the learning sciences and refers to a student's ability (or lack thereof) to apply the knowledge acquired in one setting (e.g., a Biology 101 lecture) to another setting (e.g., a biotechnology company). Since many modes of traditional schooling do not provide opportunities for students to practice transfer, the report highlights examples of how to design courses and classroom activities that facilitate both deeper learning and transfer using hands-on, problem-based activities.[17]

The report also proposes a taxonomy for "twenty-first-century competencies" that includes three overarching categories: cognitive skills (e.g., technical knowledge, problem solving), interpersonal skills (e.g., communication), and intrapersonal skills (e.g., work ethic). While the framework builds on many others offered by scholars and pundits alike, it has proven to be highly influential not only in the United States but around the world, largely because it is based on an exhaustive review of the scientific evidence available on what it takes to be successful in school, life, and work.[18]

These are but a handful of examples of researchers and pundits calling for the educational system to transform itself to pay more attention to these skill sets, whether they are called twenty-first-century competencies, inter- or intrapersonal competencies, or noncognitive skills. And the data we collected in Wisconsin reinforced this fact. Given the scientific consensus, the NRC, Heckman, and a number of other scholars have shifted their attention from studying which skills are essential for success in life and work, to thinking about how these competencies can best be cultivated in students from preschool through postsecondary education. This new focus has in turn led to another point of consensus: adequately cultivating these competencies in students takes time as well as a sophisticated approach to course design and instruction. Our study builds upon the efforts of these scholars by documenting specific instructional techniques that appear to be cultivating twenty-first-century habits of mind, as well as the fact that teaching and hiring are not simply technical problems to solve with a new curricula or screening tests, but instead are complex phenomena that implicate cultural and organizational issues. And one of the more surprising aspects of our fieldwork was the realization that what many employers were actually seeking in their employees were characteristics and habits of mind associated with a particular type of educational philosophy—that of the liberal arts.

EMPLOYERS WANT COMPETENCIES ASSOCIATED WITH THE LIBERAL ARTS

Recent headlines have said it all: "That 'Useless' Liberal Arts Degree Has Become Tech's Hottest Ticket," "Employers Want Broadly Educated New Hires, Survey Finds," and "Why Businesses Prefer a Liberal Arts Education."[19] As Michael Fromm, the CEO of an electrical manufacturing company in Pennsylvania, said, "We want task-oriented people who have disciplines in critical thinking. If someone's studied literature, they know people and have insight into themselves and customers. I find people that have a liberal arts background have a broader view of the world and will go farther in business."[20]

Of course, this is not to say that all business owners would prefer to see the labor market flooded with graduates in history, literature, and film studies, but it seems like many would not mind if students attended a postsecondary institution that required them to take some courses in these disciplines. Furthermore, recruiters from technology companies such as Epic Systems, Google, and Facebook (all red-hot companies rapidly growing in size and market value) say graduates from these fields are particularly attractive given their intellectual flexibility and ability to communicate complex ideas in verbal or written form.[21]

Yet many policy makers and employers, particularly the skills gap proponents who joke about the uselessness of French literature and philosophy, fail to recognize the value of a liberal arts education, whether it takes the form of a four-year bachelor's degree at UW-Madison or a two-year associate's degree at Madison College, both of which have "general education" requirements that touch upon disciplines as varied as English, art, and psychology.

To ensure that students acquire these varied skill sets, one instructor in manufacturing technologies at a technical college shared that his college has rigorous technical courses in four different areas of manufacturing, and also a "strong" general education program that includes two communications courses, two math courses, a human relations course, and two science courses—all of which he felt were essential to create a well-rounded student and employee.

Still, the assault on general education continues. When Turina Bakken became a dean at Madison College, one faculty team proposed essentially eliminating the general education requirements for a popular program. The goal was to accelerate students' time to the job market by focusing solely on critical technical skills in their field, trimming the program from a two-year associate's degree to a one-year degree. Turina replied to this team, "Do you guys realize what that would do to the integrity of the credential in the marketplace, given that what you're saying you're going to get rid of is exactly what employers are asking for?" The skills that would be lost once the general education courses were removed from the program, including communication and critical thinking, were competencies that English and history courses were designed to cultivate.

These competencies have been formalized at Madison College into "Core Workforce Skills" that are now a focus of each program's curriculum. This change was made not because of the arguments of a liberal arts defender, but because industry had spoken in multiple advisory board meetings about the dire need for these competencies—and the college had listened. Similarly, a respondent from Milwaukee Area Technical College observed, "Many companies will say, 'Your two-year and four-year degrees are so bloated, why would I need someone that needs English or history?' and they don't understand that that's going to make a really good employee. I don't argue, but it's happened where an employer comes back and says, 'You were right.'"

But the value of competencies such as critical thinking cannot be measured solely in economic terms. Thinkers from Thomas Jefferson to Charles Van Hise long acknowledged such habits of mind as essential ingredients for an informed and engaged citizenry in a representative democracy. Consequently, the growing emphasis on the economy and preparing students for the world of work as the raison d'être of higher education has its own critics. These voices have lamented the loss of focus on intellectual and moral development, the public good, and the broad-mindedness that Jefferson believed so important to a higher education.[22]

So it's clearly not as straightforward as skills gap proponents argue. The liberal arts, we argue, are not harming the economy. Instead, it may be the other way around—a "hyper-vocationalized" higher educational approach focusing solely on ensuring that students have a job upon graduation will ultimately inhibit the development of the nimble workforce required for the twenty-first-century economy.[23] The skills gap narrative ignores the fact that we must also think about the job the student will need five or ten years hence, and the types of industries and occupations that will exist in twenty years, which will rely on that student having developed a transferable set of durable competencies, both technical and nontechnical. Luckily, many educators are thinking about these issues and forging ahead with their work despite the constant barrage of critiques aimed at their profession.

The Distinction Between Training and Education Is Important

In the broader debates about skills, jobs, and higher education, a distinction is often made—one echoed by several of our study respondents—between *training* and *education*. Simply put, training is the direct instruction in how to perform a specific task such as pipetting, welding a T-joint, or operating Microsoft Word. It is often relatively brief, and it is unlikely to produce the full suite of twenty-first-century habits of mind that employers and educators desire. Why is this the case?

Because these habits of mind require a solid grounding in the underlying principles and concepts governing a particular task. That is, one must understand the principles of molecular biology regarding what is being pipetted, the different metals and techniques used in welding, or the grammar and compositional techniques to use when typing a document in Microsoft Word. What is often overlooked is the fact that developing this type of deep understanding in students requires an important ingredient that is often lacking in rapid training interventions: time. If the educational program involves opportunities for hands-on application and practice in different contexts, it increases the likelihood of transfer as well as the acquisition of additional competencies such as communication and teamwork. Technical skills acquired in a short-term training session, on the other hand, are less likely to be transferable or multidimensional because they are usually focused on the mastery of a single, discrete task in a limited number of situations.

Why does this distinction matter? Does it matter if states like Wisconsin focus more on rapid training for jobs instead of a longer-term, more intensive system of higher education? The answer is a definitive yes. While training has a role to play in filling short-term worker shortages, by quickly conveying new skills to adult learners, or amending an individual's skill sets with a quick bootcamp, it is a Band-Aid solution to the challenge of developing deeper learning and habits of mind that will serve students throughout their lives. As Tom Heraly said, "They're different terrains." He explained it with reference to welding. "For example, I can train you to weld that one part with this welder. It's not a hard task; it's only going to take me two weeks. But I can't educate you on the materials behind that and why you're doing it, 'cause that's the education, that takes critical thinking, the ability to evaluate and analyze." Tom noted that education beyond mere training in welding is critical, because too many people misconstrue the trade as a simple, anyone-can-do-it enterprise. In fact, Tom argued, welding is a complex craft that involves different types of welding, a variety of tools, manual dexterity, and problem-solving aptitudes that only get more refined with experience. These habits of mind are particularly important, Tom said, because when something goes wrong the welder needs to quickly synthesize information and actively problem-solve beyond merely seeing and knowing that a weld is bad. Ideally, the educated welder will understand the underlying causes of *how* or *why* the weld is bad instead of just recognizing the failure.

This is not to say, nor was Tom suggesting, that everyone needs to spend four years in college. In addition, not all training programs are created equally. Some last only two hours and focus on a single technical skill, while others may last several weeks and address a more comprehensive suite of competencies. What we and others are critiquing is the assumption that what the labor market needs is simple: technical skills that can easily and rapidly be acquired in a short-term training program.

Rather, we suggest that participating in well-designed, longer-term programs is time well spent. It allows instructors to get to know individual students, work with their strengths and weaknesses, and, most importantly, plan a sequence of courses that will lead to a deeper understanding of a field and its valued practices, habits of mind, and behavioral norms. Janet Batzli at UW-Madison described the "privilege" of having students for over two years at the college level because "they need a longer period of time to see how things start to come together . . . it takes time to develop intellectually and integrate knowledge and skills . . . it takes time to develop those skills and craft them to help you in your career pursuit."

And therein lies the rub. Adaptability is the coin of the realm in the workforce because workers have to adjust to products and processes that are in constant flux. If businesses rely only on workers trained in short-term programs, or the government begins to deemphasize longer-term programs in favor of bootcamps and certificates, the quick training focus simply will not create adaptable thinkers or worker. Instead, what is needed is an approach to education that has its origins in the craft guilds of medieval Europe, and one that is ironically favored by skills gap advocates like Governor Walker: apprenticeship.

Educators Should Approach Teaching and Apprenticeship as a Cultural Act

One of the most influential ideas in education research in the past twenty-five years is that of a *community of practice*—a group of professionals who share a trade or craft, communicate using the same technical language, and share habits of mind for how to perform tasks, engage in appropriate behaviors, and solve problems. As new members are introduced to the community, whether through a traditional apprenticeship as in the German system or via a freshman chemistry course at UW-Madison, they initially wait on the sidelines and watch experts at work, performing tasks that are designed specifically for beginners. It is only as they progress through their training that learners are gradually allowed to assume more responsibility, attempt more difficult problems, and take on the identity and ethos of the larger community.[24]

How did the idea of a traditional apprenticeship become intertwined with modern schooling? One of the scholars responsible for the integration of traditional apprenticeships models and contemporary cognitive psychology was the anthropologist Jean Lave. In her early research on apprenticeships in West Africa, Lave studied how Liberian tailors engaged in years-long apprenticeship training with their young students. In her 1977 paper, "Cognitive Consequences of Traditional Apprenticeship Training in West Africa," Lave asked whether formal schooling was the only way to acquire complex cognitive skills.[25] Clearly the answer was no, as Lave observed that the goal in traditional apprenticeships was to convey not only the technical proficiencies associated with the trade, but also other capabilities such as how to interact with customers or deal with particularly complex and unpredictable problems. Noting that many of these skills were acquired through watching and then copying a master craftsperson, Lave made the distinction between an *inductive* approach to teaching and learning (one relying more on modeling and then practicing real-world problems) and a more *deductive* approach in formal schooling (one relying primarily on verbal instruction and the transmission of context-independent material).[26]

Luckily, Lave discovered that immersive, authentic learning experiences teaching complex habits of mind could in fact be transferred to more formal, school-like settings. Learning scientists developed instructional techniques that rejected the common approach of lecturing about a topic for fifty minutes, and instead engaged students in hands-on activities that were structured so that the expert (i.e., the teacher) would gradually "fade out" his or her mentoring as learners acquired more and more experience. The takeaway here is that the apprenticeship model *is* powerful, it *does* take time, and aspects of it *can* be incorporated into the college classroom.[27]

So how might we cultivate twenty-first-century habits of mind in ways that are durable and encourage transfer to new situations, jobs, and tasks? We argue that these issues are far less about the type of institution in which teaching takes place—be it a two-year technical college or a four-year research university—and more about the kinds of instructional design and classroom teaching in which educators engage. Fortunately, there are many examples of this type of education throughout Wisconsin. Scott Cooper offers one of them.

EDUCATING WELL-ROUNDED PEOPLE
AT UW–LA CROSSE

Scott Cooper, a professor of biology at UW–La Crosse, teaches only about a mile away from Ron Petersen, but his working environment couldn't be more dissimilar.

First, changes in state policy have treated Petersen's Western Technical College and UW–La Crosse very differently. After an initial budget cut in Governor Walker's first term, WTC has been enjoying something of a renaissance in the eyes of policy makers and business leaders, who see its programs as a more efficient and straightforward way to get skilled workers into the labor market than through four-year universities.

UW–La Crosse has not fared as well, largely because the university is dealing with its share of over $500 million in budget cuts to the UW System since 2011.[28] For UW–La Crosse, that share was in the several millions between 2011 and 2014, while the latest budget enacted in 2015 has amounted to an additional $8 million cut that has affected teaching faculty, library subscriptions, equipment purchases, and student services, among other frontline activities. Though morale cannot be tallied in budget ledgers, it has been affected as well.

There are other differences between Ron Petersen and Scott Cooper's classes. Ron teaches mostly men in their twenties, thirties, and forties, many of whom have already spent a lot of time in the working world. Ron's students also get one-year technical degrees with no general education requirements. In contrast, Scott works with a mix of young men and women in an institution in which every student takes two years of general education credits—in everything from Arts and Communication Arts to Ethnic Studies—in order to graduate. Scott also has no employer advisory board, he is not particularly connected to businesses in the area, and his students, for the most part, were not far out of high school before enrolling at UW–La Crosse.

Where Ron's class is clearly linked to career pathways that lead to local and regional companies in electronic repair or manufacturing, the plans of Scott's students, like many students at UW–La Crosse, are often more ambiguous. Of the seniors in his Molecular Biology section we talked to during our study, a few thought they would pursue graduate school, some were entertaining careers in government or private industry, and others were still considering their options.

Scott's disconnection with local industry, what some might term a "misalignment" between higher education and the workforce, is not due to any ivory tower perception of academic infallibility or because he does not want to get his hands dirty. La Crosse, he pointed out, is a town of only about fifty thousand, and many graduates have to leave the area to find work. The number-one employer for UW–La Crosse graduates, he said, is the Mayo Clinic, in Rochester, Minnesota, which he had visited. Many others go to the Twin Cities, Chicago, or Madison, but either way, his relationship with La Crosse businesses is tangential at best to his students and his work, which focuses more on undergraduate research, hands-on lab training, and the intellectual calisthenics of biology.

Despite the polarization and budget cuts, he harbored no ill will for those who have made such a production of higher education's apparent impotence in recent years. He merely pointed to the fact that public universities like UW–La Crosse serve a number of interests, not just employers'. "I actually feel more beholden to the students to prepare them to do well," he said. "I think industry has a perfectly good say, just as anybody—I mean nonprofits, or medical schools, or anybody else—would. The flipside is they're really not paying for any of this." He added, "I don't know at what point public schools are no longer public. Once you get below 25 percent funding from the state, how much say should they have in it?"

In spite of the differences with Ron's experience at WTC, Scott looks at his role as an educator in much the same way Ron does. His job, he knows, is to teach the kind of content in molecular biology that is taught in colleges all over the country. But his job also entails teaching students the problem-solving, critical thinking, and adaptability skills that will allow them to succeed not only right out of college in the working world, but for the rest of their lives in jobs, relationships, and their personal lives.

And despite Scott's separation from local businesses, he purposefully runs his class like a biotechnology company so his students can tackle real-world problems, presenting the product of semester-long experiments to "clients," who are actually faculty colleagues. Scott also spearheads the campus undergraduate research programs, getting ideas for research from the local business, nonprofit, and policy-making community, which are then given to students who engage in their own research projects under the mentorship of a faculty member. These teaching strategies are not in answer to any compulsion he feels to align his teaching with workforce needs, but rather are the result of his belief that the kinds of skills acquired through practical, authentic scientific research experiences will prove valuable wherever his students end up. "What we want them to be able to do is, when they encounter something they've never seen before, kind of fall back on those fundamentals and figure it out," he concluded. "Those are probably the highest-order thinking skills . . . where they have to really sit down and think and say, 'Okay, I've never seen this before, but . . . '"

Scott also knows he is reaching the students near the end of a long road of socialization, where students have already been influenced by a number of different people and situations. "Get along with others and show up to class," he said, explaining the skills he thinks need to be taught early on. "Some of the stuff should have been instilled in them before they come to college," he continued, through "parents, and coaches, kids who went through sports. Some of the best students I've had are the ones that were on sports teams." Science, in his mind, should also be a workout, and he approaches his students and his instruction in ways similar to coaches who stress technical, social, and mental skills.

In telling us his stories about teaching in a small, public liberal arts institution in La Crosse, Wisconsin, Scott highlighted the complicated nature of the issues facing higher education in the early twenty-first century. The aftermath of the Great Recession of 2008 has made everyone aware of the need to think about employability and jobs, while the value of a broad-based education that cultivates a variety of skill sets is clear to many educators and business owners alike. Throw in the influence of parents, peers, and soccer coaches, and it has quickly become clear that a complex array of factors shapes students' career trajectories as they enroll in WTC or UW–La Crosse and then graduate into an uncertain world, making it clear that there is no easy answer to the issues raised by the skills gap.

But certainly a key aspect of preparing students so that they acquire twenty-first-century habits of mind is a well-designed and implemented educational program. Thus, in the next chapter we explore in depth some of the practices that Janet Batzli, Tim Wright, Scott Cooper, and others use in their daily work as educators, as well as the research literature behind many of these instructional techniques. Given what is known about how people learn and what competencies are necessary for success in school, life, and work, figuring out how to disseminate these practices has become a national priority.

Stories from the Field

Teaching Habits of Mind in the Postsecondary Classroom

The real process of education should be the process of learning to think through the application of real problems.

—JOHN DEWEY

The instructors we spoke with in our study strove to create learning opportunities where students mastered technical content hand-in-hand with other crucial competencies. This type of teaching was important because once in the "real" world, students will need to think critically *in a research lab*, or communicate *in a welding shop*—that is, nontechnical competencies will be embedded within specific discipline-based situations and tasks. As the authors of the NRC report on twenty-first-century competencies argue, "The notion of expertise is inextricably linked with subject-matter domains: experts must have expertise in something."[1] Thus, for our respondents and many researchers, nontechnical competencies are rooted in specific discipline-based environments, instead of standalone, generic skills that could be picked up in a workshop on critical thinking. This is why we use the term *habits of mind* in this book—as a broader description of ways of thinking, decision making, and being in the world that integrate knowledge of a particular domain (e.g., mathematics) with other skills and aptitudes.

As we traveled throughout the state of Wisconsin, we realized that many of the instructors we met were cultivating the kinds of habits of mind that business owners desired. Furthermore, some of these teachers were using instructional methods grounded in theories that we were familiar with from previous research on the learning sciences and STEM education, and their stories begged to be told. In this chapter we take a closer look at how these educators incorporated four of the most important habits of mind identified in our study—communication, teamwork, self-regulated learning, and critical thinking and problem solving—into their courses. We follow this up with a brief discussion of the broader context of instructional reform in higher education.

Some readers may ask, why do we focus on these habits of mind and not technical abilities or knowledge? Besides the fact that it would be hard for us to do justice to the core disciplinary knowledge and skills required in fields such as electrical repair or molecular biology, certain competencies are more transferable between and among occupations and industries than knowledge linked to a specific domain.[2] As a result, we limit our discussion to those habits of mind that should serve students well no matter what job they take, whether right out of college or twenty years after graduation. While you won't find instructors like the ones we profile in this chapter in every single classroom across the country, there are a number of them out there, and as you'll see, their daily work gives lie to the blanket assertion that the professoriate is out of touch with workforce needs, and that college isn't really worth it.

COMMUNICATION

Our conversations with educators and employers reiterated the fact that in the business world, both oral and written communication skills are critical for every employee, whether an hourly production worker or a high-level executive. Communication skills were deemed particularly valuable in fields like engineering that, in practice, required a considerable amount of working with others. Recalling the old joke about the difference between an introverted and extroverted engineer (the former stares at his shoes during conversation, while the latter stares at *your* shoes), the dearth of competencies in oral and written communication was a continuing concern for a number of employers we spoke with. And this even though the country's accrediting agency for undergraduate engineering programs (the Accreditation Board for Engineering and Technology, or ABET) had been requiring that programs teach communication skills for years.[3]

The focus on communication was apparent during our visit to a company that manufactures mobile hydraulic cranes. The company's president and cofounder, emphasizing the importance of speaking and listening skills, asserted that engineers couldn't lock themselves away and design fantastic machines. "What they need to do is be able to discuss during the design process, with manufacturing and sales and commercial people, what it is that's required of the product that they're designing," he said. Then, they need to "listen, understand, and make changes," something that he thought was both invaluable and sometimes missing from engineers working in the manufacturing industry. He is right, and probably would not be surprised to learn that, according to an analysis of the Georgetown Center on Education and the Workforce, five of the twelve most desired skills in the workplace are communicative in nature.[4]

Teaching these skills, however, is not easy. Research stresses the notion that each field has its own unique forms of written and oral communication, or what experts like Carolyn Miller call "genres," and that students must be immersed in specific disciplines in order to be socialized into these groups' unique professional cultures.[5] Developing skills in these fields therefore depends not on direct instruction in writing techniques or "spending a day talking about communication," but in allowing students to assimilate competencies using tools and forms closely linked to that discipline. The onus for developing writing skills should also not be placed on a single, massive paper or final project, as research shows that smaller, less grade-intensive assignments (e.g., asking students to respond to lectures, laboratory exercises, literature, or other texts via journals or reflective essays) buttress students' learning of that content as well as their technical writing.[6]

Many of the teachers we talked to used these and related tactics to develop their students' writing abilities. Timothy Paustian, Distinguished Faculty Associate in UW-Madison's Department of Bacteriology, developed his approach to writing instruction through his involvement in professional development activities for STEM faculty. Tim had won a grant in 2010 expressly to encourage communication and collaboration between students in his courses, and over time he had realized that an effective approach was to use written exercises to continuously push students in their learning through content analysis, synthesis of disparate ideas and datasets, and purposeful reflection on their own work. And this emphasis on writing continues throughout the semester. "In the first laboratories and the classes that we teach, we have them writing stuff," he said. "We have them taking their data and writing reports on it and that continues throughout." In his physiology laboratory, for example, students conduct eight lab-based experiments and then complete a series of writing-based assignments, including journaling, preparing results sections as they would appear in a scientific paper, and interpreting their analyses. Tim said he knows this decision to focus on writing is paying off, because "I've had dozens of students come back and say, 'I'm so glad. I found all the writing you made us do tiresome when we did it, but . . . I'm taking lessons from the stuff that you guys have taught us and use it all the time in my job.'"

While note taking may also appear to be an easy and commonsense practice that does not warrant much attention, it is often these seemingly simple and habituated tasks that inhibit learning and growth. Rather than simply acting as a scribe in the lecture hall and copying verbatim from slides or chalkboards, students can be taught to take notes in ways that actually aid their learning. The popular "Cornell method," for instance, is a five-step organization system for recording, winnowing, reciting, reflecting upon, and then periodically reviewing academic notes that can help students learn in multiple ways.[7] Teaching a deliberate approach to note taking can improve learning while also cultivating important skills that can be used in the workplace. UW–La Crosse's Scott Cooper sees note taking as a key part of the undergraduate research project he assigns students in his biology class. For Scott, as with many professional biologists, note taking is a basic component of good lab technique, so much so that he has students include their lab notes—with detailed, step-by-step recordings of their bench experiments—with the other materials they turn in at semester's end. His reasons for doing so are simple. "Someone's gonna use this after you leave," he tells students, meaning others will want to replicate the experiments after the students finish the work.

Because assiduous note taking is a fact of life in professional biotechnology and research labs. Scott concluded that "I think (that) adds a layer of reality and responsibility."

Oral communication skills were also crucial for many educators (and employers) we spoke with during our fieldwork. While many educators use oral presentations to cultivate their students' speaking skills, an increasing number are tweaking the traditional college presentation format—in which an individual or a small group dryly presents content-oriented material in front of the class—in favor of assignments that demand more from their students. Some educators require the use of PowerPoint slides, Prezi, PechaKucha, and other digital formats, while others assign presentations that closely follow workplace-oriented conventions, such as scientific poster presentations or product pitches to potential clients.

One example of this more demanding approach takes place in a biology course at UW-Milwaukee, where the instructor tailors presentation assignments to address the kinds of demands students will face outside the university. The communication of ideas and the defense of one's argument, she has concluded, are crucial in industry and other professional settings. Consequently, for her students' class presentations, each is required to choose an academic paper based on their interests in cell or molecular biology, to closely study the paper, and then to present its methods, findings, and conclusions to their classmates who have also read the piece. Following their presentation, the presenter stands for a defense of sorts, taking questions from their peers. "We want to kind of mimic question and answer sessions," the instructor told us, "so that they also can have a chance to practice how to ask a question and how to answer questions." The exercise not only socializes students into the unique give-and-take demanded in the discipline, but also teaches presenters and audience members alike to hone their listening skills and improve their abilities to frame good questions.

Other instructors also emphasized the role of active listening and demanded more from audience members than is often the case in a college classroom. The biology instructor at UW-Milwaukee, for example, grades both presenters and their classmates on their participation in oral presentations, as does Paul Whitaker, an associate professor of biology at the two-year UW–Marathon County. "As individual groups are presenting, all of the other students in the classroom don't get to take a nap," he said. "They have to evaluate . . . what was good about it, what was bad about it." Janet Batzli and her Biocore colleague Michelle Harris use a similar approach called "feedback presentations" specifically designed not only to have students put themselves and their ideas "out there" by doing a presentation, but to teach them how to think on their feet as they respond to audience questions. Calling these nongraded presentations "one of the most valuable learning activities students do," Janet explained that students are assigned a particular research topic and then given one week to review the relevant literature, generate a related research question, and design a laboratory experiment testing that research question. Students then present the literature review, research question, and experimental design to their classmates, who in turn ask questions, generate ideas, and more generally provide feedback. "It's not solely about the content," Janet said. "They're standing in front of their peers, in front of their instructors, and saying, 'Rip it apart. Tell us what we should do.'" The exercise creates a two-way street, she suggested, that benefits everyone. "They're really starting to hone this skill of not only asking for feedback, but giving it in a substantive way."

The overarching goal is for students to learn how to develop arguments, to critically examine one another's presented information, and to open themselves to constructive feedback, but in a low-stakes environment that helps students become comfortable with speaking in front of peers and giving one another constructive feedback. "We specifically make these presentations nongraded so we don't put [on] the pressure that they've always felt about saying the right thing or getting the right grade," Janet explained. "There's a trust and also a confidence that grows," she added, when students find out, "it's okay not to know the answer to everything, and to be able to think outside the box for a moment."

Several respondents in our study referred to these speaking and listening, physical presentation, résumé building, and writing abilities more broadly as "employability skills" that they felt should be integrated into their institution's programs. An administrator at a technical college put it bluntly when describing how he believes students should be taught certain communication skills. "How do you talk to others, how do you talk to your instructor?" he asked. He was sending graduates to advanced manufacturing companies, mostly in central Wisconsin, and his experience had shown him that even a graduate with all the technical know-how in the world could lose out on a job if they didn't know how to present themselves and their ideas to potential employers. For him, creating realistic mock-interview situations and coaching students on the social intricacies of appearance, demeanor, and articulation can make all the difference. "How do you shake hands correctly? Some students don't even realize that that makes a difference to several employers—that you know just how you shake their hand," he said. "How you make eye contact can be the difference in how you get a job or don't." These basic social skills are particularly important in light of the fact that many employers are seeking applicants who "fit" their organizational culture, much of which can become evident in these subtle, interpersonal exchanges.

In several cases we found that these competencies are taught using realistic scenarios that force students to actively think about how to present themselves in a variety of professional settings.[8] For instance, Professor Karyn Biasca, the director of UW–Stevens Point's Paper Science and Engineering program, spends class time teaching students how to compose a professional résumé to apply for work in the paper industry. When we spoke in September 2014, Karyn was in the midst of just such an assignment with her students. "By the end of the day tomorrow," she said, "they're supposed to all have their first drafts of their résumés turned in so that we can look at them and make sure that they're on the right track." The résumés that made the cut—that were not "full of grammatical and spelling errors . . . like text messages on paper," she said—would be included in the program's student résumé book and distributed to recruiters for placement in internships or entry-level positions. The same kinds of tasks are assigned in a capstone course in the biotechnology program at Madison College, where after a lesson on the proper techniques for drafting résumés and cover letters, students are asked to work on both for an imagined job in the biotech industry. "There's limitations to what we can accomplish," Lisa Seidman said, referring to how deeply they could cover communication skills in her courses. "But within those limitations, we work on them."

Speaking to the issue of what some perceive as the millennial generation's overly familiar communication habits, several instructors noted techniques they used to teach students proper e-mail etiquette. Kim Manner, a mechanical engineering instructor at UW-Madison, makes it a point to let students in his classes know when he feels their messages are unprofessional. "I have students who send me e-mails with a real casual attitude and addressing me by my first name, and yet I've never met them," he explained. "I said, 'Well, wait a minute, you got to be a professional, we have never met, and we are not on a first-name basis.'" While many would see the error of their ways with a simple reminder, Manner often makes sure they really get the message. "I usually send them an e-mail and ask them to rewrite it and send it to me again," he chuckled. "They may think it's stupid, but they learn something from it." UW-Madison Biocore instructors also emphasize the importance of e-mail etiquette and, as Janet explained, are often surprised that students need the lesson. "We say, you know, 'When you're writing an e-mail to a professor or your TA even, it would be a good idea to start with a salutation," Janet told us. "It's a professional thing. You know, it's better than, 'Hey.'"

TEAMWORK

Employers also repeatedly described the ability to work well with others as an essential (yet often problematic) aspect of their company's success. Judy Aspling, a plainspoken HR manager at a plastics manufacturer in Superior, put it simply. If you are going to work at the Charter manufacturing plant, she said, you have to show a basic aptitude usually expected of children. "They have to be able to get along with each other," she told us. "Play nice. Keep the sand in the box . . . they need to be able to collaborate."

Educators involved in the sciences also emphasized teamwork in research and design settings. Michelle Harris spoke of the value of collaboration *and* communication skills in the lab. "You're rarely working on your own," she said. "The ability to listen to others but also express your opinions respectfully, and also work together to come up with a best solution, is critical no matter what they [students] do." Scott Cooper underlined the point after referring to a poster he was working on with multiple authors. "You don't do anything all by yourself in the sciences," he remarked. To Scott's point, consider that the revolutionary finding of gravitational waves in early 2016 was reported in a paper authored by over one thousand researchers![9] Like communication skills, teamwork is considered so central to effective design work that ABET requires accredited engineering programs to demonstrate that their students can function on multidisciplinary teams before graduating.

Still, instruction in how to operate in teams is typically *not* integrated into college curricula. When it is, it usually takes the form of having students work in groups on projects, without instructors giving formal guidance on what makes teams work successfully and/or tailoring carefully crafted tasks to a group learning experience. Tim Tritch, a career services professional at UW–La Crosse, sees this as an opportunity for improvement. "I think there's been a big increase in the time I've been here in team projects," he observed. "What I'm not sure exists is instruction on how to do that well." Tim went on to make a point that researchers on teamwork are increasingly making: "You can require a group project for a class, but that's different from teaching them how to work effectively in a group."

While it may be tempting to think that teamwork is a simple matter, it is not always obvious to students. Several of our respondents described the need to explicitly discuss, prior to assigning team or group projects, what good team members are and how they behave. This is a technique that an applied engineering technical instructor in Wausau's Northcentral Technical College uses in his classroom. "I talk about team building, and . . . we start brainstorming what it is to be a successful team." After prompting students with the question of what makes teams effective, he leads the conversation toward particular practices, asking students to be as specific as possible: "They'll say something like, you know, 'One of the things that's required to be a successful team is to respect one another.' Then I'll ask them: 'Well, what does that mean? You know, specifically what does that mean . . . list specific things that indicate that you're respecting your teammates.'"

Farris Saifkani, an instructor in a Manufacturing Engineering program at UW-Stout, discussed how he assigns students to group projects regardless of personal dynamics "to accustom them [to the fact] that you don't have a choice . . . you have to be able to work with everybody." Farris, like other instructors who worked in industry before coming to teach, knows this from personal experience. "You can't just go to your manager [and] say, 'I can't work with this guy.'" Similarly, Peter Dettmer at Madison College told us he wants his students to face at least some level of conflict during group work. Without such tension, they will not learn how to overcome conflict in the future. He said he designs teams "specifically to have certain personalities . . . work with each other," as he put it, "knowing that there might be . . . at least some disagreement that they have to resolve."

In terms of assembling teams, many strategies go beyond allowing students to self-select into groups, which often results in students who know one another clustering into the same team. Ron Petersen, the electrical repair instructor at Western Technical College, told us that he uses "randomizing" software to assign students to different lab partners from class to class. "Rotating those students around, it's interesting to see how many times it works exactly the way I wanted it to," he grinned. "You get two very strong-willed leaders and they'll get paired up, and you'll have two coattail-riders that get paired up." Ron said the partnerships seem to continually spur not only interpersonal skills but also, and perhaps more importantly, harder work.

Another critical aspect of effectively cultivating teamwork skills suggested in the research literature is to carefully design tasks that require collaboration and support their transfer to novel settings. Ideally, a well-designed team project or assignment should actually *require* teamwork and interdependence in order to be completed, while also relating to the course's content so students can identify the exercise's larger purpose.[10]

First of all, assignments that involve more complex decision making or collaborative task performance reduce the chances of teams simply dividing up the workload among individual students and cobbling a final product together at the end.[11] There are mixed opinions regarding how strictly an assignment should be structured, but it's important to provide some loose parameters to guarantee the team members work together on an assignment while also setting well-defined expectations for students of what constitutes successful performance.[12] For example, several educators in our study described using *think-pair-share* activities that prompt students to solve a problem by pairing up with a classmate to discuss their ideas and then share their solution with the rest of the class. A variation of this widely used technique is to combine pairs to form a larger group and then engage in a similar process of brainstorming, discussing, and sharing solutions.[13]

Second, in order to encourage the transfer of both course content and teamwork competencies, these tasks and assignments should reflect authentic, real-world situations that the learner may encounter in the workplace, social situations, or other out-of-class venues. One educator, for instance, described how his welding classroom is set up to reflect an actual foundry, where teamwork is a natural and integral part of the daily work. "There are duties set up within the class," he said. "Somebody is in charge of putting the supplies away, of sweeping the floors . . . emptying the waste baskets, but also taking the scrap metal and making sure that it goes into the bins for recycling, and those duties are rotated." During each class period, students work through their welding lessons together, carrying out their maintenance and cleanup responsibilities under a newly assigned "boss" who is held responsible for others' conduct. While this kind of authenticity might be too elaborate to achieve in many classrooms, educators can experiment with structuring teams and tasks so that they provide realistic practice in discipline-specific tasks.

Yet despite the payoff that seems self-evident to many educators, it's no secret that some students simply don't enjoy teamwork. Often, this apprehension is the result of previous experiences working with peers who coattail-ride for a better grade with minimal effort, known in social psychology as *social loafing*. To deter such behavior, a professor at UW–La Crosse uses graded peer evaluations through the course of team projects. His physics students work in teams of three to complete lab and activity exams, and each team is required to submit one set of answers on which each member is graded. To ameliorate the fear of social loafing, his solution is a peer evaluation system. "They take the exam and (then) we give them a ballot," he explained. "Each one evaluates the other two on their contribution on the exam or the project . . . was this person an active participant in all the activities?" He said the ballots give him a good idea of the effort of individual group members. "If someone did not (do the) work, I do see the students will punish (that student)." If students understand going into the teamwork process that peer reviews will partly determine their grade, the increased accountability may result in higher motivation and greater contributions from everyone involved.

SELF-REGULATED LEARNING

Self-regulated learning, or the desire and ability to engage in a goal-directed, self-monitoring process of learning, is another highly valued skill that we heard consistently discussed by both employers and postsecondary educators.[14] Closely related to concepts like grit, conscientiousness, and work ethic, many educators see self-regulated learning as something of a "Holy Grail" for student success.[15] In the twenty-first century, with technology and the nature of work itself changing so quickly, this ability is widely viewed as essential for anyone hoping to build a successful career. It is so important, in fact, that labor economist Anthony Carnevale stated in a 1990 study of employers' skills needs that self-regulated learning, or what he called "learning how to learn," was *the* foundational skill upon which all others were based.[16]

Though they rarely mentioned the term *self-regulated learner*, employers also placed a particularly high value on the ability to continually learn and adapt. This sentiment was often called *trainability*, or the willingness and ability to learn new procedures and techniques on the job. A supervisor at Field Logic, a company in Superior that manufactures foam targets for archers, spoke about not necessarily looking to hire people with a specific skill set. Instead, he was "looking for someone that's willing to say, 'Oh yeah, that'd be great. I'd love to give that a try. I'm willing to learn; please teach me.'" The desire for such an employee was not solely about personality types he and others wanted on staff, but about the company's need to remain nimble in a business environment that often required new strategies and approaches. Judy Aspling underscored this point. "That's our business plan; that's how we work," she said, discussing her company's need for workers who could be trained in a number of different competencies after they were hired. Competitive pressures in the marketplace demanded nothing less.

Educators were cognizant of these dynamics as well. With reference to the biotechnology industry, for example, one career advisor at UW-Madison said that because the field evolves so rapidly, educators needed to "make sure that [students] have the ability to be active learners, continuous learners, [so that] they're seeking new information and new training all the time." Karyn Biasca of UW–Stevens Point agreed. "What we're after," she explained, "is that they . . . know how to learn, and then they can take their career in whatever direction they want to go." College education, she suggested, is just the beginning.

Given the importance of having students and employees who are willing, able, and prepared to continually learn throughout their academic and professional careers, the question turns to how, and where, people learn self-regulation skills. Do they come from parents? From places of worship, sports, or other afterschool activities? Can educators at the college level even make a dent after a student has reached adulthood? Setting aside for the moment the extent to which self-control, goal setting, and responsibility should or could be learned in the home, grade school, or various other cultural fields during childhood, the fact remains that it *is* possible to teach some aspect of work ethic, via self-regulatory competencies, in the college classroom.[17] According to educator Linda Nilson, teachers can always—no matter what has come before—have an impact on their students. "It really doesn't matter who or what may be at fault," she wrote. "We have these young people now."[18] Indeed, there exists considerable evidence from educators in the field as well as the research literature that it is possible to teach students how to improve their self-regulation skills.

As Nilson argues, becoming an effective learner entails a "sequenced series of practices that virtually any learner can understand and develop."[19] One of the more significant things an instructor can do to begin to foster students' self-regulative behaviors, and perhaps a sense of work ethic, is to create a classroom environment with high expectations and a low- to zero-tolerance policy for irresponsible behavior. Tim Wright, the aerospace composites instructor at Wisconsin Indianhead Technical College, is one of a number of instructors who uses such an approach. For him, building a serious, workplace-like learning climate begins on the very first day of class with a simple admonition. "You are in college," he tells the students. "You're an adult and you're expected to act in every way like an adult." Tim's opening day speech involves setting out important, non-negotiable rules such as his "ten commandments," as well as other expectations including "respect for the school community, peers, staff, instructors," which means not arriving late or leaving early, and not using cell phones in class.[20]

A biology instructor we spoke with also feels that students will not learn how to self-monitor without such rules enforcement in college, which is why self-regulation is built into the program. "We have a rule, which I enforce in my classes very rigidly: if they do not hand in everything that is due, even if they have an A on their test, they still do not pass the course," she said. "No employer is going to say, 'Well, I told you to do these three things, and you only did one, but that's okay!'"

Like many other educators we spoke to, she docks students for tardiness, absence, and late or sloppy assignments, saying that completing her program demands a strong sense of conscientiousness. "They need to come on time . . . their grades start to drop if they're not here, and at a certain point they won't pass their courses," she explained. "Most students have a good [work] ethic to make it through the program, and either they come in with it, or they change their mind partway through and decide they're going to make it."[21]

Self-regulated learning instruction is not just about curbing irresponsibility or a slack work ethic, though. It is also about setting clear, challenging, yet attainable, goals for students. For Tim Wright, this not only means expecting them to succeed if they truly put their mind and heart into the course, but also expecting them to treat their work with the care it deserves. This idea is represented in one of his commandments: "Thou shalt exercise the highest degree of craftsmanship in everything you do," it reads, "regardless of its ultimate significance." In explaining this particular tenet, he said that besides preparing students for the world of work, it also conveys his conviction that being disciplined, self-regulating, and motivated is essential because a true craftsperson should constantly strive for excellence. Or in Tim's translation: "Good enough isn't good enough." As he spoke about this idea of craftsmanship, it was clear that it plays a major role in his vision of education. "Attention to detail," he said, "that really goes hand-in-hand with craftsmanship." And over time and with practice, students will hopefully develop the attitude that goes with true craftsmanship.

For many of the educators we spoke to, cultivating self-regulation entails facilitating a cultural shift in how young people think about their own progression and development in their lives. Tom Klubertanz, a biology professor at UW–Rock County, spoke about some students' failure to recognize that by "sticking your neck out" and engaging in serious, difficult, time-consuming academic work, they can open new doors, get better jobs, and perhaps improve their lives. This is especially important in Tom's case, because UW–Rock County is a two-year transfer institution located in Janesville, a city that has had more than its fair share of bad luck in recent years. Closed factories and shuttered businesses are an all-too-constant sight in town, he noted, and have a way of quashing the kind of confidence successful pupils need to develop. Consequently, Tom feels that cultivating a sense of ownership over one's own learning and success is critically important for his students' success not only in school, but also in life. Self-regulated learning is not a silver-bullet solution, especially considering systemic issues such as stagnant local economies and structural racism, which can make it extremely difficult for even the most hard-working and enterprising young person to launch a career. Still, cultivating in college students this essential habit of mind can give them one more tool for adapting to a rapidly changing world.

CRITICAL THINKING AND PROBLEM SOLVING

To the general public and many educators, critical thinking centers on identifying and challenging one's assumptions, critically analyzing texts or historical events, constructing logical arguments, and so on. In our study, we found that more four-year educators spoke of critical thinking in these terms—as the cultivation of a habit of mind that is proficient in assessing complex situations and framing problems, evaluating multiple sources of information, and arguing for the best alternative. In this way, critical thinking is often thought of as an attitude, a habit of mind that is informed and always skeptical, and an approach "in which the thinker improves the quality of his or her thinking."[22] Put another way, critical thinking for many university instructors is about opening oneself up to the exploration of new ideas and examining problems from various perspectives to shed light on one's blind spots.[23]

In contrast, when critical thinking was discussed by employers or by educators in two-year technical colleges, it was referred to as a process of thinking pertaining to physical and technical problems instead of human affairs or verbal argumentation skills. This interpretation is consistent with the common notion of school-based problem solving, where students are confronted with tasks and situations that involve phenomena such as numbers or machinery—not themselves and their own thinking.

For instance, when Tom Heraly thinks of the one critical competency he needs to convey to the students in his automated systems class at Milwaukee Area Technical College, it is the ability to deal with ill-defined problems, because that is the nature of many tasks and projects that students will encounter in the world of work. In real factories, shops, or offices, problems are rarely neatly bounded and solvable with a single calculation. Instead, in the course of working on a project, people inevitably encounter unanticipated problems whose parameters and causes are unclear. Random events such as cost overruns will impact the work, and in some cases, something will go disastrously wrong with a piece of equipment or the work site. So Tom gives students ill-defined problems and tasks, such as class projects that have multiple solutions or even no solution, drawing inspiration from perhaps the most famous ill-defined task of them all: the Kobayashi Maru.

In the second *Star Trek* film, *The Wrath of Khan*, all aspiring Starfleet commanders were presented with the challenge to rescue a civilian ship that was under attack by the Klingons. Because the ship, the Kobayashi Maru, was in a Klingon Neutral Zone, a Starfleet ship entering the zone attempting a rescue would be interpreted as an act of war, thereby putting the Starfleet crew and ship in danger. But to ignore the plight of the civilian vessel would result in a death sentence for that crew. The test is designed to present a no-win situation to the students, and a test of their character and decision-making prowess. (Note: James T. Kirk cheated on the exam.)

Tom referred to this famous test when he described the types of tasks and problems he likes to present to his students. He presents them with a broken circuit board or a predicament where the solution is not readily obvious. Ideally, the students test various hypotheses, run into dead ends, and then rework potential solutions. "If there's a little pain in what you're doing, so you run into some problems and have to back up and try another route and back up and try another route . . . you remember that a lot of it is just thinking through what the procedure is, and that is critical thinking."

Along similar lines, David Jonassen spent much of his career at the University of Missouri studying how people solved ill-defined problems. Jonassen started out advocating for a constructivist approach to instructional design and technology use, where learners' active construction of their own knowledge and understanding is given primacy over the dominant mode of direct instruction. Later, this interest in constructivism led to problem solving because, as Jonassen put it, "it is probably the more constructivist form of learning . . . in order to learn to solve problems, learners must necessarily construct understanding of problem types and solution alternatives."[24] His later research on workplace problem solving shed important light on the disjuncture between formal education and the world of practice.[25]

Peter Dettmer at Madison College also spoke at length about a similar skill that he has heard many employers complain their job applicants lack: the ability to thoroughly, creatively, and critically work through a problem that has no simple solution. Known to Peter as *troubleshooting*, this competency is remarkably similar to both critical thinking and problem solving, and has become one of the central foci of his teaching and professional activities. Peter emphasized that troubleshooting "really isn't a hard skill" but instead a set of "mental tools and attitudes" that anyone can be trained to master. He teaches his students how to define problems, collect and analyze the information, determine if the information is sufficient, propose and test solutions, and finally make repairs once the cause of the problem is isolated. It's a habit of mind, Peter said, that is virtually guaranteed to get someone a job in manufacturing, and in his field, several of his students have been hired out of his classroom *before* they finished their coursework.

As evidence of its value in the business community, Peter shared how one of the local employers who sat on his program's advisory board was so impressed with his one-credit troubleshooting class that he asked Peter to come out to his facility to teach the course to maintenance mechanics, process technicians, and manufacturing engineers at his company. Peter condensed the course into a weeklong training for staff, which went so well that the company flew Peter to their out-of-state facility for another staff training.

What this employer recognized in Peter's course was what his instruction does *not* do. It does not focus on well-defined problems that can be found in under half an hour and which draw on a single, bounded type of knowledge. His instruction also does not focus on problems with no real-world constraints to consider, such as time or uncooperative colleagues—all features of how problem solving is usually taught in school. Certainly, facts and procedures are essential to fixing an electrical short in an industrial oven or updating a project with a client's new specifications, but what employers want and need from their employees is the ability to think through and address incipient and ill-defined situations.

In the world of practice that we encountered in our study, there certainly were instances where critical thinking, problem solving, and troubleshooting were used in different ways. For instance, the problem of making the numeric calculations required to recalibrate a laser cutter differs from that of estimating the number of parts to stockpile at the end of an assembly line, and both challenges are more technically oriented than the managerial problem of a supervisor needing to figure out how he should navigate a work group split by infighting. Despite their differences, however, underlying these tasks and situations—particularly because each is unpredictable and emergent—is a similar habit of mind. Indeed, in the literature we found that others also see a significant overlap between problem solving and critical thinking, such that "the skills used, especially in the application of logic, are quite similar and certainly complementary."[26] In any case, no matter what it is called, several of our study respondents referred to both critical thinking and problem solving as habits of mind or mental tools that they hoped *all* graduates entering the world of work would have acquired in college.

KEY ELEMENTS FOR TEACHING TWENTY-FIRST-CENTURY HABITS OF MIND: BACKWARD DESIGN AND ACTIVE LEARNING

Teaching twenty-first-century habits of mind, of course, is much easier said than done. It takes careful forethought and planning, and as anyone who has put together a course syllabus that didn't simply track the chapters in a textbook knows, this is a complex task. When the goal of cultivating teamwork or critical thinking skills in students is added to the equation, whether for two hundred freshmen in Chemistry 101 or fifteen second-year students in electrical repair, teachers' tasks become even more challenging. However, it is possible, and educators like Peter, Janet, Scott, and Tom have successfully embedded these competencies into their disciplinary, content-rich courses by drawing upon two key ideas that have strongly influenced postsecondary education since the 1990s: backward design and active learning.

Backward Design

Integrating twenty-first-century habits of mind into a course or academic program should be one of the central goals of educators, but how can it be done? For the instructional designer, the challenge comes in integrating skills like problem solving, oral and written communication, and teamwork into courses that are primarily focused on academic or technical content such as molecular biology or English composition.

Janet Batzli at UW-Madison recounted how she learned to effectively design a course with her post-doc mentor. Janet said, "We had a lot of fun teaching together, but [were asking] constantly, 'What is the goal? What do we want [students] to know and be able to do?'" Their thinking about curriculum and instruction revolved around their goals of what students should learn in the course. Scott Cooper at UW–La Crosse also referred to this strategy, known in educational circles as *backward design*.[27] When designing a course in this way, Scott said he "reverse-engineered" the course, starting with goals such as learning how to read a scientific paper. In many colleges and universities, identifying student learning goals is becoming a necessity to comply with institutional mandates or accreditation requirements. Whether or not it is required, however, the entire course planning process starts with the simple exercise Janet described, where the instructor asks, "What is the goal? What do we want students to know and be able to do?"

The onus of establishing these goals need not fall only on the educator's shoulders, as there are many parties who can and possibly should be involved in identifying them. As noted, the institution or accrediting agencies may have something to say about these goals, but one party should not be overlooked—representatives from the local community. For instance, Scott canvassed local businesses, nonprofit groups, and policy makers to identify pressing questions or issues that they thought should be answered.

The next step in the backward design process is identifying the types of evidence that would reliably indicate students' accomplishment of the desired goals. If a goal relates to students understanding effective team processes, what assessment would provide evidence on this point? On this issue authors Grant Wiggins and Jay McTighe counsel educators to not just rely on the standard midterm or final exam, but to also consider other forms of student work including lab notes, peer and self-evaluations, homework assignments, and participation in discussions (both online and in person).[28] Whatever the source of evidence, the important thing is to clearly link each assessment to a specific learning goal.

Next, Scott and Janet crafted activities that would help students reach these goals. Describing this approach as embedding "stealth learning objectives" within the course, Scott ensured that every learning activity, such as closely reading the methods sections of research articles, served the course's overarching goals.

This approach to instructional design is being widely adopted, largely due to increased pressures on educators to improve the quality of teaching and learning within the college classroom. In fact, it is this growing movement toward teaching reform that informs much of our thinking about the limitations of the skills gap narrative, and the overlooked role of teaching in cultivating twenty-first-century habits of mind.

Active Learning

One of the more prominent critiques of undergraduate education in recent years came from sociologists Richard Arum and Josipa Roksa in their 2011 book *Academically Adrift: Limited Learning on College Campuses*.[29] They found that 45 percent of college students did not demonstrate any learning gains in their first two years of college, and after four years, that level was an unimpressive 36 percent. In a summary of their findings, the authors responded to the question of how much students are learning in contemporary higher education with a devastating answer: "The answer for many undergraduates, we have concluded, is not much."[30]

The former president of Harvard University, Derek Bok, is also an outspoken critic of the traditional mode of instruction in US higher education, where faculty stand in front of students and lecture, with nary a pause for questioning or engaging with the audience. Bok singles out the lecture method as a teaching technique that is particularly ill suited for cultivating twenty-first-century competencies.[31] Critiques of the lecturing method have even made their way to the White House, where a 2012 report by the President's Council of Advisors on Science and Technology took the lecture method to task.[32]

In fact, much of the national movement in reforming how postsecondary faculty design and teach their courses has come from the STEM fields, with some science faculty themselves leading the charge. In his widely cited paper titled "Farewell, Lecture?" in the journal *Science*, Harvard physicist Eric Mazur observed that when he began his academic career he never asked himself how to best educate his students. Instead, Mazur noted, "I did what my teachers had done—I lectured." But after recognizing that his students were not learning basic concepts of physics from his brilliant lectures, he took a closer look at his teaching. Mazur observed that:

> The traditional approach to teaching reduces education to a transfer of information. Before the industrial revolution, when books were not yet mass commodities, the lecture method was the only way to transfer information from one generation to the next. However, education is so much more than just information transfer, especially in science. New information needs to be connected to preexisting knowledge in the student's mind. Students need to develop models to see how science works. Instead, my students were relying on rote memorization.[33]

This was a problem both of the instructor's mode of crafting learning opportunities (or the lack thereof) in the classroom, as well as students' habitual reliance on memorization. In response, Mazur began to "turn this traditional information-transfer model of education upside down." Instead of lecturing in each class, he started to "teach by questioning" and engaging students more directly in the learning process.[34]

Mazur was not alone in this quest to find a more effective way to teach in the college classroom than the "straight lecture." Researchers from many disciplines—including cognitive psychology, educational research, cognitive science, and human development—have been exploring how to best teach students for decades. These diverse fields are sometimes lumped together into the "learning sciences," and scholarship in this area spans research on the nature of children's problem-solving processes to neuroscience studies that explore the relationships among the brain, emotion, and learning. Based on extensive research in both K–12 and postsecondary classrooms, researchers have documented that certain teaching methods are more effective in cultivating what the National Research Council called *deeper learning*, or teaching for transfer.

These teaching methods are known as *active learning*, and they are grounded in the idea that instead of passively receiving information from a teacher via a didactic lecture, students actively engaged in constructing their own understanding of course material will learn better, retain more information, and be more adept at transferring their new understandings to different situations.[35] Given that interactive classroom activities such as small-group work exploring physics or engineering problems also require students to work in teams, communicate with one another, and actively problem-solve, many active learning techniques also cultivate critical thinking, communication, and teamwork skills. Hence, the federal government is pouring millions of dollars via the National Science Foundation and the Department of Education toward disseminating these methods across the country. It is not an overstatement to say that learning scientists have hit upon an approach to teaching that provides a road map for cultivating the types of cultural capital (the twenty-first-century habits of mind) that are valued by both educators and business owners. Consequently, we argue that instead of systematically defunding the higher education sector, it would be more productive to leverage our society's scarce resources to support postsecondary instructors' professional development and training in evidence-based instructional practices.

Challenges with the Widespread Adoption of Backward Design and Active Learning

As with most educational reforms, however, it is much easier to identify a "best practice" than it is to implement it on a wide scale. This has proven to be the case with efforts to promulgate active learning in the college and university classroom, where factors like four-hundred-person classes, a poorly paid and overworked teaching staff (especially non-tenure-track adjunct faculty), and change-resistant disciplinary and institutional cultures have stymied the vision of Derek Bok, Eric Mazur, and the federal government.

Further complicating matters is the fact that most postsecondary educators are not required to take formal courses in learning theory or instructional design throughout their training; thus, simply put, some do not know how to teach very well. To become a professor in many colleges and universities, one needs to demonstrate expertise in one's discipline, the idea being that a PhD and an illustrious research record are qualifications enough to stand in front of a room full of students.[36] Consequently, too often the course preparation process is a perfunctory matter of handing a new instructor a textbook or weathered notes and PowerPoint slides from the previous term.[37] In these cases, the course itself is essentially a week-by-week tour of the chapters of a textbook that need to be "covered"—this is especially true if the course is part of a required sequence.

Perhaps one of the biggest issues facing the reform of teaching in higher education, however, is not a matter of how many faculty are trained to use small-group work or problem-based learning techniques, but instead, how faculty think about the very nature of teaching and learning itself and their role in these processes as instructors. Indeed, evidence suggests that active learning methods can (and are) sometimes used to very poor effect, resulting in classroom experiences that may be just as ineffective as a fifty-minute PowerPoint lecture.[38] This implies that, as education writer Parker Palmer observes, "Good teaching cannot be reduced to technique; good teaching comes from the identity and integrity of the teacher." Unfortunately, the focus on professional identity and how educators think about themselves in relation to their students—not just in terms of the research versus teaching dynamic, but in terms of the self—is rarely heard amidst the clarion calls for change and charges that people who lecture are engaging in the "pedagogical equivalent of bloodletting."[39] Palmer is correct in his conclusions that, "In every class I teach, my ability to connect with my students, and to connect them with the subject, depends less on the methods I use than on the degree to which I know and trust my selfhood—and am willing to make it available and vulnerable in the service of learning."[40] The issue of vulnerability is also one raised by Bourdieu in his analyses of power dynamics within the classroom. While his focus was largely on the reproduction of social inequality through forces such as the structure of the educational system itself, he also paid close attention to the idea of "pedagogic authority," manifested in how the curriculum and classrooms are organized.[41] Often, the teacher maintains complete authority and dominance by controlling the pacing, organization, and techniques by which knowledge is conveyed in the classroom. Consequently, the aforementioned active learning techniques represent a challenge to this singular source of control in that they devolve a significant amount of control and power to students.[42]

Thus, the question of identity becomes a key issue in educational reform, as faculty must negotiate the institutional and disciplinary pressures to focus more on research and less on teaching, and also their own personal comfort level when it comes to standing in front of a classroom and no longer operating as the sole arbiter of knowledge.[43] It involves viewing the course not as a venue for providing instruction (the means), but instead as a site of producing student learning (the end).[44] To fully realize the vision of an active learning classroom requires faculty to not only learn these new techniques and slowly wean themselves off of the fifty-minute straight lecture, but also to make fundamental changes in how they think about the nature of teaching itself, shifting from a paradigm focused on instruction to one that emphasizes student learning instead.

Creating learning opportunities like those described here is neither easy nor simple. Various elements influence the ability of educators to design such environments: budgets, educators' professional training and experience, organizational leadership, students' aptitudes and interests, and the curriculum itself.

In the final chapters of this book, we explore each of these factors from a systemic perspective, considering which parts of the educational system *and* the business community are the most important for facilitating the effective instruction of teamwork, communication, self-regulated learning, problem solving, and critical thinking such that they are transferable to the workplace and other parts of students' lives. If we can figure out how to facilitate such teaching within the nation's colleges and universities, then students will be in an excellent position to acquire the habits of mind that will serve them well as they graduate and seek employment, meaning, and service in the twenty-first-century world.

Building a Skills Infrastructure

Leverage Points for Change

*It is not possible to improve quality without a thorough
understanding of how the system works.*

—H. WILLIAM DETTMER[1]

For those committed to ensuring that students graduate with twenty-first-century habits of mind as well as some expertise in a field that will lead them to a satisfying career, figuring out how to integrate those competencies into the design of a course and classroom activities is a top priority. This, of course, applies to all venues for learning that are now available for students, whether eighteen or forty years old, such as one-year technical diplomas, four-year bachelor's programs, distance and online courses, and workplace training, to name but a few. As the educational pathways available to students continue to proliferate, maintaining this focus on high-quality curriculum and instruction that truly facilitates student learning will be essential. But effecting change in how educators go about their daily work involves not just minor tweaks, but a wholesale transformation in how our society thinks about, organizes, and supports educational practice, but also how institutions structure the very nature of work for their employees. In fact, even if one could wave a magic wand and instill in the world's instructors the knowledge, capabilities, and drive to teach for transfer with a focus on technical content and twenty-first-century habits of mind, it might not be enough, because no educator operates in an institutional vacuum.[2]

Instead, classrooms are located within complex organizations like Milwaukee Area Technical College and the University of Wisconsin–Madison, each with its own unique policies, valued forms of cultural capital, workplace procedures, budgets, and leadership. Thinking back to our theoretical framework, also consider the broader fields of state and national politics, the thousands of colleges and universities that shape the field of US higher education, and even the global economy. Further complicating matters are the students themselves, who each walk into the classroom with different stages of preparation, expectations, and life experiences, thereby altering the already complex calculus of the instructional space.

We don't offer a silver-bullet answer to magically transform the college classroom into an active learning paradise, because there simply isn't one. Instead, looking at these issues from a systemic perspective, we argue there may be certain factors exerting an outsized influence on the rest of the system. Consider the well-known "butterfly effect" from chaos theory, where the flapping of a butterfly's wings in South America could conceivably affect the weather in Texas, based on the idea that a tiny change in the initial conditions of a complex system could have unpredictable and far-reaching impacts. This early work on weather patterns helped to set in motion a new paradigm that eventually reached fields as disparate as population health, engineering, logistics, and criminology, which ultimately led to the rejection of linear, input-output models for thinking about the world.[3]

While systems-oriented thinking has also influenced education, particularly those engaged in understanding why decades of reforms in K–12 education have borne only spotty fruit, the framework has had less of an impact on how higher education researchers think about and approach problems such as college completion, access and affordability, and instructional reform. Of course, the reliance on linear models also afflicts the thinkers behind the skills gap narrative—those leading organizations like Wisconsin Manufacturers and Commerce (WMC) and the Wisconsin Policy Research Institute (WPRI), as well as many politicians in the

US—which has led to an inaccurate, misleading, and in some cases, a purposeful misdiagnosis of this complex situation.

In the remainder of this book we describe the results of our systems-oriented analysis of the higher education–workforce fields in Wisconsin, and how it led us to identify six leverage points that are closely linked to the goal of seeing our nation's graduates enter the workforce and society at large with twenty-first-century habits of mind.

A CLOSER LOOK AT COMPLEX SYSTEMS AND WICKED PROBLEMS

Consider problems such as endemic poverty, climate change, global terrorism, inner-city food insecurity, or mysterious viral outbreaks. Do these have a single solution that a policy maker can simply legislate away, or are there individual programs that can be funded to address their root causes? For instance, some may look to mandating kindergarten for four-year-olds, harnessing solar power, invading countries that harbor terrorists, building more supermarkets in so-called food deserts, or inoculating entire populations to deal with these complicated problems. Others may ask, as systems researcher Barry Richmond once said, can we just "pull out a big stick and beat a nasty problem into submission?"[4] While some of these solutions may be on the right track, and some may be addressing underlying causes, looking only to unilateral solutions—or the big stick approach—is usually a mistake.

That is because issues like poverty and climate change are what some call "wicked problems," or a type of real-world problem that lacks clear and sufficient information about its origins and manifestations, involves multiple actors with sometimes conflicting goals, and is itself embedded in other, equally complicated situations and problems.[5] Wicked problems also tend to include situations where there are multiple variables at play. The problem of hunger and food insecurity, for instance, implicates not only the availability of grocery stores (and subsequently, fresh fruits and vegetables), but also generational differences in cooking habits, transportation systems, crime and poverty, food advertising that pushes unhealthy processed foods, and so on.[6]

In fact, this type of systems-oriented thinking is becoming more and more prevalent in research on health disparities, largely because the traditional focus on magic-bullet solutions has proven so ineffective.[7] Other disciplines taking up the mantle of systems thinking to tackle intractable, complex problems include sociology, where agent-based modeling is being used to understand issues as diverse as social identity and innovation diffusion, and business, which is being forced to account for global systems of finance, transportation, and capital.[8] Even the field of education, which some characterize as the poster child for magic-bullet solutions, has adopted frameworks for studying how and why reform efforts falter by examining the systemic relations among teacher cognition, sociocultural forces within schools, and policy dictates coming from district-level offices.[9] In each of these situations, one of the analyst's primary tasks is to adopt a systems-oriented mind-set wherein the problem solver first documents and defines all problem elements and interactions, and then acts to "identify in the complex causal network (where) the trouble really lies." Essentially, this is what Peter Dettmer is talking about when he teaches troubleshooting to local employers and students in his courses. He is seeking to cultivate a habit of mind that allows one to see systems in their entirety, that is open to possible solutions for (and sources of) the problem, and that utilizes all available information to logically and systematically arrive at an optimal solution.

Of course, this approach makes things immensely complicated, and doesn't lend itself to a repair manual, a single law, or a 140-character tweet. Unless we get past a magic-bullet, unilateral view of these problems, little progress will be made on the pressing social, economic, and environmental issues facing the world today or in the future.

The issues raised by the skills gap narrative represent such a wicked problem. In particular, the central question of how to cultivate twenty-first-century competencies in college students implicates a variety of factors from parents to teachers, labor markets to guidance counselors, K–12 schooling to state and national politics. The skills gap narrative frames this as a simple matter, something that can be addressed with the "big stick" of aligning education to workforce needs.

This framing of the issues, however, did not arise from an innocent misdiagnosis of the problem. After carefully analyzing the postsecondary legislative agenda in Wisconsin, the Walker administration's rhetoric, and the work being advanced by think tanks such as the WPRI regarding the managerialist reforms of university rules and the dangers of the liberal arts, we conclude that those advancing the skills gap narrative are in fact intentionally assigning blame for economic problems—from sluggish job growth to Bucyrus International's relocation to Texas—on a single entity: public educators.[10] By promoting this agenda, skills gap advocates are not only able to force institutions long thought to harbor left-wing activists and "political correctness" to abide by a more market-centered mission, but also, as some observers such as Peter Cappelli argue, to shift much of the cost of workforce training from the private to the public sector. The critiques of public higher education that the narrative portends have been so closely linked to a neoliberal agenda, both rhetorically and legislatively, that these conclusions are difficult to avoid.

It is important to note that we do not ascribe these intentions to the entire business community in Wisconsin. In fact, many of the business owners we interviewed for this study voiced a far more nuanced perspective on the higher education system and the state of the labor market and economy than many skills gap proponents. Instead of pinning the blame solely on liberal arts programs, many employers accounted for their roles in exacerbating hiring problems, expressing balanced opinions about issues ranging from the merits of four-year college degrees to the influence of global competition and outsourcing on their companies. Instead, the framing of the skills gap critiqued here has been advanced by a relatively small but influential group of analysts and policy makers who have interpreted business owners' struggles with the labor market through an exceedingly narrow lens.

Of course, not all of the diagnoses of the skills gap advocates are incorrect. For instance, WMC highlights the role that internship and apprenticeship programs can play in bridging the gap between school and work for many students, and more of these articulated career pathway programs certainly would be a welcome addition to the educational system. The problem is that these analyses are too selective in their approach, and highlight but a few aspects of the much more complicated, multifaceted system that comprises the relations between higher education and the labor market.

ROOT CAUSE ANALYSIS

Consequently, because a corrective to the skills gap idea is needed, we engaged in an analysis of higher education–workforce dynamics that views the situation in terms of a complex, closed-loop system with inter-dependencies between and among elements. Of course, this analysis was made more challenging by the facts that multiple, constantly evolving fields are in play, and that it includes cultural factors instead of focusing exclusively on technical or structural elements.

In conducting this analysis, we realized that simply mapping out the complexity of the system would be an interesting but mostly academic exercise. While such documentation could provide educational leaders and policy makers with a "road map" of sorts displaying the different career pathways available to college students and cross-field linkages (or lack thereof), we felt that because the system under consideration was being actively altered and manipulated with certain goals in mind, an analysis with *our version* of change in mind would be both viable and useful.

Inspiration for next steps came from two sources. First, the ideas of systems theorist Robert Axelrod rang true, in his notion of "harnessing complexity," where analysts use their understanding of system's complexity to deliberately and strategically change specific components of that system. The aforementioned use of systems thinking to identify key leverage points for change in educational systems also came to mind, as a way to illuminate those policies, people, or organizations that would most likely lead to systemic change.[11]

Second, using a technique from continuous improvement called *root cause analysis*, we "mapped" the key components of the fields (and their interactions) that are implicated in the skills gap argument using data from this study and various reports and publications. The primary purpose of root cause analysis, which is not dissimilar to the troubleshooting techniques used by Peter Dettmer and outlined in the previous chapter, is to identify the various factors that are essential for the successful (or unsuccessful) realization of specific goals (see figure 7.1).[12] This process can be broken down into three steps.

Articulate the Goals of Interest

The first step in a root cause analysis is to articulate the goals of interest. Here, we listed three goals that have been articulated by various parties as the ultimate purpose of higher education. One is espoused by skills gap advocates and is driving much of the contemporary discussion about higher education: to *meet workforce needs* and bolster the economy.

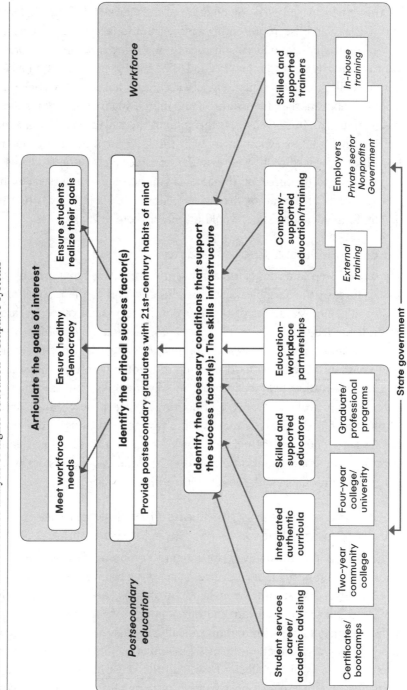

Another goal is based on a combination of the views of Thomas Jefferson and Charles Van Hise, representing a more traditional and public-oriented view of higher education's role in society: to *ensure a healthy democracy* and to primarily serve the public good. The final goal is based on a concern for college students themselves, who are understandably concerned about the labor market, their futures, and increasing income inequality: to *ensure students realize their goals* throughout their lives. While some may see this final goal as synonymous with the goal for a healthy economy, they differ in whose well-being is under consideration—the student's or the business's. Of course, all three goals can be seen as interrelated, but for the sake of this analysis they were treated as separate goals that the system, in its idealized state, would ultimately help to realize.

Identify the Critical Success Factor(s)

The second step of a root cause analysis involves identifying critical success factors, or the variables that most directly lead to the realization of these goals. The single factor that our data, and that of other researchers, indicate leads to these goals is *providing graduates from all postsecondary programs with twenty-first-century habits of mind*. Specifically, the ideal graduate would be a hard-working individual with rigorous technical training in their field, solid problem-solving skills, and the ability to communicate, work in teams, and continually learn new things. Interestingly, even if the analysis removed the two goals dealing with democracy and students' well-being, and focused only on the need for a skilled workforce, its conclusions would remain the same—the system would still require graduates with these habits of mind.

Identify the Necessary Conditions That Support the Critical Success Factor(s): The Skills Infrastructure

In the third step of the analysis, we sought to pinpoint the necessary conditions that support the sole critical success factor we identified in the previous step. These are the policies, programs, and institutions that actively reinforce and sustain the development of students with twenty-first-century habits of mind. Specifically, six distinct factors stood out as conditions that directly influenced students' abilities to acquire these habits of mind, which collectively we call the *skills infrastructure*. Much like a city's health care or transportation systems rely on an infrastructure of human resources, programs, funding, and physical materials, a similarly complex and multifaceted infrastructure is required to craft educational experiences for college students that produce the diverse skill sets and ways of thinking that will serve them well in life and work. The next subsections will detail the six component parts, or *leverage points*, of this skills infrastructure.

Skilled and supported educators

One of the obvious, yet often overlooked, conditions required to produce well-rounded, skilled college graduates is a good teacher. Educators like Janet Batzli, Tom Heraly, and Ron Petersen are critical resources that should be valued and supported by the political leadership in this country, and the fact that the teaching profession is not highly valued in the United States is one of the biggest issues impeding progress in this country.

Instead, what is needed is a national movement to not only ensure that the training and certification processes for K–12 *and* postsecondary educators are of the highest quality (and where such procedures do not exist, that situation must be remedied), but also to provide higher wages, autonomy, and rhetorical support, and therefore a bit more respect, to a profession that is much more highly regarded in countries like Japan, South Korea, and Finland than in the United States. If we are serious about generating a more skilled workforce, engaged and informed citizens, and graduates who can earn a decent living, then we must pay much more attention to supporting those professionals who are best positioned to make that happen—teachers.

Integrated, authentic curricula

Next, as we emphasized in chapter 6, having real-world, authentic situations in which content-specific learning activities can be embedded is strongly associated with students' acquisition of course content and other twenty-first-century habits of mind. Identifying situations and real-world problems that are appropriate for a particular course, and adeptly integrating them into the syllabus, is a challenging skill that educators will need to master. Regardless of its difficulty, however, ensuring that the curriculum utilizes as many authentic problems and situations as possible, while carefully considering how the range of student backgrounds and identities may make certain problems more or less appropriate, should be a national priority. Furthermore, in order for students to develop these habits of mind in nontechnical situations, it is essential that educational programs continue to maintain general education requirements. This is the liberal arts tradition at its core, and it is clear that when well delivered, it cultivates in students a combination of competencies that are valued in the labor market and make for informed, critically thinking citizens.

That said, the liberal arts tradition is evolving, and many advocates note that more attention will need to be paid to the vocational needs of students than in the past. Higher education institutions can accomplish this goal by providing career counseling or requiring additional technical courses (e.g., computer programming) as part of a liberal arts program, but for longer-term associate's and bachelor's degree programs, the fundamental notion behind the general education and liberal arts movements should be maintained, supported, and even celebrated.

Company-supported education and training

One of most influential thinkers in US vocational education, the educational economist Charles Benson, spoke of the "responsibility" that employers had to "establish high quality training programs in the workplace in which students may participate." Back in 1992, Benson argued that the willingness of employers to do so was an essential part of what he called "the new vocationalism"—a view of higher education that integrates academic and vocational studies—but that the lack of concern about training by many companies was troubling.[13]

While employers spend $177 billion a year on formal workplace training, which includes contracts to external training companies, tuition reimbursements, and structured in-house training, the majority of these dollars are spent on bachelor's degree holders in the service industry between the ages of twenty-five and fifty-four.[14] In our own study, we also found that larger companies tended to have formal training programs, whereas small to mid-size companies (which represent the majority of manufacturing companies in the United States) lacked such programs and relied on informal shadowing, which supports the ManpowerGroup's conclusion that "employers are not doing enough to address talent shortages," followed by recommendations that they "foster a learning culture" within their companies and increase investments in training and development.[15]

Overall, the evidence suggests that the business community needs to become much more committed to developing its internal labor market. It can do so by providing well-designed training programs either on-site or through local providers, and clearly communicating opportunities for employees to acquire the credentials or skills needed to advance their careers. Whether employers provide financial assistance and/or paid time off, or require employees to essentially go to "night school" and acquire new competencies on their own time and dime, the business community's role in skills cultivation must no longer be ignored. Too often, in discussions about whether college is preparing students for the jobs of tomorrow, the employers' responsibility in continuing this preparation is overlooked, with the postsecondary sector being singled out as the primary (if not the only) venue where students acquire valuable skill sets. The main point is that for the skills infrastructure to function effectively throughout people's working lives, employers need to be more actively involved in supporting their employees' desire and need for learning throughout their working lives.

Skilled and supported trainers

Once workplace training provided by the business community is part of the conversation about skills and the cultivation of twenty-first-century habits of mind, the same issue regarding the quality of curriculum design and classroom teaching in colleges and universities comes into play. Whether the in-house trainers or private firms enlisted to train a group of employees are adept at the active learning methods outlined in this book is an open question, and if the answer is that direct instruction, rote memorization, and decontextualized teaching is the norm, then another part of the higher education–workforce system is in need of improvement. In any case, the point is that those professionals providing workplace training must be as skilled and supported as postsecondary educators in order for the entire skills infrastructure to adequately cultivate twenty-first-century habits of mind.

Student services: Career and academic advising

Students in both high school and college need to have access to two distinct, yet related, types of support services. The first pertains to their need for access to high-quality and up-to-date data about trends in the labor market, local job and internship opportunities, and programs in employ-ability skills such as résumé writing and interviewing. The second would provide support for their academic success, including tutoring services, workshops on study skills, and other tools that can support students in their scholarly pursuits. This is particularly important for students who may be the first in their family (or hometown) to attend college, and students from underrepresented minority groups who may be facing a particularly alienating learning environment. Essential components of the skills infrastructure, both career and academic advising services, unfortunately, are also some of the first units on the budgetary chopping block when fiscal crises hit colleges and universities. Deprived of these critical support systems, college students are then left to their own devices to figure out how to navigate an increasingly complicated labor market, and to discover effective study practices that many of their caregivers and high school teachers may be unfamiliar with.

Education-workplace partnerships

Finally, for the skills infrastructure to effectively function there must be education-workplace partnerships in place so that information can be shared and collaborative programs designed and implemented. In our research we identified several types of partnerships that facilitated and supported other elements of the skills infrastructure (authentic curricula, skilled teachers and trainers, and student career services), a fact that points to the importance of cross-field partnerships as a foundation for many of the recommendations offered in this book.

Partnership work, however, is not easy, and involves managing the different (even conflicting) goals, expectations, cultural norms, and self-interests that each party will bring to the table. Issues surrounding education-workplace partnerships are explored in greater depth in chapter 10, but here we briefly outline the different types of programs and initiatives that can have considerable impacts on strengthening the skills infrastructure, and considerations for engaging in these partnership activities that must not be ignored.

First, a *limited partnership* involves very little coordination and generally includes work where one party simply provides another party with products or services, but with the recipient party (i.e., the "home" organization) maintaining complete autonomy over the work. An example is a manufacturer of auto parts providing Toyota with components for transmission systems. In terms of the skills infrastructure, we highlight one type of limited partnership: (a) the collection, analysis, and dissemination of labor market data, where one party (e.g., a state government) provides these data to career counseling units. Of course, these campus-based offices could collect and analyze their own data, but with increasing investments in state and regional labor market data systems, tapping into this resource makes a lot of sense.

Second, a *coordinated partnership* involves horizontal coordination where different parties both contribute something to the work in a more integrated fashion, but each continues to operate according to its own internal goals, norms, and procedures. For example, an independent team of engineers may be hired by Toyota to help design a new line of light-duty trucks. For the skills infrastructure, a variety of coordinated partnerships hold great promise, including: (a) educators providing their expertise to design workplace training programs; (b) both parties working on curriculum advisory committees to provide insights regarding course redesign and authentic curricula; (c) employers providing suggestions for student research projects and/or capstone courses; and (d) employers serving as local "experts" or mentors for advanced students.

Finally, a *collaborative partnership* is one in which two parties come together to create a "new" initiative that involves consensus-based decision making. Of course, while these types of partnerships are the most difficult to manage, they may hold the greatest payoff since the product is a truly collaborative work that reflects mutual interests and needs. Following our Toyota example, imagine the company collaborating with Volkswagen to create a new company specializing in electric cars. In the skills infrastructure, these more closely knit collaborations include: (a) expanding academic program capacity in coordination with specific industries; (b) creating community coalitions (e.g., educators, employers, government) to pursue new programs or initiatives; and (c) expanding student internship and cooperative programs.

We do not claim that ours is the definitive account of the higher education–workforce system. There are too many constantly shifting variables at play to map out the entirety of the inputs, outputs, and feedback loops that compose the relations among the global economy, the labor market, the higher education sector, and college students' lives. We also do not address issues of technology transfer from universities to the private sector, trends in employer "upskilling" where bachelor's degrees are increasingly required for middle-skill jobs, the dramatic rise in online badges and competency-based credentials that are shifting the postsecondary landscape, or a myriad of other important developments that affect these systems. Perhaps someday a cabal of anthropologists, critical sociologists, labor economists, systems engineers, and data analysts will convene to create a comprehensive account of field dynamics that incorporates each of these elements, but today we are in the early stages of such an endeavor.

Additionally, we suggest that in terms of effecting changes in the higher education–workforce system, a more productive approach than those taken by skills gap proponents builds on the ideas of cultural anthropologists such as Melville Herskovits and Alfred Kroeber, both discussed in chapter 4. Their view on cultural change was that besides the external "forcing" of change by outside agents, subtle alterations of beliefs, practices, and social structures can unfold when new cultural forms are closely mapped onto the existing ones. Effecting change by "meeting people where they are" is becoming a tried and true approach in fields as diverse as public health and education, and the beginning point of such a strategy is some sort of map or documentation of existing systems, such as the one outlined here.

In the remaining chapters of the book we highlight three of the elements required for cultivating twenty-first-century habits of mind—skilled and supported educators, student services, and education-workplace partnerships—and discuss ways that policy makers, researchers, educators, and employers have found to create and support these critical pieces of the skills infrastructure.

Teacher-Centered Reform

Support Systems for Improving Postsecondary Instruction

> *Teaching is impossible. If we simply add together all that is expected of a typical teacher and take note of the circumstances under which those activities are to be carried out, the sum makes greater demands than any individual can possibly fulfill. Yet, teachers teach . . . How is the impossible rendered possible in practice?*
>
> —LEE SHULMAN[1]

EDUCATOR SUPPORT SYSTEMS

The Latin origins of education (*educere*) illuminate what role teachers play in society. Ideally, they "bring out" the innate capacities and talents of students through skillful instruction. They "lead forth" by providing a model of expertise and behavior for a particular craft, discipline, or profession. They also can cultivate in students the habits of mind that allow them to carefully, critically, and creatively solve problems and address dilemmas, whether in the workplace or at the dinner table. Imagine a nationwide cadre of highly skilled postsecondary educators, proficient in learning theory and active teaching methods, who bring out student talents and skills in these ways. Clearly, it would be a core—if not essential—part of the "engine" that drives graduates to acquire twenty-first-century habits of mind. This is why the first, and possibly the most important, part of the skills infrastructure is teachers.

So a pressing question for the nation—if not the entire world—is how to cultivate and support a highly skilled workforce of professional teachers. There are many countries that do this rather well, at least at the K–12 level. Some countries, such as Japan and Finland, are regularly held up as paragons of teacher development, and part of what fuels much domestic educational policy is the fear that these countries will ultimately surpass the United States, not only in innovation but also in the kind of workforce capacity that has made the United States the envy of the world. One would thus expect the United States to model its teaching workforce systems after these countries, but that is not the case.

For the sake of comparison, let's first specify what nations with high performing school K–12 systems do. A review of the literature by Stanford researchers found that they:[2]

- provide universal, high-quality teacher preparation and education that includes extensive mentoring for beginners (induction programs) and professional development;
- allocate only a small percentage of teachers' time to teaching (35 percent at schools in Japan, Singapore, and South Korea), and build in time for collaborative planning (e.g., the Japanese model of *kenkyuu jugyou*—lesson study—is world famous);
- decentralize educational decisions and give local schools and teachers autonomy to make many decisions (Sweden and Finland)—instead of prescribed teaching methods, teams of teachers focus on local, classroom-based problems; and,
- provide competitive salaries that are comparable to other professions.

Now, for a blueprint of how *not* to cultivate a highly skilled, supported teacher workforce, let's take a look at the United States, where:

- different, nonuniform types of teacher preparation exist depending on the state and institution;
- teachers are poorly paid compared to other professions with high turnover;
- very little mentoring or on-the-job preparation time is provided—development of professional learning communities is difficult; and,
- educational decision making takes a top-down approach where teachers have little autonomy and must comply with federal or state standards.

As the Stanford report concludes, because extensive research has shown what it takes to develop and sustain an effective teaching workforce, "the United States is squandering a significant opportunity to leverage improvements in teacher knowledge to improve school and student performance."[3] It is simply a fact that in the United States, we are not doing it.

While "other nations, our competitors, have made support for teachers and teacher learning a top priority with significant results," the United States takes a different approach, particularly when it comes to cultivating and supporting another actor in the educational ecosystem—the postsecondary educator.[4] And in Wisconsin, being an educator during the administration of Governor Walker is another challenge altogether.

UNDERMINING THE TEACHING PROFESSION AND MORALE IN WISCONSIN

From the perspective of Wisconsin educators at all levels of the profession, the spring and summer of 2015 was a period of profound disenchantment. Between budget cuts that resulted in a 15 percent reduction in state support for public K–12 education from 2008 to 2015, and a corresponding increase in funding for the ongoing privatization of education via voucher programs, teachers were not feeling particularly hopeful in the Badger State.[5]

"They have been called lazy and greedy on blogs and website comment boards," an article in the *Milwaukee Journal-Sentinel* noted. "Their motives and commitment to their profession have been questioned. They have been told they're paid too much money."[6] The article went on to illustrate the recent experiences of several area teachers. One was Linda Kerr, a kindergarten teacher in North Lake who also volunteered evenings and Saturday mornings with afterschool programs. "We care about kids with a passion that's hard to put into words," she said. "And so it really hurts when people look at you and say you don't deserve the pay that you take home."[7] Erin Parker, a high school teacher in Madison, told another reporter that the criticism she'd seen and heard, in which teachers were excoriated as "glorified baby sitters" who "deserved minimum wage," had taken a toll.[8] "You feel punched in the stomach," she said.

The mood began to permeate postsecondary institutions as well, though 2011 was just the beginning for Wisconsin colleges and universities. Despite the fact that the UW System was already reeling from the $250 million in budget cuts passed a few years earlier, Governor Walker proposed another round of reductions in January 2015, this time to the tune of $300 million.[9] In remarks to the press, he shrugged off criticism, suggesting that offsetting the proposed cuts was as simple as having university instructors teach more. Campus governance was the focus of further recommendations in February, when Governor Walker's office proposed removing faculty tenure protections from state law and relegating future tenure decisions to the politically appointed Board of Regents.[10] While the uproar over the changes to the Wisconsin Idea forced a retreat by the governor's office, the new tenure policy sailed through the legislature and was signed into law in July, along with another $250 million cut to the UW System budget.[11]

Postsecondary educators across the state, many of whom believed recent pay freezes and changes in tenure policies would lead to a mass faculty exodus, were crestfallen. "In barely a week," one local columnist wrote, "Walker managed to do to university morale what he's already accomplished among Wisconsin's elementary and secondary public school teachers. The entire system feels under attack."[12] UW-Madison professor Grant Petty argued that the perception was understandable. Speaking of his military background, Petty pointed out that commanding officers always paid close attention to team morale. It was, after all, a crucial facet of any organization's productivity. "What we've been hearing over and over again from our public leaders has been mostly denigration of public servants, public employees, public teachers, professors, and so on," he said.[13] "And it does wear down the morale after a while. It makes people wonder a little bit why they're working so hard."

Another military voice was that of Colonel John W. Hall, who wrote that in his military training the goal was to create "curious, agile thinkers, capable of using an array of disciplines and methodologies to solve complex problems." Unfortunately, upon returning from his service to Wisconsin, Hall was disappointed to find that his state's government did not share "the military's appreciation for higher education or academic expertise" or the commitment to something "bigger than oneself" that was enshrined in the Wisconsin Idea.[14] The feeling was widely shared from one end of the state to the other. Kristine Butler, a French professor and chair of the modern language department at UW–River Falls, put it bluntly: "Morale on campus is lower than I've ever seen it. In fact, morale is lower than it has been at any job I've ever worked, including waiting tables at Pizza Hut in high school and de-tasseling corn when I was 14."[15]

Faculty and staff sentiment reached a low point, however, in early March 2016 at a somber meeting of the UW System Board of Regents that garnered national attention. This meeting amended the long-standing tenure policies of the system, which previously had stipulated in state statute that tenured faculty could be fired only for just cause or in the event of a financial emergency. Now, faculty could be dismissed due to "program discontinuance" based not only on educational considerations but also "student and market demand and societal needs." These changes were inspired by the view that higher education was "out of step" with the private sector, where people can be fired for any number of reasons. Echoing language commonly used by Wisconsin Republicans and advocates of a market-driven approach to educational policy (i.e., neoliberalism) such as the Wisconsin Policy Research Institute and Wisconsin Manufacturers and Commerce, the Regents repeatedly mentioned "flexibility" and "accountability" during the meeting. Some board members, implying that academics were insufficiently aware of fiscal challenges buffeting the nation, even told the audience "welcome to the twenty-first century" and "sometimes the market is cruel."[16]

Of course, the types of academic programs that were deemed insufficiently market-oriented were clear to observers of Wisconsin politics, with the WPRI famously singling out Renaissance art and film studies. The writing seemed to be on the wall regarding which departments and faculty would be cut when—not if—campuses began to balance increasingly dire budgets (hint: education, arts, and humanities). But these changes were not solely about job security. As the American Association of University Professors (AAUP) argued, they represented a blow to academic freedom, as outspoken faculty and/or those engaged in politically unpopular research, like climate change or studies using human stem cells, could now be conveniently silenced by having their programs discontinued.[17] Ultimately, the AAUP sadly concluded that, "The policy appears to be only the latest step in an ongoing attack on the University of Wisconsin as a public good that exists for the benefit of all citizens of the state."[18]

The implications of recurring demoralization, reduced job protections, and public belittlement for the teaching profession are considerable. As Parker Palmer wrote, changes to our educational systems will never occur, regardless of new curricula or restructured schools, if "we continue to demean and dishearten the human resource called the teacher on whom so much depends."[19] But the impacts weren't just rhetorical. The budget cuts imposed on public education in Wisconsin had real impacts on programs that helped prop up some of the skills infrastructure discussed in the previous chapter. While the complaints of some pundits about bloated university budgets—including highly paid administrators and dormitories with lazy rivers and high-speed Internet—created a perception that there was lots of "fat" to cut from the postsecondary budget, the truth was far different. After three cuts at or above $250 million, the system was being cut to the bone. Here are but a few of the hard decisions that UW System campuses had to make in the aftermath of the $250 million cut in the 2015–2017 biennial budget, with their share of the cuts in parentheses:[20]

- **UW–Madison ($63M).** The College of Engineering halted plans to expand their student advising services, and now has only 17 advisors serving 6,600 students. The Summer Science Institute, a program that exposed high school students to research careers, lost 48 faculty and 44 staff (including academic advisors). The College of Letters & Sciences eliminated student online course support and increased by 15 percent the number of students each advisor must take on in the Office of Undergraduate Advising. While the university has spent over $9 million to retain faculty being poached from other institutions (colleges and universities with better statewide political environments than Wisconsin's, mostly), some faculty are still leaving due to budget cuts and changes to tenure policies.[21]
- **UW–Eau Claire ($7.7M).** Fifteen percent of the entire workforce was cut (179 full-time positions), 25 faculty resigned their positions (a 150 percent increase over the previous year), and the entire general fund was used to meet the revenue shortfall. In addition, the university eliminated two academic affairs and three student affairs staff positions, with cuts representing a 26 percent reduction in the annual operating budget.

- **UW–Green Bay ($2.4M).** State support of the budget has declined from 41 percent of the total budget in 1995 to 17 percent in 2015. Due to recent cuts, the university eliminated multiple campus positions, leading Chancellor Gary Miller to say, "That's a significant reduction in our workforce; we are losing some key people and some key knowledge." UW–Green Bay also cut $500,000 from academic support programs (including university outreach and adult learner access), reduced staff and activities at the Center for Advancement of Teaching and Learning, and eliminated virtually all programs for faculty and staff development.
- **UW–Parkside ($2.1M).** Parkside, after spending down reserves contributing to a $2 million structural deficit, increased course loads for instructional staff to four courses per semester.
- **UW–River Falls ($2.8M).** River Falls' cuts resulted in larger classes (two to three times larger than previous year), fewer sections for many courses (which increases students' time to graduation), and additional functions and workload for faculty and staff. The administration has also noted that prospective students and families are asking about the impacts of budget cuts, with some current students thinking about transferring out of the system. Other impacts include reduced hours at the library, reductions in music and foreign language courses, and fewer opportunities to partner with local businesses due to reduced staffing.

Such reductions in student support services, career advising, and the basic educational functions of a university do not advance the goal of creating a more highly skilled teaching workforce. Instead, they inhibit the ability of teachers and institutions to cultivate twenty-first-century habits of mind among students. In short, they undermine the skills infrastructure in the name of austerity and accountability.

Unfortunately, cuts to public higher education are not limited to Wisconsin, but have taken place across the country and the world. In many, if not all, of these cases, these cuts have been accompanied by rhetoric regarding the need to invest in workforce development, spur economic growth, and balance budgets.

Yet few recognize the contradiction in slashing funding for public higher education on the one hand, and talking up the skills gap narrative and workforce development on the other. In Kentucky, after Republican Governor Matt Bevin proposed a substantial cut to address the "skills gap," the response by Southcentral Kentucky Community and Technical College President Phil Neal highlighted this seemingly obvious disconnect: "It is puzzling that at a time when workforce development is one of the Governor's top priorities, there are proposed cuts to the very engine fueling workforce development."[22] Of course, the same can be said for the actions of the Wisconsin legislature, the administration of Governor Walker, and even the UW System Board of Regents. During the debate about altering tenure protections in the UW System, which was based largely on the purported need to provide administrators with the "flexibility" to deal with fiscal crises, Regent Jose Vasquez heatedly pointed out, "Let's be clear, folks, it was not a financial crisis internally created. The fiscal crisis we have has been imposed on us."[23]

Perhaps the only silver lining in this situation is that the general public is realizing that these massive budget cuts are compromising the quality of education in Wisconsin and throughout the country. In a survey by Wisconsin Public Radio, almost two-thirds of the respondents were opposed to UW System cuts, and 23 percent felt that education was the most important issue facing the state.[24] Coupled with the momentum across the United States and internationally for introducing hands-on, experiential, and active learning into the college classroom, it is possible that a growing public backlash against the perpetual disinvestment in higher education is leading to a moment of opportunity.

While this is an optimistic stance to take in the face of rhetorical attacks and truly destructive budget cuts, it is undeniable that governments and institutions are starting to understand what learning scientists have long been arguing—that students learn better through active engagement with the material instead of passively sitting in lecture halls for hours on end. In fact, the National Science Foundation in the United States has made the widespread adoption of active learning a central feature of its portfolio, based on the belief that the STEM workforce and national scientific literacy will be in jeopardy if changes are not made in the way undergraduate education is conducted.[25] As a result, there are more tools available now than ever before for policy makers and educational leaders to begin setting in motion a system for preparing college and university educators to master sophisticated approaches to instructional design and classroom teaching.

HOW TO ENCOURAGE THE ADOPTION
OF ACTIVE LEARNING TECHNIQUES

While there are many dedicated and talented educators working in higher education—some of whom have been profiled in previous chapters—many factors appear to be discouraging the widespread adoption of active learning techniques in the nation's colleges and universities. They include the facts that many instructors are underpaid and overworked adjuncts with no job security, that entry requirements are such that most faculty have no formal training in how to teach, that many faculty work such long hours that seeking out professional development for teaching is simply untenable, and finally, that some faculty are simply uninterested in improving their teaching skills. Basically, there are a host of institutional, cultural, and personal reasons why many faculty members will not become adept at techniques such as problem-based learning or Socratic lecturing.

This begs the question: how do we change the status quo from faculty lecturing over years-old PowerPoint slides to one in which teachers utilize teaching methods based on evidence about how people really learn? From the federal government to college deans, the quality and efficacy of teaching in higher education is being questioned, scrutinized, and examined in unprecedented ways—many of which are increasingly focused on one of the central issues in this book: how can we better prepare and support educational professionals so that they can cultivate twenty-first-century competencies in our students?

This is a question, of course, that has long vexed education reformers at the K–12 level. If one thing is clear in the complicated policy debate about "teacher quality," it is that too many adopt the silver-bullet approach. Fortunately, a systems-oriented perspective is beginning to creep into discussions about improving both K–12 and postsecondary teaching, where analysts are recognizing that schools, colleges, and universities are complex and multifaceted institutions. Given this reality, the educational reformer needs to think across levels, take the systemic nature of the organization into account, and start to pinpoint exactly which aspects of the organization are supporting or inhibiting reform.

But it is not enough to simply map these elements out into models with lots of boxes and arrows; instead, what is needed are accounts of how specific organizational elements collectively impinge upon the decision-making processes of faculty as they sit in their offices, design new courses, and plan next week's lecture. In other words, what the field needs are accounts of how educators make decisions in the real world, or what cognitive scientist Edward Hutchins called "cognition in the wild" and what anthropologist Clifford Geertz famously called an "outdoor psychology."[26]

In our own research on instructional decision making, we studied the belief systems that STEM faculty had about student learning, the habits of mind they developed about classroom teaching, and the specific steps that faculty took when planning a course, all so we could provide policy makers and postsecondary leaders with detailed accounts of the subtle dynamics among cognition, culture, and context as they influenced educators in their daily work.[27] In particular, we focused on *perceived affordances,* or schemata that over time cement associations between environmental cues (e.g., a struggling student, a syllabus) and particular behaviors or responses, which ultimately start to act as cognitive shortcuts for decision making.[28]

Why are accounts of perceived affordances and other localized cognitions useful? Because it is through these perceptual lenses—the complex matrix of dispositions and prior experiences that Bourdieu called the habitus—that people interpret new events and information, frame problems in certain ways, and decide on subsequent behaviors. In other words, if a new policy mandating the wholesale adoption of problem-based learning across *all* disciplines were enacted by UW-Madison or Milwaukee Area Technical College, then the first wave of reactions would likely be a product of people's opinions regarding this mandate, past experiences with active learning, ingrained perceptions about what type of teaching was possible (and socially acceptable) in their department, whether their disciplines were appropriate for certain teaching techniques, and so on. Research on reform implementation in K–12 schools has found that ignoring these preexisting cognitive frameworks, local cultural norms, and habituated school routines is simply a recipe for disaster, like trying to introduce a new professional sports league in Brazil or Spain without appreciating the fact that soccer is a core feature of the national identities and daily recreation in these countries.

This is also why an agent-centered approach is a mainstay of disciplines such as medical anthropology, where the goal is often to meet local populations where they are in terms of belief systems and existing practices, and then to design initiatives from that foundation.[29] This strategy was borne in part out of a reaction to the tendencies of governments and aid agencies to use a top-down approach, such as telling people they *have* to boil water or *have* to start eating more vegetables, without dealing with contributing issues such as the lack of stoves, access to fresh produce, or cultural food habits.

So instead of viewing the slow—some say glacial—rate of reform in postsecondary teaching as the fault of stubborn, recalcitrant faculty resistant to change, we argue that it is more productive to advocate for these methods without demonizing either the lecture format or colleagues who are slow to change.[30] Why do we make this case? Because teaching itself is sufficiently complex to belie the simplistic, binary descriptors of "active learning" and "lecture." Furthermore, the act of verbally conveying key ideas to students (i.e., the lecture) plays a critical role in many active learning techniques, such that some cognitive psychologists recognize that there is indeed "a time for telling."[31] This fact prompted physics educator Noah Finkelstein at the University of Colorado–Boulder (CU-Boulder) to say, in response to charges that lecturing was akin to bloodletting in the age of antibiotics, "I don't think there should be a monolithic stance about lecture or no lecture—there are still times when lectures will be needed, but the traditional mode of stand-and-deliver is being demonstrated as less effective at promoting student learning."[32] Thus, it is possible to recognize the power of engaged, active instruction while also acknowledging that the dominant and habituated practices of the professoriate may indeed have some role to play.[33]

Whether or not the lecture has a major role to play in the college classroom of the future remains to be seen, but at the very least this nonconfrontational stance translates into a strategy for change that is consistent with the "meet them where they are" approach being taken in public health and other fields. Recall, too, Alfred Kroeber's theory of cultural change (discussed in chapter 4), where older cultural forms may stand a greater chance of evolution and change when they come into contact with new ideas, artifacts, and practices that resonate with the traditional.

Fortunately, this more nuanced approach to teaching reform is being promulgated in colleges and universities throughout the country. We now turn to several illustrative examples that we think point the way toward sustainable, long-term change in how faculty design and teach their courses.

PROMISING EXAMPLES OF TEACHER-CENTERED REFORM TO IMPROVE POSTSECONDARY TEACHING

There are many examples of teaching-related reforms that take into account the systemic nature of postsecondary institutions and educators' unique cultural norms, practices, and perceptions of the world. In the remainder of this chapter, we highlight a few initiatives and campus-based programs to illustrate that a systems-oriented approach that places educators at the center of reform is not only possible, but also appears to be one of the most promising for effecting change in how faculty plan and teach their courses.[34]

Engaging the Entire System:
The University of Colorado–Boulder AAU Initiative

As previously mentioned, the typical way to effect change in faculty teaching is for outside reformers to impose a new idea in a top-down approach, or what Steven Pollock, a physicist at the CU-Boulder and a colleague of Noah Finkelstein's, calls the "push model" of educational change. In that model, content specialists develop materials, collect data about their efficacy to prove that they work, and attempt to convince colleagues to adopt the new curricula. After decades of observing this approach fail at CU-Boulder and elsewhere, Pollock concluded that "push models are a sales pitch and nobody likes that; it doesn't feel right, and it doesn't work." Instead, STEM educators at CU-Boulder developed an approach that starts "from the ground up" where local educators articulate the goals and develop the materials and assessments for a new curriculum or teaching approach. Then, the education experts can take over, do experiments or observations, and evaluate the curriculum's ultimate efficacy in promoting student learning. This approach, in Pollock's view, is based on "a response to local needs" instead of being imposed from outside the system.

Building on these realizations and several successes in biology and physics, a tight-knit network of discipline-based education researchers at CU-Boulder secured a grant from the American Association of Universities (AAU) to implement what they called a "top-down, bottom-up, middle-out" theory of systemic change.[35] The goal of the initiative is to "improve student learning and engagement across campus by professionalizing faculty roles, practices, and cultural norms around education." Clearly, then, in an academic milieu where faculty expertise and achievement is truly the coin of the realm, the designers see faculty (and their roles and professional identities) as the primary agent for change. But instead of focusing on changing only faculty practices, the approach also targets other levels of the system. Overall, the four-level approach targets the following leverage points: (1) faculty practice (bottom up); (2) departmental culture (middle out); (3) administrative support (top down); and (4) background technology and infrastructure. Importantly, the cultural element of the approach depends on building and expanding a close-knit community of faculty who excel in both research *and* teaching, which is essential in an institution that is at heart a research university.

Whether or not this approach will be successful in transforming teaching and learning at CU-Boulder remains to be seen, but this multipronged approach is remarkably similar to the preferred strategy of Lee Shulman, a renowned expert on reform (or lack thereof) in K–12 education, who also supports a combination of a top-down and bottom-up approach to change.[36] In any case, this systems-oriented approach is a vast improvement over the old push model of reform.

Articulating Learning Outcomes: Accreditor or Institution Mandated

As we mentioned in chapter 6, backward design is a core principle in the development of high-quality, learner-centered instruction. This deceptively simple concept places one's goals for student learning (e.g., a grasp of genetics, teamwork skills) at the heart of how a course, specific learning activities, and assessments should be designed.[37] These outcomes can, and often are, developed solely by the instructor, but increasingly, institutions or accrediting agencies are getting into the game by mandating the articulation of learning outcomes. While not explicitly a teacher-centered reform, these directives set in motion a student-centered approach to planning.

In the case of the national engineering accrediting agency, or ABET, there are eleven competencies that future engineers are expected to acquire through their education. These include an ability to communicate effectively; to apply knowledge of mathematics, science, and engineering;

to understand professional and ethical responsibility; and to grasp the impact of engineering technology solutions in a societal and global context.[38] Interestingly, when a proposal was put forth to eliminate the "global competency" learning goal, an outcry arose from the engineering community because the increasingly international nature of many projects made staff who could competently interact with other cultural groups indispensible to engineering firms. One argued that this would create a competitive disadvantage with engineers coming from China, Russia, and India, because "the thing that has made American-trained engineers stand out is that they can think critically and ethically and they can write."[39] Of course, this particular competency is also a hallmark of the liberal arts tradition.

By making accreditation contingent upon engineering programs proving that their courses focus on these competencies, ABET essentially mandated that all engineering programs in the United States use a backward design approach. While the impacts of such mandates on how individual courses are designed and executed on a day-to-day basis may vary considerably, at the very least instructors' planning is focused not only on covering a textbook but also imparting in students skills that are remarkably similar to the twenty-first-century competency framework.

Institutions can also require their instructors and programs to identify and address these outcomes, a tack that was taken at both Madison College and UW-Madison. These strategies can be remarkably effective, as evidenced by the efforts of Janet Batzli, who designed the program goals of Biocore to be responsive to "the essential learning outcomes of the university," which included not only technical mastery but social and ethic responsibility as well. Janet's colleague Michelle Harris added that "aligning our student learning objectives with those program goals, and with what students do in class and with what they're evaluated on, is really important." Of course, in the midst of an actual course, new learning opportunities may emerge from student interest or serendipity, and in such cases, adherence to learning outcomes should not stifle student learning.

Training the Next Generation: The DELTA Program

Given the lack of training most graduate students receive in learning theory, classroom management, or even in basic instructional techniques, many institutions are developing workshops, brown-bag lunches, and lecture series focused on teaching them how to teach. An innovative strategy, however, is to influence faculty before they even enter the professoriate. The DELTA program at UW-Madison aims to train graduate students to become effective educators while they are still young and in the early phase of their careers and professional identity development. Given that not all graduate students work as teaching assistants (TAs) and that orientation programs (when they exist at all) for these positions are necessarily brief, providing high-quality instruction on teaching is quite revolutionary.

The program includes courses such as "The College Classroom," taught by Nick Balster, a professor of soil science, where graduate students discuss education research, learning theory, and classroom management issues. Twice a semester the students give twenty-minute mini-lectures to their peers, which are videotaped so that the students can provide a self-critique of their teaching. Then, Balster and other students give critical feedback, which can be a challenging experience for some, as students are generally supportive yet brutally honest. Balster says that the first time the students do this exercise, most are thinking about a specific teaching technique and/or the material they'll be teaching. The course, however, emphasizes backward design, and students discover how to articulate learning outcomes and create their next mini-lecture accordingly. The second time they teach their peers is quite different, and can be a formative experience that many early career educators never get to experience.[40]

FOSTERING CULTURES OF ACCOUNTABILITY: WHAT ARE THE COSTS?

With these promising examples of systemic reform in mind, it is worth turning to another reality facing higher education: the cresting wave of accountability that is crashing on colleges and universities across the country. This movement, if allowed to continue unabated, has the potential to hinder much of the progress being made by programs like the CU-Boulder initiative or UW-Madison's DELTA program.

While accountability has been part of the wider market-centered ethos since the 1960s, much of the educational establishment has spent the last few decades wrestling with the issue of teacher quality: how to measure it, how to cultivate it, and what to do when it falters. At first these debates and policies largely unfolded in K–12 schools, but in the 1990s policy makers and postsecondary leaders began to speak about introducing a "culture of evidence" into higher education, and holding institutions and faculty accountable for the taxpayer and student tuition dollars that were being sent their way.[41] For example, the Wisconsin Policy Research Institute released a report in early 2016 with an article titled, "How the Regents Can Make Professors Accountable to Taxpayers and Students."[42]

Whether one agrees with the merits of operating universities more like businesses, the hitch with these approaches is that they do not seem to be concerned with supporting high-quality teaching or building a skills infrastructure. Instead, they are borne out of a desire for control and to hold people accountable for their professional shortcomings. That is, postsecondary policies are being designed with the overarching goal of forcing compliance with accountability measures rather than on supporting education professionals in performing their jobs.

While there may be a middle ground between these two goals, in Wisconsin the focus is clearly on accountability alone.[43] Consider the message being sent to professional educators when the focus is on ensuring compliance with accountability measures rather than on providing support, funding, and workplace conditions that foster instructional excellence, as countries such as Japan and Finland do for their K–12 teachers. In the former situation, morale plummets and people feel worse than a bunch of teenagers working under an incompetent manager at Pizza Hut. In the latter, professionals are inspired to craft the most effective learning opportunities possible for their students, and they are provided with the resources and leadership support to do so. The fact that many doctors, whose profession has also embraced accountability metrics with a vengeance, are beginning to question whether these metrics encourage practice more concerned with completing checklists than providing quality patient care, should raise some red flags among those foisting an accountability policy on higher education.[44]

Are these policies truly supporting systems that help teachers cultivate twenty-first-century habits of mind? Again, we do not suggest that the higher education sector is blameless. Instruction can be improved, performance review is often spotty at best, and the student debt crisis is making the dream of a college education unattainable for many young people, particularly those from low-income and underrepresented minority groups.

It's not just about teachers, however. While students should be an obvious part of the teaching and learning equation, they are often invisible in these debates about the future of higher education. Are they prepared to fully engage in the classrooms, laboratories, and discussion sections that are part of rigorous postsecondary programs? Are the nation's colleges and universities fostering academically challenging yet socially and culturally welcoming environments for learners of all backgrounds? We can't forget that even if educators design the perfect learning opportunities, students bring in their own unique expectations, experiences from K–12 or the workplace, and personal situations and travails. That is, their own habitus becomes introduced into these new systems, and the impacts of this dynamic between the institution and students on their ultimate success should not be underestimated.

Millennials Face the Future

Support Systems for Today's College Students

> *We want to raise a generation of kids who have a mouse in one hand and a book in the other.*
>
> —HENRY JENKINS[1]

DON'T FORGET ABOUT THE STUDENTS

A critical yet frequently overlooked element of the skills puzzle, surprisingly enough, is students themselves. Aside from wishing that they
wouldn't become art history majors and would instead go into skilled
trades, proponents of the skills gap narrative don't talk much about students. It is as if they are simply chess pieces to nudge in certain desirable career directions and away from others, with little attempt made to
understand their preferences and needs for successfully earning a certificate, associate's, or bachelor's degree. It is a bizarre and unfortunate
aspect of the skills gap narrative.

Yet a considerable amount of attention has been paid to the current
crop of students, the so-called millennial generation, as a group of young
people with certain expectations about school, work, and the nature of
learning and community, as well as unique communication practices

acquired amidst an era of digital devices and a continually streaming Internet. Regardless of the veracity of these generalizations, it is indisputable that educators and policy makers engaged in discussions about the future of education and the workplace should at least *think* about students when shaping the very world that they will inhabit. As a result, it is worth investigating how this generation thinks about school, learning, and work as an important part of the twenty-first-century habits of mind equation.

The paradigm shift from a focus on teaching to a focus on student learning, as discussed in chapter 6, highlights the importance of this issue. Such a shift implies an emphasis not only on the disciplinary knowledge or skills that a student should master by the end of a course, but also on how instructors can design learning activities to most effectively engage them in the learning process. This is not to say that the fundamentals of welding or physics should be ignored—or, as many faculty fear, "dumbed down"—but simply that educators should think deeply about the unique cultural backgrounds, goals, and predilections that their students bring into the classroom. A basic concept of adult education is that teachers need to be aware of whether their students are electricians or hedge fund managers, because instruction should be linked to their frames of reference in order to encourage the transfer of new ideas and concepts to wherever a student may need to apply it.[2] Plus, it makes the class more interesting and engaging for the students.

It's critical to point out, however, that there exists no single monolithic group of college students, a misconception that terms like "the millennial generation" risk conveying. The stereotype of mostly white eighteen- to twenty-year-olds partying in on-campus dorms or fraternity houses, cemented into popular culture through movies like *Animal House*, unfortunately remains a dominant conception of what college students are like. Instead, colleges and universities are becoming increasingly multiracial and multicultural, only 14 percent of college students in the United States live in on-campus housing, and many adults are increasingly attending college in person or via the Internet. The average age of students at Madison College, for example, is twenty-nine. So, while there may be some commonalities among certain generations, there is no single "type" of student, and educators would be remiss in not paying careful attention to the unique situations, backgrounds, and talents of the different students in their classrooms.

This chapter also addresses one of the key components, or leverage points, of the skills infrastructure that pertains to student success: academic and career counseling services. Academic supports are essential in the face of evidence suggesting that many students are neither using effective study habits, nor are they particularly good at managing the manifold digital distractions that constitute our everyday environments. Furthermore, many colleges have recognized that career services could be better, providing students with up-to-date and accurate information about the labor market, internships, and basic competencies such as how to write a résumé. This, of course, raises the important issue of whether well-paying jobs will be waiting for students upon graduation.

However, there is still a limit to what colleges and universities can and should do in terms of shepherding students through molecular biology courses, choosing a major, or charting a career trajectory. While evidence suggests that many students do in fact seek academic programs that are linked to "hot jobs" of the moment such as computer science or engineering, there still is (and should be) a considerable amount of free choice involved in the matter. As Matt Reed, a community college dean, noted, "Students aren't widgets, they have preferences of their own and those preferences don't always align with local employment markets." Matt has found that students in his college persist in choosing to be social studies teachers even when told they will have more job opportunities by teaching math or science. So even though his college works closely with employers and aligns its curriculum to labor market needs, Reed observed that "at the end of the day, students want what they want."[3]

COLLEGE STUDENTS IN THE EARLY TWENTY-FIRST CENTURY

Millennials. Gen Why. Nexters. Generation Me. Net Gen. Echo Boomers. Digital Natives. While many stereotypes about millennials are repeated in the popular media (e.g., that they're overly reliant on parents, lazy, and uncommitted), more and more researchers are studying this generation because in many ways they are a fascinating experiment in social and cultural change. This generation, born roughly between 1980 and 2000, is the last to know life before the Internet began to dominate the economy, alter the face of education, and shape how we communicate with one another. They are also growing up and facing adulthood in a rapidly changing economy that was rocked by the Great Recession of 2008, are experiencing soaring amounts of student debt, and are in many cases living with their parents out of a lack of job prospects or indecision about their career trajectories.[4]

Throughout our study we heard many stories and opinions about millennials, particularly how they approached the world of work and their academic pursuits. Some were positive, others less so, but regardless, understanding a bit more about how this generation is thinking about and experiencing school and work needs to be part of the conversation.

How Millennials Think About the World of Work

Researchers are finding that in the world of work, millenials want many of the same things they expect from college: feedback and recognition, a clear trajectory to success, well-defined objectives, and a safe working environment with a mentor (or boss) they can also call a friend.[5] They also prefer flexible work environments and the ability to telecommute, lots of team-oriented tasks, and a relaxed workplace atmosphere.

Some researchers have also found that millennials highly value work that is intellectually stimulating, with pay and benefits coming in a close second to a satisfying career.[6] Building on this idea, this generation highly values a work-life balance, or the ability to set one's job aside and pursue family time or hobbies, although what sets them apart from other generations may be their "confidence and conviction to demand it from their employers."[7] Consequently, millennials are often portrayed as a group that, when dissatisfied with working conditions or their career prospects within a company, has no qualms about quitting and seeking other opportunities, in contrast to older generations, who may have felt committed to a single company for their entire working lives out of responsibility, obligation, or a sense of duty.

Supporting some of these findings, employers in our study had much to say about millennials, although it is important to point out that criticisms about "young people" have probably been uttered by every generation of adults throughout human history. Several business owners felt that many of their young hires have been entitled and narcissistic, and failed to understand that they have to "pay their dues." Malik Surani, HR manager at Tigre-ADS USA, Inc., explained, "people want immediate results . . . and people have very limited tolerance to waiting for something to happen."

This perspective often translates into what some employers feel are unrealistic expectations for wages and benefits. For instance, some referred to millennials' need for "instant gratification" without understanding that before raises and promotions comes "earning your stripes," and several observed that salary expectations were simply way out of line with the local labor market. Reflecting on why the new generation tended to overestimate their abilities, a manufacturer in Oshkosh, Wisconsin, said, "They see themselves at a higher level than what they really are . . . everything is hand-fed to that generation now." This, of course, is an interesting observation when set against Ron Petersen's criticism of employers offering his students $12 an hour for technical positions. Should skilled younger people be happy with such a wage and simply work their way up? Or does the wage reflect problems with employer expectations?

Another critique pertains to the younger generation's work ethic. Todd Larson, an HR manager at Swanstrom Tools USA, elaborated on this point, saying, "We've got guys that are seventy-five years old still working here and just knocking things out, and I've got guys that are in their first year of college that'll be standing around or talking and they really don't seem to care—we've seen them sleeping on the job and stuff like that."

On a more positive note, as part of our study we also held focus groups with students enrolled in courses taught by some of the educators featured throughout this book, as well as with recently hired employees at selected companies. While they are a small sample of students and employees, many of whom were enrolled in (or were graduates of) four-year degree programs, almost all recognized the importance of hard work and cultivating both technical and nontechnical competencies. For instance, when we asked some of Scott Cooper's students what skills they felt were important for success in the workplace, one senior said, "Keep studying, study hard, and never stop being interested to learn more every day." Others pointed out that since they would likely hold multiple jobs throughout their careers, the ability to carefully read the labor market, acquire new skills, and adapt with the economy was particularly important.

While this is a necessarily brief overview of how millennials are thinking about the workplace, and how they are viewed by some employers, it highlights the fact that this generation does have different views about what work means to them, what the workplace should look like, and their approach to labor itself than previous generations. Many are also aware that they are facing a rapidly changing labor market and that some of the older rules—"get that first job, and you'll be taken care of for life," or "go to college and leave with little/no debt"—have gone out the window. At the very least, such realities underscore the importance for these students to develop a strong sense of self-regulated learning, whether on their own or through explicit instruction by their teachers and mentors. As the chairman of AT&T told his 280,000 employees in early 2016, "There is a need to retool yourself, and you should not expect to stop."[8]

How Millennials Think About Education and Studying

The way that millennials approach higher education and studying itself also sheds light on how and why this generation may need to be handled differently than past cohorts. First of all, having grown up during a time of economic dislocation via one of the largest recessions in US history, many seek higher education for private, economic reasons. A survey of freshmen attending four-year institutions found that the top reasons for attending college were to get a better job, learn about things of interest, be trained for a particular career, and earn more money.[9] Following these mostly economic rationales for going to college was obtaining "a general education and appreciation of ideas," which in previous years students had rated more highly.

Research on whether students make career decisions in response to the economy also indicates that students do pay attention to labor market signals; post-recession enrollments in programs considered "marketable," such as STEM fields, have increased, while those in the arts and humanities have decreased.[10] While there is considerable debate about whether this is a problem of the liberal arts not adequately advertising the vocational merits of their programs, or whether higher wages and increased job security await graduates of STEM and profession-oriented programs, enrollment patterns do appear grim for fields that do not provide students with a clear pathway to the workforce.

Beyond career decision making, researchers are also investigating how college students are approaching learning itself, with often discouraging results. Educational psychologists studying the learning strategies used by college students found that the most common approaches—rereading, highlighting, and summarizing text—are ineffective.[11] Further inhibiting student learning is the fact that many students begin to study only when explicitly directed by their teachers, which is called *cue-seeking* behavior, in contrast to students who are *cue deaf*, or self-initiate studying when they recognize on their own that they need to hit the books.[12] Of course, cue-seeking behavior indicates a lack of self-regulated learning aptitudes.

The amount of time one puts into hitting the books is obviously an important component of studying as well, but studies suggest millennial high school students spend only about three hours per week, and they expect to put forth a similar amount of effort in college.[13] Furthermore, in 2009, over 50 percent of college freshmen and seniors reported spending ten hours or less per week studying, which is a far cry from the general rule of thumb that many instructors give their students—to expect to study about two to three hours per credit hour per week.[14]

To summarize, many college students are not studying as much as they need to, initiate the studying process only when told to, and use ineffective strategies when they do study—all of which indicate the need for more explicit mentoring on how to study, particularly in the early stages of a college career.

Finally, millennials' information-seeking behavior relies on the Internet for ease and convenience. In a study of 102 students at a small, private college, 98 percent of students reported frequently using Google when doing their assignments, and 58 percent frequently consulted Wikipedia.[15] However, while technology can aid them in their studying, it can also take away from the larger goal of learning.[16] For example, technology is also used in class, but not always for class-related purposes—one survey found that digital devices were used an average of 11.43 times during school days, and this accounted for an average of 20.9 percent of students' class time. While over half of the students claimed usage was "a little distracting," the two biggest disadvantages were related to not paying attention and missing instruction.[17]

Of course, smartphones and the Internet are not inherently antilearning, and advocates of online education, educational gaming, and the use of digital media for instructional purposes emphasize the positive uses of these new tools. In a world where millennials and even younger generations are participating in what Henry Jenkins calls digital "participatory cultures"—such as podcasting, fan fiction, and Wikipedia—young people easily form online learning communities where they create, share, and learn from one another. Jenkins argues that the competencies being gained through these seemingly "noneducational" pursuits are in fact rather profound. "Through these various forms of participatory culture, young people are acquiring skills that will serve them well in the future," he writes, adding that "participatory culture is reworking the rules by which school, cultural expression, civic life, and work operate."[18]

In any case, millennials will need to be careful to observe the cultural norms of the workplaces that they enter upon graduation, particularly if they are "old school" companies like John Deere, which Tom Heraly spoke about. This process of adapting to the cultural norms of a new field, as represented by a small family-owned company or large corporation that hires the college graduate for her first job, is inescapable. And adapting oneself to the unique milieu of a new workplace may be one of the primary barriers young people have in entering the workforce today. Tom observed that: "We have students that will be text messaging while you are lecturing. Now can you imagine text messaging while your manager's talking to you on the tasks you need to complete today? It's hard to show them the relevance—that what you do in class reflects on what you're going to do out in industry, and this is not acceptable behavior in industry."

These observations raise the question: setting aside for a moment the role that family, K–12 schools, and other parties play in cultivating awareness about studying and career decision making, is there anything postsecondary institutions can do to help students make more successful transitions to college?

ACADEMIC ADVISING

One of the two student support services that are a core part of the skills infrastructure is academic advising. Generally speaking, academic advising units offer study skills training and tutoring to students—two things that could mean the difference between success and failure. Although it varies by school, such training can focus on specific learning strategies, time management, and effective note taking. For example, at the Greater University Tutoring Service (GUTS) at UW-Madison, there are two types of services offered—individual advising sessions and workshops that cover basic study skills, multiple-choice test taking, and finals week study strategies.[19] Given the fact that many first-generation college students or graduates of underresourced high schools where these skills were not taught attend our colleges and universities, providing such learning opportunities can be particularly important.

However, these services tend to be underutilized on many campuses. In a 2012 survey at the University of California–Los Angeles, only 44 percent of students used the campus writing center, and 43 percent took advantage of study skills advising.[20] More frequently, students meet with their program advisors to talk about which courses to take or what to major in. While such advisors, as well as individual faculty, may play an important role in providing tips about studying and career paths, there simply are not enough such advisors (or faculty) to provide rigorous advice on these issues to all students. Not using such services may be a result of the proximity of the service to the student, students not feeling that their behaviors need to change, a lack of awareness of such opportunities, or a lack of time.[21] Regardless, research-based learning and self-management strategies, taught by trained academic support staff, can help students become self-regulated learners and better transition, academically speaking, from high school into *any* college program.

CAREER ADVISING

The second student support service in the skills infrastructure—and one that is certainly on the radar screen of skills gap advocates—is career advising. In our fieldwork, we found some highly sophisticated, industry-specific career services, such as UW-Madison Engineering Career Services, whose staff oversees internship placement, conducts one-on-one counseling, assists students with the job search process, and facilitates employer-student matches via career fairs. Yet, in other cases, students had less robust services at their disposal; they were sent to a college- or university-wide career services office, which in some cases had limited staffing. Unfortunately, in times of fiscal duress, as in Wisconsin during our study, these are the types of units and services that are often the first casualties of budget cuts.

Inhibiting the efficacy of these services, like academic advising, is the fact that many students don't use them. A 2012 survey of 593 college career service directors found that 35 percent felt that the main factor impeding the success of their programs was simply getting students to use them. Further, 47 percent felt that a lack of student motivation was a major problem in students' utilization of these programs. Almost half believed that a required career class would ameliorate relationships between career centers and students.[22]

Recognizing that many of its students lacked structured guidance in career selection and how to market a liberal arts degree to employers, UW-Madison's College of Letters and Sciences (L&S), which offers degrees ranging from biology to art history, created a "Career Initiative" in 2013.[23] The initiative includes ramped-up career advising services and a course for second-year students that guides them in exploring different career prospects and how to make critical life decisions (L&S 210). Sophomore Ryan Kielczewski observed that making decisions about majors and careers is complex: "Some people do already have it planned out, but to be honest, I really don't." Taking L&S 210 made sense for Ryan, especially given the economic and political climate. There he picked up on the predominance of the skills gap debate, saying, "Everything's so job-related these days; everything's leading up to the job and how to get one . . . so why not take a class like that?"[24]

It is highly likely that the college developed the initiative partly in response to the skills gap debate, which explicitly questioned the value of liberal arts training provided by colleges like L&S. Regardless of the motivation, the dean of L&S, John Karl Scholz, touted the program at a meeting of the UW System regents, stating that it "represented a new standard for career preparation" in a public research university. Scholz further stated that one of the goals of the initiative was to teach L&S students how market a liberal arts training, because "students in the College of Letters & Science have the skills employers want, but many of them don't know how to talk about the value of their degrees to employers."[25]

Another important service that career advising offices need to provide is up-to-date information about the labor market, which students can and should weigh against personal choice when making decisions about majors and career pathways. For instance, it would be a disservice to not inform students that the median earnings for majors such as art and music education ($36,000) and psychology ($41,000) are much lower than electrical engineering ($87,000) and management information systems and statistics ($80,000).[26] However, they should also be provided with data that contradicts the popular notion that liberal arts graduates are unemployable.[27] Further, to demonstrate the difficulties of picking "winners" among different majors, contrary to the popular assumption that STEM-related majors are recession-proof, students should also be informed that the major that had the highest unemployment rate in the aftermath of the Great Recession was architecture, not art.

In addition, students should be made aware that the career pathways for different disciplines and their connections (or lack thereof) to specific occupations vary considerably from field to field, thus raising questions about claims that some majors really are a road to lifelong unemployment. For example, nursing is a discipline with tight connections to an occupation, as graduates from associate's or bachelor's degree programs are well prepared to obtain industry-mandated certifications, which lead directly into a specific job (i.e., registered nurse). In contrast, biology programs, particularly in four-year universities, have loose connections to occupations and no industry with which to link program curricula to specific credentials, primarily because students are on a variety of career pathways including graduate school, government and nonprofit organizations, and private-sector jobs in industries ranging from biotechnology to health care. While this may suggest a need for such programs to provide students with more articulated pathways, it may make little sense given the diversity of careers available to the holder of a biology bachelor's degree.[28]

This highlights one of the problems with skills gap advocates' preoccupation with steering high school and college students into certain careers and away from others. While Jim Morgan's assertion that "today's high school student does not even know what a CNC operator is or does" suggests the need for more career counseling about the opportunities available in the skills trades and advanced manufacturing, his more problematic argument is that students are being "pushed" to "get degrees in subjects that do not necessarily prepare them for jobs that exist in the market." Naming history and political science majors, Morgan overlooks the fact that students educated in these fields enter a variety of occupations and fields, not just a single job like CNC operations.[29] Again, the data do not support the oft-cited contention that liberal arts majors are unemployable, as 90 percent of UW-Madison liberal arts graduates report being employed full-time and/or attending graduate school.[30]

Furthermore, it is worth reflecting on the vagaries of the labor market and how problematic it is to predict "winning" and "losing" occupations for the next five, ten, or even twenty years. Consider the field of law, which until recently was a "hot" field for many young people. But only 60 percent of the class of 2014 were employed in full-time positions requiring the bar exam, leading to a decline in law school enrollments and an oversaturated market of young, indebted lawyers.[31]

So, while providing such information is a critical service that all college students should receive, these projections are far from a crystal ball, especially with the swiftly changing currents of technology and the rapid change in corporate needs. Thus, the notion that government should get into the business of legislating students' career choices—which has been explored by states such as Florida, where differential tuition would be charged to students attending public institutions based on whether their intended major was "market-ready" or not—is exceedingly short-sighted and dangerous.[32] The irony of castigating society for the heavy-handed "college for all" movement while advocating for students to flee the liberal arts and pursue the skilled trades is lost on skills gap advocates.

Instead, the better strategy is a combination of broad educational preparation that fosters twenty-first-century habits of mind *and* a focus on some sort of technical skill that can easily and readily be marketed on a résumé or during a job interview. Carefully cultivating the habits of mind described in chapter 4 is thus essential, so that students are prepared to continually reshape themselves in an economy that will inevitably change in the coming decades. But this approach to career guidance must also be balanced against something that lies at the heart of a free society: personal choice in regards to one's career and life course.

Returning to the educational philosophy of Thomas Jefferson, many have argued that students should also be allowed and encouraged to explore different career interests until they find something they truly enjoy—whether Renaissance art, biology, history, or CNC operations—because personal enjoyment in work increases their prospects for long-term job satisfaction while also engaging them in a process of personal growth. Given the fact that many Americans will have more than ten jobs in their lifetimes, it is critical that students be taught how to make tough career choices, and not assume that they should be locked into a job that a career aptitude test decided for them at age eighteen or that the government projects will be a hot occupation.[33]

Vice Provost Turina Bakken of Madison College said that one of the roles of technical colleges is to "be a place where people can come in and explore and deepen and be transformed" through exposure to 140 occupational programs. Turina observed that many students, particularly those just out of high school, might not know what exactly they want to do. Allowing these students to "come out the other side with a credential and a career that wasn't even on their radar screen when they walked in the door" is something that must be "preserved" in higher education. As Turina noted, even with a shortage of welders, if a student isn't interested, he won't become a welder. This echoes Matt Reed's earlier observation that, "at the end of the day, students want what they want."[34]

Besides allowing students to explore multiple options, providing them the space and guidance to think about which programs and careers they are interested in may ultimately benefit both them and the economy. Considerable evidence exists linking job satisfaction and employee engagement with company productivity, and thus, profitability.[35] Consequently, many executives counsel college students to really think deeply about questions such as "What do I want to do for the next twenty years?" and "What makes me happy?" These observations from the business sector point to the need for students to really think through their career choices in terms of qualities like happiness and satisfaction, as well as hard-nosed analyses about what the labor market data indicate for the future.

THE OTHER ELEPHANT IN THE ROOM: WHAT JOBS AWAIT THESE GRADUATES?

Finally, there is another issue that is too often overlooked in discussions about skills gaps and the future of higher education: what jobs are waiting for college graduates? While skills gap proponents constantly refer to the large numbers of "family-supporting" jobs that are awaiting well-trained applicants, it is a fact that the fastest-growing jobs in Wisconsin are low-wage, low-skill service positions. The top five occupations with the most projected openings between 2012 and 2022 are as follows: retail salespersons (3,070 average annual openings), food preparation workers (2,910), cashiers (2,790), waiters and waitresses (2,440), and customer service representatives (2,320). The only occupation in the top fifteen that pays an average salary that is above the living wage for a family of four is registered nurses (1,920), with others, such as personal care aides (1,590), paying well below that.[36] Indeed, analyses of Bureau of Labor Statistics data indicate what some call a "hollowing out" of the labor market, with jobs in the middle-wage category (here measured at $12.51 to $24.99 an hour) decreasing in Wisconsin while jobs in the low- and high-wage categories are increasing.[37]

This is not to suggest that no decent jobs are being created in today's labor market. Many living-wage jobs can be found in the advanced manufacturing, biotechnology, and high-tech industries throughout Wisconsin, but the numbers simply do not represent the majority of available jobs. Educational historians W. Norton Grubb and Marvin Lazerson made an observation in 2004 that remains true today: "Many jobs in our economy are structured so that they don't encourage the development of serious competencies. The jobs of the youth labor market are virtually all low-skill, repetitive service jobs, and they present young people with an image of work in which even basic academic and personal competencies—never mind the complex abilities forecast for the 21st century—are all but irrelevant."[38] This is no small matter, as the other part of what some call the school-to-work "pipeline" is a job that pays a living wage and benefits. This is part of the social contract that involves a student and his or her family investing considerable time and money into acquiring certain forms of cultural capital (i.e., a degree, a skill set) that ideally will be highly sought after in the labor market. Given that the average student debt at graduation rose 56 percent, from $18,550 to $28,950—more than twice the rate of inflation (25 percent) from 2004 to 2014—a well-paying job is essential for many students' financial futures.[39] While the price tag of a college certificate or degree obviously plays a huge role in this state of affairs, the presence (or absence) of well-paying jobs is too often overlooked as a factor that inhibits graduates' abilities to pay off their debt, save for the future, and enter the middle class.

This raises the question of whether UW-Milwaukee economist Marc Levine was right in arguing that the "skills gap" problem was less about education and more about "a sputtering job creation machine, in both the quantity and quality of jobs created."[40] The sluggish creation of jobs in states like Wisconsin, and the fact that many large companies, such as AT&T, plan to shed at least 30 percent of their workforce by 2020 due to automation and increased efficiencies, paints a gloomy picture on the employment front.[41] Of course, this raises the not inconsiderable issue that we really don't know what the jobs of 2020 or 2030 will look like. What is clear is that we should be educating *all* students with an eye toward the ever-changing and unpredictable nature of the labor market not just for today, or even tomorrow, but for the middle of the century.

These issues of jobs, student debt, career advising, and the unique nature of millennials collectively point to the need to be proactive in reshaping a skills infrastructure that can cultivate the types of competencies and habits of mind that will serve them, the economy, and society at large well now and into the future. As the next chapter will discuss, one of the principal components of this infrastructure, and a precondition of sorts for many programs like career counseling services, is cross-field partnerships. Whether these partnerships are focused on creating a new internship program or designing problem-based learning lessons for a machining class, such collaborative work is both essential and much easier said than done.

10 A Shared Responsibility

Strategic Education-Industry Partnerships

When you sing with a group of people, you learn how to subsume
yourself into a group consciousness . . . That's one of the great
feelings—to stop being me for a little while and to become us.
That way lies empathy, the great social virtue.

—BRIAN ENO[1]

PARTNERSHIP WORK AS A CULTURAL PROBLEM

One of the primary arguments of the skills gap narrative is that the two fields of education and the workplace need to be more tightly integrated and aligned, not disconnected spheres of learning and commerce. While some may argue that basic research or philosophy courses that have no obvious link to the working world do in fact connect to it—by enabling discoveries that will chart the course of the culture and economy ten or twenty years hence, and by cultivating in students valuable habits of mind—there are growing efforts to link all educational programs more clearly and immediately to the workforce.

From the University of Maryland's partnership with Northrup Grumman to create new programs in cybersecurity to Georgia Tech's well-known engineering cooperative programs with local businesses, more and more partnerships are being created to provide students with clearly articulated career pathways from their educational preparation to specific jobs and industries. Overall, the idea is that through such strategic partnerships, the issues raised by the skills gap narrative can be addressed; the pipeline can be tightened, the alignment improved.

Our analysis suggests this focus on partnership is on the right track: more coordinated efforts to support student career advising, generate authentic curricula, and foster school-to-work pathway programs like internships and apprenticeships are key aspects of a skills infrastructure. Creating such collaborative endeavors, however, should not solely be the responsibility of higher education in terms of altering their practices and programs. It is also up to the business community to commit time and resources to these efforts, and state and federal governments to create the environment in which they can flourish. The importance of building bridges to knit together a stronger skills infrastructure is, of course, the central argument in this book.

That said, our data indicate that alignment between fields is not dependent upon programs, policies, and structures that closely link an academic program and a specific occupation or industry. Consider the example of Scott Cooper at UW–La Crosse, who has no ties to industry and whose students have no single, clear career pathway to travel upon graduation. Yet through laboratories operated like a mini-biotechnology company—complete with client presentations at the end of the semester—and instruction that fosters problem solving, communication, and teamwork competencies along with principles of biology, Scott is educating his students in precisely the way that David Mead and Jeff Williams from Lucigen desire. Essentially, Scott is cultivating the exact sorts of competencies that businesses want and need in new employees.

This is not to suggest that cross-field partnerships are not important, or that clearly articulated career pathways are undesirable. As we discuss in this chapter, both are essential components of the skills infrastructure. Still, this is where we diverge from the skills gap narrative, with its overemphasis on partnerships and career pathways as well as its reliance on assumptions about who is aligned, who is not, and how technical, programmatic solutions are the best approach to "fixing" supposed (educational) deficiencies. Instead, a more comprehensive and systemic perspective is needed that touches upon *all* components of the skills infrastructure. Indeed, the myopic focus on programmatic solutions is shortsighted not only because it ignores classroom teaching and the cultural aspects of skills development, but also because it assumes that expanding or creating new programs, which by definition require cross-field partnerships, is an easy and unremarkable task.

As with developing teachers conversant with teaching twenty-first-century habits of mind, partnership work is no simple task. Too often it is viewed as a simple technical problem: just create a new certificate or degree program to meet high-demand occupational needs, or tweak the curriculum to better match specific skills demands in the labor market. What these directives mask are hard, potentially divisive questions about *whose* voice and perspective will be the most influential in crafting new syllabi and programs and *whose* interests and needs constitute the primary framing of the endeavor.

Further complicating matters is the fact that there are at least three different types of partnerships—limited, coordinated, and collaborative—that vary depending on the nature of the work, degree of partner investment, and desire for autonomy. Breaking the notion of partnership down into these categories is necessary because too often, organizations become involved in collaborative work with little planning or recognition of its difficulties. By keeping in mind these different forms of partnerships, postsecondary leaders, employers, and government agencies can be better prepared (and informed) when embarking on the rewarding, yet often simultaneously difficult and contentious, process of working collaboratively. Considering differences in the types of partnership and their corresponding levels of institutional commitment is essential, given the evidence from research on interorganizational collaboration demonstrating that many partnerships fail.[2] This is because crossing organizational boundaries to engage in collaborative work is not only a technical issue—as simple as signing an agreement and launching an initiative—but also a political and cultural one, implicating different organizational norms, routines, and self-interests. The key to understanding these dynamics is to recognize that collaborative work takes place in the intermediary zone between fields, where new ideas are forged, new understandings emerge, and new challenges crop up—what we call the *third space* of partnership work.

OPERATING IN THE THIRD SPACE

The concept of the third space is often used to describe learning communities in classrooms where students and teachers from different backgrounds and perspectives came together to transform what could have been zones of conflict and misunderstanding into spaces of collaboration and learning.[3] This is the interstitial space between fields and groups, where educators and employers bring their own unique habits of mind, needs and goals, and resources to bear upon a new problem or activity. In field theoretic terms it is where distinct strategic action fields come together, either in conflict or coordination, to compete over scarce resources as each vies for power or control.[4]

We use the third space as a metaphor to talk about education-workplace partnership work because it highlights the uncomfortable fact that working in this zone can be a tricky and challenging business, where different goals and interests must be negotiated alongside the problem of simply dealing with two, often quite different, cultural groups. In particular, unless the work is simply a matter of delivering a product or a service, with no real collaboration necessary or desired, then the different goals and self-interests of each potential partner must be carefully negotiated so that one party's needs do not run roughshod over another's.

Understanding partnership work in terms of the third space is also important because after the work is performed, the outcomes often will return to one of the partner organizations, or what we call the *home organization*. For instance, a biology course that was collaboratively redesigned by a group of local educators and employers will ultimately affect only one party—the college or university where the course will be based. This fact raises important issues, particularly that of self-interest, because it is in these situations where change can be foisted upon a group by external agents who have a limited understanding of (or investment in) how the new product or process will operate.

Because many partnerships fail to address these issues and reconcile differences in perspective and goals, we highlight these matters here in the hopes of improving practitioners' understanding of how these differences influence partnerships and how they can be managed. As Clyde Kluckhohn (1949) said, "Anthropology provides a scientific basis for dealing with the crucial dilemma of the world today: how can peoples of different appearance, mutually unintelligible languages, and dissimilar ways of life get along peaceably together?"[5]

So, what strategies did we see in Wisconsin for forming partnerships or engaging in collaborative work in this third space so that college students could best be prepared for life and work? How did different cultural groups represented by business and higher education work to ensure that each party's interests were carefully considered, and establish some sort of common ground?

THE WISCONSIN APPROACH TO PARTNERSHIP: ONE-SIDED DELIBERATIONS IN THE DEAD OF NIGHT

In the legislative process it is not uncommon for new laws or rules to be enacted with little to no consultation with those affected, and of course, this habit crosses political party lines at both the state and national levels. But the administration of Governor Walker took this habit to a new level in Wisconsin during the time of our study.

Act 10—the "budget repair bill" that included massive changes to collective bargaining agreements for public employees—was released with scant public input or debate. Some hearings on the legislation were announced with little public notice, held late at night and in some cases behind closed doors.[6] This practice of developing legislation without consulting with the public or the opposition party became something of a trend with the state government. A proposal to exempt all government communications from open record laws was unveiled with no public debate, as were the failed changes to the UW System charter. When these proposals saw the light of day, the public backlash was so fierce that Governor Walker and his GOP colleagues were forced to back down.

However, the approach proved more successful when it came to higher education policy. Act 55, which included changes to tenure rules as well as the budget cuts for 2015–2017 biennial, contained 135 non-budget policy items that were slipped into the legislation, which is another unfortunate bipartisan trick used to pass laws that have little or nothing to do with government finances (e.g., tenure reform). In addition, none of the expert hearings that are a normal part of the deliberative process were held regarding this legislation that unleashed significant changes to the UW System.

While one could chalk these moves up to politics as usual, there have been some real casualties and loss of trust along the way. Chancellor Becky Blank of UW-Madison, noting that the UW System and Board of Regents have a "long tradition of inclusive and transparent review, input, and discussion" bemoaned the fact that changes to tenure protections included in the 2015–2017 biennial budget were "put into proposed law without any public discussion or input from the higher education community."[7]

This approach effectively sends the message that one party (i.e., education) is not valued and its voice is not being considered when legislation and policy is being crafted. This is a textbook case of how *not* to engage in partnership work—unless, of course, one is uninterested in truly acting as a partner. This raises the question about whose interests are being reflected and considered in regard to postsecondary policy, if not postsecondary administrators' and educators'? In the case of Wisconsin, where the skills gap narrative ruled the day, the answer is clear and unabashedly so: certain segments of the business community. To put the situation in perspective, imagine a scenario where the tables were turned, and higher education leaders were the sole voice being heard regarding workforce and economic development policy, with the business community relegated to the sidelines. The cries of indignation would be deafening.

In response to the unwillingness of the Walker administration to engage in a dialogue with the postsecondary community, and to offer legislation that reflected the best interests of public higher education in the state, the national American Association of University Professors (AAUP) and the Wisconsin branch of the American Federation of Teachers (AFT) released the following statement in February 2016:

> Since 2011, the governor and the legislature of the state of Wisconsin have been engaged in an attack on the UW System as a public good that exists for the benefit of all citizens of the state. This vision of higher education has shaped the UW System since the formulation of the Wisconsin Idea in 1904. The attack began with the assault on collective bargaining in the state through Act 10, and continued with legislative changes to tenure, due process, and shared governance, changes that threaten to undermine academic freedom. This attack jeopardizes the working conditions of faculty and academic staff as well as the learning conditions of students in the UW System.[8]

With these critiques in mind, we return to a central issue implicated in the skills gap narrative and the overarching question regarding the ultimate purpose of higher education: whose interests should be served? The private gain of students and the economy, the public good of society at large, or the basic pursuit of knowledge and learning for its own sake? Or perhaps a combination thereof?

The answer to this question was clear during the years of our field study in Wisconsin. The interests of the "economy" were by far foremost in the minds of policy makers and many pundits, meaning that the health and vitality of the private sector was being prioritized. Besides ruffling the feathers of the AAUP and AFT-Wisconsin, the implications of this stance are far more deleterious than skills gap advocates appreciate, because when the playing field is tilted so severely to favor one side, the prospects of true collaboration, trust, and productive relations are jeopardized, if not made impossible. Consequently, one of the principal strategies for strengthening the school-to-work pipeline—to cultivate more partnerships between higher education and the business community—becomes rather difficult to set into motion.

THE PROBLEM OF CONSIDERING THE SELF-INTEREST OF ONLY ONE PARTNER

Consider for a moment a historic example of a partnership between a university and the private sector. In the early 1900s, L. R. Jones was recruited to the Plant Pathology Department at UW-Madison, where he embarked on a research program to study cabbage diseases. Instead of concocting research questions on his own, however, Jones asked Wisconsin cabbage farmers to identify varieties that were likely to be disease resistant. Later colleagues observed that "the concept of a professor building on what the farmer already knew was fundamental in an effective partnership."[9] Thereafter, whenever the legislature held hearings on the university budget, the farmers who had partnered with Jones would travel to Madison to support university-based research.

Whose self-interest was being pursued here—that of the farming community, the university researcher, or the state as a whole? The question of self-interest is critical in partnership work, as research in the administrative sciences has shown that the inevitable tension between each partner's self-interest has the potential to torpedo collaborative work from the beginning. Unless the partnership has an element of interdependence, where "parties to a network agree to forego the right to pursue their own interests at the expense of others," the prospects of a productive relationship are dim.[10] Another key ingredient in productive collaborative work is trust, because it paves the way for reciprocity and more efficient interactions with the other.[11]

Thus, the tension between self-interest (which is natural, necessary, and good for partnership work) and collective interest must be managed and negotiated carefully so that trust can be developed, and the real work of creating new apprenticeship or internship programs can follow. However, there are considerable problems with the way partnership work is being promoted and designed, not just in the state of Wisconsin but across the United States. Joint efforts are often framed strictly in terms of the self-interests of one partner. Even technical colleges where attention to jobs is a core institutional mission, there are other interests (e.g., students and society) that must be given equal consideration.

Charles Isbell, an associate dean in the College of Computing at Georgia Tech, a university renowned for its close ties to industry, underscored this point when he spoke of the fact that some companies (with their short-term needs foremost in mind) will ask for a wholesale change in the curriculum, and then come back three years later with new ideas. Isbell noted that such fickleness is at odds with the long-term mission of the university, which aims to provide students with long-lasting competencies. In regards to partnership, Isbell observed that "the two sides are always going to be pushing back against one another—universities have the responsibility to push back."[12]

Until and unless a respectful coordination of self-interest is addressed and negotiated, it is not partnership, but simply a top-down imposition of change. In the case of employer-centric perspectives, this is particularly problematic given the fact that businesses play a considerable role in skills-related debates (i.e., via workplace training and hiring for cultural fit), though their responsibilities are neither discussed nor the focus of policy makers. It is clear that in this higher education–workforce system, some form of engagement across fields is essential, and if done well, can yield results that single organizations acting on their own would be unable to effect. The question, then, becomes how to best engage in partnership work.

IT'S HARDER THAN IT LOOKS: RULES FOR DESIGNING EFFECTIVE PARTNERSHIPS

Partnerships and collaborations between and among organizations have long been studied in administrative science, and the evidence suggests that between 60 and 80 percent result in failure.[13] This was evident in prior research we conducted on education partnerships, where shared work is often entered into on the basis of a handshake or an e-mail agreement, with little conversation about critical matters such as goals and objectives, expectations for work, and perhaps most importantly, who has the authority to spend money and make decisions.[14] Fortunately, we and other scholars have identified aspects of designing and implementing partnerships that, if considered, should increase the prospects for success.[15]

Identify the Type of Collaboration That Best Suits the Activity

Too often people assume "partnership" is one thing; it is not. There are at least three distinct types: *limited* partnerships, in which one organization clearly directs the actions of others; *coordinated* partnerships, which involve horizontal coordination but no centralized governance; and *collaborative* partnerships, in which partners are tightly coupled and employ a consensus-based governance system. The collaborative type of partnership deserves special attention. Barbara Gray captured the core idea that distinguishes this type of arrangement when she wrote, "Collaboration is a process through which parties who see different aspects of a problem can constructively explore their differences and search for solutions that go beyond their own limited vision of what is possible."[16]

It is this potential for constructive exploration of differences and development of solutions that makes collaborative partnerships so attractive and yet so challenging at the same time, as they are difficult to manage and generally fail more often than they succeed. In regard to crafting partnerships to support the skills infrastructure, partnership types should be carefully matched to the nature of the task at hand and the degree of trust among potential partners. In some cases, a limited partnership may work well (e.g., a campus internship office directing employers to submit position openings), while other cases may demand something more collaborative (e.g., creation of a new degree program tailored to an emerging local industry).

Get Acquainted and Honestly Appraise Self-Interests at Stake

Researchers agree that partnerships should begin with a careful planning stage, where all potential partners meet and get acquainted with one another and clearly discuss the proposed work. This involves not only getting to know the key personalities in the other organizations and developing a sense of familiarity, but also learning the basics about how their organizations operate. In particular, honestly assessing what each organization hopes to gain from the partnership (i.e., its self-interest) is essential in order to better understand people's motivations and actions. Research indicates that some degree of self-interest is a key ingredient to successful collaboration, as without it, why put much energy into the work? But if only one party's self-interest frames and informs the work, the chances for a truly synergistic partnership are low.

Potential partners should then discuss these issues openly in pre-partnership planning meetings that bring representatives from different organizations together. This is a good way to start things off on an informed and, ideally, a positive footing. At these meetings, critical issues need to be discussed, such as goals and objectives for the partnership, the nature of the problem at hand, and so on. Based on the results of this meeting, the parties can decide whether moving forward is in everyone's best interests. In the event that the work must continue based on legislative mandate or a leader's directive, this early stage is perhaps doubly important, as there are no "escape clauses" if things go awry.

Engage in a Careful Design Process

Once the parties have agreed to proceed, it is time to begin designing the organizational structure for the partnership. Because newly initiated partnerships in the third space lack structure and procedures, starting them is akin to creating entirely new organizations: hierarchies, policies governing task delegation and accountability, and other features of functioning organizations must be established. Further, because the organizational structure of a partnership will guide these policies and procedures, if these features are at odds with the existing cultural dynamics of the partner organizations, a smoothly operating partnership is unlikely. Thus, choosing the organizational structure and designing its procedures are among the most important activities in the third space of partnership, and these are not simple tasks. Unfortunately, this is the stage that many administrators cite as their worst experience with collaboration. If the partners fail at this early point to demarcate boundaries and create effective structures and procedures, it likely will exacerbate, rather than address, the inherent tensions in partnership work.

Cultivate Personnel Who Are Boundary Crossers

Finally, once the partnership is designed, successful implementation depends on the presence of staff and leaders who are both flexible and able to cross organizational and cultural boundaries—these are *boundary crossers*. At all organizational levels, these individuals will need to contend with boundaries that separate different organizations, cultural groups (e.g., disciplines), and stakeholders. Failure to effectively navigate these boundaries may result in misinterpretations of events or documents, or even outright conflict. Effective boundary crossers can anticipate and mitigate these tensions, largely because they tend to be good listeners, can empathize, take careful notice of others' views and tacit assumptions, and can find common ground among different parties. These individuals are particularly important in navigating education-workforce partnerships, as the cultural divisions, goals, self-interests, and power dynamics can be particularly stark.

EIGHT TYPES OF PARTNERSHIP WORK TO SUPPORT THE SKILLS INFRASTRUCTURE

Now that we know some ground rules about how to engage in partnership work, the question remains: what types of partnerships can ensure that students are acquiring twenty-first-century habits of mind? There are many different possible strategies, and many different initiatives under way around the United States and the world: apprenticeships, education-workplace clusters, an articulation of career pathways, stackable credentials, specialized colleges for specific companies, and so on.[17]

In our own study and through a review of the literature, we identified eight efforts that appear to be particularly influential in "hitting" or shaping critical aspects of the higher education–workforce system that are centered on student learning. Each of these strategies can be mapped onto the aforementioned categories of partnership (i.e., limited, coordinated, collaborative) so that it is clear what types of investment and commitment will be required for each one.

Student Career Services: Limited Partnerships to Provide Up-to-Date Labor Market Data

One of the simplest, and most common, types of education-workplace partnerships is where employers provide information about job openings, internship opportunities, and other information to campus-based career services. This is clearly a low-risk partnership type that involves limited investment in time or resources. While this is a good start in facilitating lines of communication across fields, and increasing opportunities for students, the coordination can and should also extend to state government, regional workforce entities, and others who have access to cutting-edge labor market information. Such data, which are becoming increasingly available from both public and private sources who scour online job postings and labor market statistics to discern trends in hiring, need to be readily accessible for students through campus career services.

Knowing whether or not biotechnology technicians or art teachers are commanding high wages due to a skills shortage could be important information to students as they make decisions about their academic and career trajectories. Of course, students should also be provided with information about job projections so that they can plan for getting not just that first job, but also that tenth job decades hence.

Workplace Training: Coordinated Partnerships for Educators to Design Programs

When employers invest in the training of their employees, it behooves them to take advantage of local educators who are conversant with their industry and adept at designing hands-on learning activities. For example, while "Megotronics University" (a pseudonym) may sound like a four-year college, it's actually a corporate training program at a plastics company in Superior, Wisconsin. Judy Aspling, the HR director at this company, described the partnership with their local technical college as follows: "They had the skills to develop the curriculum, and we knew what we wanted to teach and how it needed to be learned; we just didn't know how to do this [curriculum design] part of it."

The collaboration with the school resulted not only in a unique online training program but also a relationship with the school where she and her contact still exchange information. "This is the kind of thing that I would argue manufacturers should be going toward," Judy said, ". . . working with the technical colleges or whatever educational institutions that might be out there in order to come up with plans to specifically train their people in what they're doing rather than trying to fit somebody's generic instruction into their different-shaped hole."

Program Advisory Boards: Coordinated Partnerships to Support Course Redesign and Authentic Curricula

Many professional programs and two-year colleges are required to have a curriculum advisory board comprising local businesses, faculty, and administrators who regularly meet to discuss the curriculum and program changes. Through these boards, a considerable amount of information about industry trends, real-world problems, and job opportunities is conveyed to program faculty and staff. Thus, these advisory boards could be a venue where educators glean information about authentic situations and problems that could then be incorporated into learning opportunities such as PBL exercises. At the very least, such boards would provide a regular conduit for the sharing of information across sectoral boundaries where for many, particularly in nonprofessional programs, very little coordination or contact currently takes place.

Employer-Provided Guidance Regarding Student Projects: Coordinated Partnerships to Provide Ideas for Student Research and Capstones

One of the most interesting and promising examples of education-workplace partnerships we encountered in our study was the undergraduate research program at UW–La Crosse managed by Scott Cooper. Whether they are semester-long research projects, senior capstone courses, or mini-projects, self-directed courses of scientific inquiry are one of the richest learning experiences that can be provided for students. In the course of articulating hypotheses, reviewing the literature, gathering and analyzing data, and communicating results, students have the opportunity to practice many of the twenty-first-century habits of mind discussed in this book.

In order to make student projects at UW–La Crosse more realistic, and ultimately meaningful beyond the confines of the classroom, Scott canvasses local business owners and other community members for ideas about issues and problems that they feel are important to address. For example, a local antihunger group might want to know their return on investment for their fundraising activities, which could be taken up by an accounting class for further study. Students then take these ideas— called "course-embedded projects"—and conduct independent research throughout the course, followed by presentations to the idea's origina- tor. This is an excellent example of a coordinated partnership that brings the "outside" world into the classroom in the context of a rich learning opportunity.

Employers and Other Community Members Serving as Expert Resources for Student Projects: Coordinated Partnerships to Support Student Learning

One of the central ideas of the cognitive apprenticeship approach to instruction is that students do not rely exclusively on their instructor for guidance and expertise. They also rely on peers and outside experts, and many problems and projects explored through classroom assignments can be enhanced through the input of local business owners, government employees, or others who can be considered experts and practitioners in their field. This type of coordination would involve the instructor estab- lishing standing relationships or contacts with a cadre of experts in the area that their students could contact.

This type of relationship will make a student's experience with a proj- ect a far richer and more multifaceted experience than if they just relied on textbooks, research papers, and Google. Additionally, they will make a personal contact, get a glimpse of the working world, and see the topic through the eyes of another person whose perspective is unlike their own.

Expanding Academic Program Capacity: Collaborative Partnerships to Create or Expand Academic Programs in Response to Student/Workforce Demands

One of the more common recommendations for partnerships dealing with skill-related workforce issues is for educators to be more "respon- sive" to local, regional, and statewide occupational shortages by opening up more courses and positions for incoming students. Of course, matters are complicated when educators' hands are tied with budget cuts, limited space, and the complex nature of adding programs, but paying attention to demands in the labor market and student interest is something that most colleges and universities should be doing. In the case of UW-Madison's computer science department, student demand and a large donation from local philanthropists allowed them to expand their lower-division courses and admit more students. Such responses could be made more efficient and nimble if relationships with the local business community already exist; otherwise, educators will only learn of mounting demand several months or even years later.

A cautionary note must be issued regarding educators' response to labor market demands, however, as those demands may shift and change rather quickly, and educational programming should not be a reaction to fleeting needs or trends in the economy. Programming decisions should also not be made based on legislative fiat or the recommendations of industry groups or others whose interests in the situation may not be exactly objective. Educators should conduct a careful analysis of how a new or expanded program would serve students' short- and long-term needs, as well as how it would work with existing courses and programs, before going down this path.

Creating Community Coalitions: Collaborative Partnerships to Open Lines of Communication

Another common form of partnership is a regional "cluster" or coalition of educators, employers, government, and community representatives that convene in order to talk about economic and community development. One example is the University System of Maryland–Business Higher Education Forum Undergraduate Cybersecurity Network, a coalition of educators, businesses, government, and others who work together to create new educational programs in cyber-related degrees and certificates. Besides generating programmatic outcomes, these coalitions open lines of communication among parties who often have not been in contact with one another in a concerted and strategic effort. At the very least, community-level forums, annual conferences (such as those sponsored by Wisconsin Manufacturers and Commerce about the skills gap), and similar types of meetings can be invaluable for sparking conversations among the key players who are responsible for different parts of the skills infrastructure.

Expanding Student Out-of-School Learning: Collaborative Partnership to Expand and Enhance Internship and Cooperative Learning Opportunities

Finally, one of the more common responses to skills-related concerns is to create or expand internship, apprenticeship, and cooperative learning programs. Each of these three distinct types of out-of-school training includes employment in a local business as part of a student's academic program. Internships typically last a summer and may or may not be tied to program curricula, whereas cooperative programs may last longer and are closely tied to a student's coursework and learning expectations. Apprenticeships last years and typically involve working four days a week and attending school for one.

Whatever the program, these experiences offer students the opportunity to apply their classroom-based learning in new situations, which should allow for ample chances to transfer new concepts and ideas into real-world settings. The stronger the link between the classroom and the internship or co-op site, the better it is for the student. In any case, establishing such programs requires a considerable amount of collaboration, as many involve site visits, employer reports, and coordination of curriculum with job-site activities, all of which will require time, trust, and resources.

CONCLUSION

A New Vision for the Role of Higher Education in Society

But the Wisconsin tradition meant more than a simple belief in the people. It also meant a faith in the application of intelligence and reason to the problems of society. It meant a deep conviction that the role of government was not to stumble along like a drunkard in the dark, but to light its way by the best torches of knowledge and understanding it could find.

—ADLAI STEVENSON, MADISON, WISCONSIN, 1952[1]

THE PERVASIVE CULTURAL GAP

As we've traveled around Wisconsin and the rest of the country, giving talks and presentations about our study, the question inevitably comes up. *Is* there a skills gap? The question itself, while understandable, is flawed. The skills gap narrative, as it is framed and promoted in the state of Wisconsin and elsewhere, amounts to an elaborate *story*, a manufactured narrative designed to advance a particular ideology about the role and purpose of higher education in society.

Yes, there do appear to be skills shortages, which are occupation- and region-specific skills mismatches. In our fieldwork we heard firsthand of the need for nurses throughout the entire state, electrical engineers in western Wisconsin, and machinists in the eastern industrial regions of the state. Can the educational sector play a role in addressing these shortages and in better preparing college students for the working world? Certainly, and the skills infrastructure described in chapter 7 addresses the expansion or creation of academic programs that could deal with the "supply" side of the equation, as well as the provision of career services so that students are not left on their own to figure out how to market their art history or biology degrees.

The other questions that usually arise, especially after the political back and forth of the last few years, are telling. Is education to blame for employers' hiring problems and sluggish job creation? Do liberal arts programs not produce employable graduates who can contribute to the economy? Is the educational sector the sole party responsible for instilling in young people skills like work ethic and complex problem solving, and for keeping working adults' skills up-to-date? Is the best solution to cut education budgets and focus on short-term training programs? The answer to all of these questions, based on the evidence we collected from 145 interviews, numerous factory and research lab tours, and an extensive review of the academic and popular literatures, is no.

There does exist a pervasive gap between the habits of mind that many (but not all) postsecondary educators *and* employers are cultivating via classroom instruction or employer training, and the types of competencies required for students to excel in school, the workplace, and public life. But it is a failure on behalf of a variety of parties—not only academic programs that do not discuss careers with their students or professors who recite textbook chapters in the lecture hall, but also employers who do not provide their employees with training or professional development and who fail to craft continual learning environments within their organizations. Taking a broad perspective, there are also soccer coaches, parents, 4-H leaders, peers, K–12 teachers, legislators, and journalists that play a role in cultivating skills, knowledge, abilities, and habits in young people. But, apart from those students who have a small Years Off the Farm (YOTF) quotient and those who graduated from programs such as Tom Heraly's, Janet Batzli's, and Peter Dettmer's, it is likely that a gap will remain between what employers want out of college graduates and what competencies those young people actually bring into a job interview.

These competencies can be summed up as a combination of a strong work ethic; rigorous technical training; the ability to solve complex technical problems and interpersonal dilemmas, engage in teamwork, and communicate effectively; and the ability and desire to continually learn.

These are the habits of mind that are necessary for innovative and competent workers that the business community craves; for citizens who can contribute to a healthy democracy; for thinkers who can creatively solve the environmental, social, and economic challenges of the twenty-first century; and for students to have the best opportunities for securing employment throughout their working lives.

Rather than talking about education and jobs as a technical issue to solve with more programs and career aptitude tests, we need to be talking about these issues in cultural terms: how challenging yet transformative it is to cultivate twenty-first-century habits of mind, how hiring is often a highly subjective (yet important) matter of finding a good "fit," and how family, peers, educators, employers, and society at large collectively "brand" a person through a slow and subtle process of socialization and apprenticeship into different cultural groups. Putting culture in the foreground forces us to think more deeply and systemically about the relationships among skills development, education, and employment.

In his listening sessions with manufacturing executives throughout Wisconsin, Jim Morgan of Wisconsin Manufacturers and Commerce had put his finger right on the cultural underpinnings of the skills gap idea. Focus group respondents told Jim that they valued a complex combination—embodied in the notion of YOTF—of interpersonal skills, technical expertise, and a strong work ethic. These results were not dissimilar to our findings. But just as Morgan considered Marc Levine's claim that the skills gap was a myth to be a matter of the "right information, wrong conclusion," WMC's diagnosis of the situation and policy recommendations are similarly off the mark.[2] Our data support their views on the skills employers need as well as the fact that these skills come from a combination of various formal and informal experiences—such as school and working on a farm—but we disagree that educators alone can (or should) be responsible for instilling these skills, especially in a climate in which they are disparaged and underfunded.

Instead, there exists a yawning gap between the skills gap narrative—which takes an exceedingly narrow view of skills, ignores the role of teaching, overlooks employers' part in contributing to hiring problems and skills deficiencies, ignores the systemic nature of education-industry dynamics, and sees accountability and short-term training programs as the primary solution—and the real needs of the labor market. In other words, pursuing the path set forth by Governor Walker's administration, leaders of WMC, and the Wisconsin Policy Research Institute, among others, will ultimately hinder the talent development that these parties so desperately wish to support.

How will this trend affect the cultivation of valuable competencies? In the spirit of the systems analyses advanced in this book, where simulations are often run from starting conditions to see how different scenarios may unfold, in the next sections we seek to answer this question by imagining possible futures for our educators Janet Batzli, Tom Heraly, Scott Cooper, and Tim Wright.

WHAT DIRECTION WILL WE TAKE? IMAGINING DIFFERENT FUTURES

These hypothetical stories do not follow only one of two options—a skills gap–dominated era or one grounded in the Wisconsin Idea and the liberal arts tradition—because there are so many variables at play. Instead, they are but a few of the endless number of possibilities, even if their starting conditions have been delimited by the skills gap narrative.

Janet Batzli's Story at the University of Wisconsin–Madison

The price to attend universities such as UW-Madison continues to increase, not only because of tuition but also expenses related to books, room and board, and the daily necessities of college life. The average debt of graduates from public four-year institutions in Wisconsin, with which 70 percent of students graduate, is projected to rise from $26,210 in 2014 to $34,200 in 2020, with no relief in sight. With wages not keeping up with rising inflation, middle-class students across the country who hope to acquire a bachelor's degree begin to seek out other options for their education. These include amassing Advanced Placement credits in high school so that few, if any, general education or foundational courses are needed in the freshman and sophomore years, or taking these courses at local community colleges and then transferring in their junior or senior years.

Janet observes all of these developments with some trepidation, as the effects on Biocore and other programs at UW-Madison are clear: declining enrollment in these early undergraduate courses. Since tuition dollars are one of the most important revenue streams for public institutions, given the precipitous drop in state support, this decline has considerable costs. But these costs should be measured in terms of hits not only to the university, but also to the growing numbers of students, particularly those from low-income and underrepresented minority groups, that are able to afford a postsecondary education. Another impact on students is related to the rush to finish college as quickly as possible, which leads students away from two-year foundational programs like Biocore that are designed to prepare them for advanced coursework in any bioscience major, and four-year programs whose curricula are carefully designed to cultivate specific habits of mind and integrate disparate fields of knowledge over time.

Instead, a new three-year degree option and a state-mandated cut to general education course requirements results in students not being exposed to disciplines (and ways of thinking) outside of their chosen major; not having time to develop critical thinking, writing, and collaboration skills, and other twenty-first-century habits of mind; and not being adequately socialized into authentic disciplinary settings, such as a biological research laboratory. While Janet continues to teach her students how to be professional biologists, as well as competent writers, thinkers, and problem solvers, Biocore exists as a boutique program for the very few students who understand how critical these skills are for life and career preparation. Perhaps most distressingly, programs like Biocore become limited only to those students who can afford the time and cost to attend a four-year university. Due to regular budget cuts by the state, continuing fiscal pressures slowly chip away at the number of students who leave campus fully prepared for the economic, social, and environmental challenges of the twenty-first century. Employers, in turn, notice even less evidence of the kinds of twenty-first-century skills they need in job applicants.

Tom Heraly's Story at Milwaukee Area Technical College

The governor and state legislature shift course and embark on a well-resourced campaign to retain educational talent in the state. While providing pay increases to better align state faculty salaries with peer institutions across the country, the state institutes professional development programs specifically designed to train faculty members how to teach twenty-first-century competencies. State leaders also ask the Department of Public Instruction to organize a public effort to actively promote the teaching profession.

Commercials are filmed where K–12, Wisconsin Technical College System (WTCS), and UW System instructors are shown hard at work, and then showered with praise by famous Wisconsin citizens such as Bob Ueker (of Milwaukee Brewers fame), Greta van Susteren (of Fox News), and actor Willem Defoe. Tom Heraly is featured in a commercial catching a forty-yard spiral from Aaron Rodgers, the Green Bay Packers quarterback, at the historic Lambeau Field. As a part of these initiatives, Tom's school, MATC, launches a campaign in collaboration with WMC to inform the public that a combination of technical and nontechnical training in two-year colleges will better prepare students for the future.

Tom's version of the Kobayashi Maru approach to problem-based learning, recognized by fellow educators nationwide and supported by several empirical studies of student learning, is written into a new national curriculum for electronics courses. State funding for education-workplace partnerships, especially for internship programs that closely link programs like Tom's with on-the-job experiences, strengthens the pathways for students in the WTCS into the workforce as well as further educational opportunities. Shortly thereafter, regional businesses, which had been struggling to find skilled writers, communicators, and problem solvers, notice an upward shift in the applicant pool for their middle- and low-wage jobs.

Scott Cooper's Story at the University of Wisconsin–La Crosse

After several of his students present excellent research at the annual Posters in the Rotunda event in Madison, Scott Cooper's efforts supporting undergraduate research get statewide and then nationwide press attention.[3] The president of the UW System, duly impressed by what Scott and his colleagues have managed to do on a shoestring budget, holds a press conference at the state capitol building where he and several legislators hold up undergraduate research as a prime example of how twenty-first-century competencies *and* workforce needs can be met through traditional liberal arts programming. The *Chronicle of Higher Education* and *Education Week* cover the event, and soon NPR Marketplace picks up the story.

With this media coverage, the issue of how the nation prepares its post-secondary educators begins to be discussed in coffee shops and around water coolers, and soon a movement is under way to require that all instructors in colleges and universities take *at least* two courses in teaching methods and learning theory. Scott's example of breaking down the walls between the university classroom and the business community also inspires campuses around the country to institute a similar approach for gathering research ideas and embedding them within courses where students engage in independent research. The state even crafts legislation to allocate funding for "research experience offices" at each campus, where staff gather community-based ideas and team up with faculty, administrators, and students to share the ideas and coordinate final research presentations for original "clients." This single change effectively transforms the town-gown dynamic in many communities around the nation, giving residents and business owners a better understanding of and appreciation for what goes on behind university walls, and helping many educators become more attuned to the needs and concerns of their region.

Tim Wright's Story at Wisconsin Indianhead Technical College

Unlike the previous scenarios, this story, unfortunately, is true. As it turns out, it was a good thing that Tim Wright didn't think of his courses solely as an external training program for Kestrel. The company that had provided the impetus for the new Aerospace Composites program continued to struggle economically. In September 2013 Kestrel employees began reporting that paychecks were late and vendors were going unpaid.[4] In early 2014 news broke that the company was behind on months of loan payments to the Wisconsin Economic Development Corporation (WEDC), and by the summer of 2014 only 24 jobs had been created out of the promised 665. To make an already grim situation worse, in the summer of 2015 it emerged that the WEDC had given over $124 million in awards to companies across the state without formal review.[5] Some of these rewards, it was reported, had gone to now-bankrupted companies and well-placed donors to Governor Walker's gubernatorial campaigns.

Kestrel merged with Eclipse Aerospace and formed a new company called ONE Aviation in 2015, but by early 2016 the company still had created only thirty jobs in Superior, most of them engineers, and the owner still didn't know where the company's marquee plane—the Eclipse 500—would be built. Given the uncertainty around these jobs, student enrollment in the Aerospace Composites program slipped. With capacity for sixteen students, in January 2016 there were only seven, and WITC made the decision to shutter the program. As administrator Bonny Copenhaver said, "If we have no students coming in and no large employer on the back end, it creates a stranglehold."[6]

This story is a case study in the limitations of creating educational programs exclusively to "meet workforce needs" and satisfy an employer's expectations for skilled labor. It also is an illustration of the government's limited abilities to predict trends in the labor market, including which "hot" jobs students should devote their limited time and tuition dollars to pursuing. Finally, it is also a cautionary tale for those who would narrow the curriculum to focus exclusively on cultivating technical acumen alone, and ignore the development of habits of mind that will serve students well regardless of the job they ultimately land. As Tim and others have observed, a student who graduated from this program with a well-rounded education should be employable in the marine repair, windsurfing, or aerospace industries, not just a single company.

Tim retired in 2015 after devoting decades of his life to the aerospace industry and being an educator at the community college level. In our last conversation with him, he had wistfully noted that enrollment was down in the program and WITC was actively seeking ways to broaden its attractiveness so that it wasn't seen as a one-way ticket to a company whose fortunes were in question. While most of those who graduated under Tim's tutelage have found other jobs in the area, the critical missing link in this picture was the 665 family-supporting jobs that Kestrel promised the Superior region.

A NEW VISION FOR THE ROLE OF HIGHER EDUCATION IN THE TWENTY-FIRST CENTURY

And so we return—after thinking of teaching, partnerships, skills, and politics—to the central issue underlying this book: the ultimate role of higher education in the twenty-first century.

First, employability *is* a central concern. Educators owe it to their students to give them the skills to acquire a satisfying career and to be lifelong learners so they can grow with and adapt to an economy that no one can predict. Students from underprivileged backgrounds, especially, deserve the kind of education that will enable them to earn that associate's, bachelor's, or graduate degree to catapult them into the lives and careers they dream about.

All postsecondary educators and leaders need to think about and actively prepare students for the world of work. With these points taken as a given, however, they cannot be the *only* rationale and vision for higher education, whether a one-, two- or four-year program. A broader, more far-sighted vision is necessary for the benefit of students, the economy, and society itself that pairs a focus on employability and economic growth with the traditional focus on learning, knowledge creation, and public service.

Sometimes called the *new vocationalism*, this vision is based on recognizing not only which way the neoliberally inspired political winds are blowing, but also (as generations of learning scientists have concluded) that overly academic, decontextualized schooling needs to cease. Instead, education needs to be more grounded, more authentic, and more transferable. This is the assessment of Lumina Foundation President Jamie Merisotis, who in explaining the foundation's investments in postsecondary education, argued: "We need to abandon our historic view in higher education that we don't train people for jobs. That doesn't mean it is the only thing we do, but to deny that job skills development is one of the key purposes of higher education is increasingly untenable. Education also must equip people with the skills they need to adapt in whatever way is necessary as their lives change, jobs evolve, and new opportunities arise."[7] Author Michael Roth, in sharing Merisotis's observation, notes that these goals are similar to the traditional goals of a liberal education, even though they represent a "contemporary version" that highlights more vocational-oriented goals. While Roth recognizes the current realities of higher education, he is nervous about these developments. If they entail a narrowly conceived view of education, focused primarily on employability and workforce issues, he worries that we risk a "self-defeating path to conformity and inflexibility—just the kind of traits that will doom one to irrelevance in contemporary culture and society."[8]

Why? Because the goals of a liberal education—which at its heart aims for the "liberation" of the individual—are to prepare students to challenge conformity in their own and others' thinking and to "create habits of action that grow out of a spirit of broad inquiry."[9] In liberating the student from old ways of thinking, stereotypes, and stale ideas, an education should ideally be a transformative experience that awakens learners of all ages to the complexity of the world.[10] This entails a learner experimenting with new ideas and disciplines, studying music, string theory, photosynthesis, or Cezanne's early paintings, all out of curiosity. This notion of a broad inquiry recalls the vision of Charles Van Hise, who hoped that students would be free to explore the world of knowledge "with their tastes and aptitudes as varied as mankind."[11]

Such a spirit of broad inquiry across the disciplines has the added benefit of helping people to get a job. Perhaps the most famous example of the role and value of liberal arts training, and specifically the arts and humanities, in the world of commerce is that of Steve Jobs and Apple. When Jobs introduced the iPad 2 in 2011, he famously said, "It is in Apple's DNA that technology alone is not enough—it's technology married with liberal arts, married with the humanities, that yields us the results that make our heart sing." Beyond Silicon Valley's heart, Apple made the pocketbooks of its shareholders sing on the way to becoming a $500 billion company, due in part to Jobs' careful study of calligraphy and historic typefaces when he designed the first Macintosh computer.[12] As a chemist said, "If American STEM grads are going to lead the world in innovation, then their science education cannot be divorced from the liberal arts."[13]

What the labor market and society need, however, are not just STEM-trained technicians with an art class under their belt. In fact, the very notion of STEM has come under considerable fire, not just for being too expansive and ill defined an acronym (biology alone has numerous subfields), but because it "undermines the unity between the humanities and the sciences" in their common pursuit of creativity, knowledge, and refined thinking.[14] In fact, there are roles in industry for those trained in fields such as art history, French literature, and anthropology. For instance, while the Big Data movement may bring to mind a host of computer scientists, many in the field are arguing for "small data"—from interviews and surveys as well as the insights of social scientists—to contextualize and interpret the results of complex calculations.[15] As a result, throughout Silicon Valley companies like Facebook have sought out people trained in many apparently nonmarketable fields, because these companies' algorithms and data mining analyses need psychologists, anthropologists, and sociologists to find what simple measures and numbers cannot.[16]

This is not to suggest that any of these disciplines—chemistry, psychology, art, or biology—should be seen solely in terms of the labor market, business, or profit. To insist that research on gravitational waves, Tarantino's films, or the ancient mating habits of blue whales must provide an immediate and obvious economic return is shortsighted to say the least, and devalues the basic pursuit of knowledge itself. In fact, the division may not be between science and the liberal arts, but instead "between respect for human intelligence and creativity, and contempt for it."[17]

But there is something else that should be part of the discussion. Colonel John W. Hall, a military historian at the University of Wisconsin–Madison, described it as being involved in something "bigger than oneself."[18] Speaking of military service and the Wisconsin Idea in similar terms, Hall pleaded with the state assembly to "close this breach" of trust that recent politics and disparagement of higher education had opened in the state, and we, too, hope that our political leaders will chart a more moderate path. When the notion of serving the public good, or pursuing interests that are not grounded in self-preservation or maximizing profit, is eliminated from the public dialogue about higher education—as it has been in Wisconsin and increasingly around the world in recent years—students are given an impoverished vision of life and public service.

This is because the issues of our time demand the skills, ingenuity, and creativity of the next generation. "We are making choices that will affect our grandchildren's grandchildren and beyond," said Harvard University's Daniel Schrag about climate change, arguing that it is therefore essential to "think carefully about the long timescales of what we are unleashing."[19] A narrow focus on jobs, education for private gain, and technical STEM fields ignores these matters, which is counterproductive in regard not only to the changing climate, but also to the economy. As Fareed Zakaria has written, the focus on STEM at the expense of the liberal arts "puts America on a dangerously narrow path for the future," largely because automatization will eventually mean that "critical thinking is, in the end, the only way to protect US jobs."[20]

Innovation and twenty-first-century habits of mind, or lack thereof, have implications not only for the economy but also for the health of democratic societies. Citizens exercising their rights and abilities to critique unjust laws, from taxation without representation to institutionalized violations of civil rights, is one of the things that has made the United States such a vibrant, productive, and pluralistic society. Given the persistence of problems such as structural racism and income inequality, and an increasingly polarized political arena where reasoned debates often lose out to sound bites and reality television stars, we need more critical thinkers and advocates for the public good than ever before. And once again, arguments for the retention of the democratic and liberating aspects of higher education are not grounded solely in idealism, but have a market-based rationale. Since employers need culturally competent staff to interact with clients and colleagues from other countries, ethnicities, and backgrounds, eliminating those seemingly useless courses in multicultural awareness or gender studies could ultimately come back to haunt the society *and* the economy.

The higher education sector around the world is undergoing massive changes and pressures at the beginning of the twenty-first century, such that a hundred years from now institutions like UW-Madison and MATC may not be recognizable in how they approach teaching and learning, in how courses are delivered, and in how they are supported/funded. The push continues to conceptualize higher education solely as a job training enterprise for the so-called knowledge economy and to make college graduates "profit centers, not insightful human beings and citizens."[21] It is true, as the *LA Times* observed in early 2016 after the world-renowned University of California–Berkeley announced a massive restructuring initiative, that "things do have to change." But when making decisions about what those changes will look like, administrators, educators, legislators, and policy makers "should focus most on how students' education will be affected," not on ill-conceived notions like the skills gap.[22]

NEXT STEPS: A LEGISLATIVE AND PROGRAMMATIC PLAN FOR CHANGE

A new legislative vision is required if we as a society are serious about creating a skills infrastructure that supports students' acquisition of twenty-first-century competencies. It will take the visionary leadership and commitment of multiple actors—politicians of all parties, educators, educational administrators and Boards of Regents, faculty, and students themselves. It involves changing minds—that is, shifting habituated assumptions and stereotypes about the world, which admittedly is not easy. But, if the following recommendations were enacted, it would begin to knit together a more robust and responsive skills infrastructure, a more collective approach to society's challenges, and a more thoughtful and expansive framing of the problems facing our world than the skills gap narrative provides.

Government is not always the solution; some policies and changes are best managed at the local level of educational systems and institutions. Thus, we first discuss policies to enact within education itself, follow with suggestions for state and federal governments, and conclude by presenting a shift in thinking for everyone—the media, government, educators, business owners, and you the reader.

Recommendations for Educational Administrators and Systemwide Leaders

First, we make three recommendations for policy makers within the educational field, which includes the presidents of systems and institutions, regents, chancellors, deans, and faculty leaders. These recommendations pertaining to teacher certification, curriculum, and student services are intended to strengthen student experiences in ways that will improve the quality of their education as well as their long-term prospects in the workforce.

Provide mandatory, paid training in teaching methods for incoming instructors

It is, at best, contradictory that most K–12 teachers are required to have extensive training in classroom management, learning theory, and human development to become certified to teach in an elementary or secondary school, but instructors in many universities have never taken a single course in these topics. Institutions such as the technical college system in Wisconsin recognize this, and besides requiring academic instructors to have a bachelor's degree and extensive work experience (two thousand hours), they require instructors to complete the following seven courses (which are known colloquially as the "Magic 7") in order to obtain the standard five-year certification: curriculum or course instruction, philosophy of vocational/technical/adult education, teaching methods, educational psychology, educational evaluation, guidance and counseling, and educational diversity. But in the UW System, where the primary credential required to land a teaching job is a PhD, it is possible that teachers have not taken a single course in these topics.

While we are hesitant to add yet more bureaucratic requirements and criteria to an occupation that has been subject to constant policy changes, declining budgets, and intense and growing workloads, it is clear that a key linchpin to improving instruction in higher education is to require that all teachers become conversant in topics addressed by the Magic 7. Thus, we advance this policy recommendation: that all institutions of higher education (public and private) provide paid training in teaching methods to incoming instructors, whether tenure-track faculty or not.

Ensure all academic programs include an employability seminar and technical skill requirement

One of the ideas commonly discussed about how to modernize or update the liberal arts tradition is to add some sort of career-oriented course and/or technical coursework to program requirements. This is precisely what the UW-Madison Letters & Science Career Initiative did, with the mini-course on career decision making and employability skills like interviewing. This approach is exactly what is required for nonprofessional tracks such as those in liberal arts programs.

Others recommend that technical-skill requirements like computer science be integrated into the liberal arts curriculum so that those students will have at least one market-ready skill—and, in the case of programming, one that arguably will be essential for many careers in the twenty-first century. While this would necessitate a difficult decision about what to remove from existing course requirements, it may be a necessary trade-off.

Defend and maintain the liberal arts/general education core

That said, one of the strongest aspects of many associate's and bachelor's degree programs is the general education requirement. These programs tend to require nonmajor courses such as English, psychology, or history—or courses to "round out" a student. Given the centrality of a broad suite of competencies, and the fact that many disciplinary courses simply don't have the time to properly deal with communication or team-work, maintaining this core is critical. In addition, given the merits of practicing newfound habits of mind in both technical and nontechnical venues, as well as creativity, courses in the arts and humanities are par-ticularly important. This is a hallmark of US higher education that needs to be maintained.

Ensure that robust academic and career counseling services are available to all students

All college students, whether in a two- or four-year institution, big or small, urban or rural, should have access to high-quality support services. These include, at the least, an academic support unit that provides tutor-ing for students struggling with their coursework and workshops on study habits, time management, and so on. In addition, a career counseling office, particularly in nonprofessional programs and colleges, should be available for students as they think about their academic and career tra-jectories. These services should tap into the increasingly high-quality and real-time labor market systems being developed by states and private ven-dors. In addition to labor market reports and projections, students should be provided with one-on-one counseling, tips about available intern-ship and apprenticeship opportunities, and workshops on topics such as résumé writing and professional etiquette.

Recommendations for Government at the State Levels

Next, we make three recommendations for legislators and governors who oversee higher education and workforce development initiatives at the state level. In a decentralized system such as we have in the United States, this is the level at which most of the decisions are made that influence funding, provide a welcoming (or hostile) climate for public employees, and create the conditions for cross-field partnerships.

Increase state funding for public higher education

Some estimate that state support for public higher education will reach 0 percent by 2059, or even as early as 2019 in states such as Colorado.[23] This scenario keeps college and university administrators awake at night, wondering where the revenue will come from to pay faculty, keep the lights on, and so on. If state governments are serious about supporting a skilled workforce and educated populace, then, quite simply, they must allocate the funds to do so. If not, then policy makers will be directly responsible for undermining the engine of workforce development, knowledge creation, and the cultivation of twenty-first-century competencies for many years to come.

However, the current experimentation with performance-based funding, where state support for public institutions is allocated based on whether certain metrics are met—including graduate employment and wages—should not be applied to all types of postsecondary institutions. This recommendation is based on growing evidence that this approach simply does not lead to improved student outcomes, and the fact that the institutional missions of comprehensive and research-oriented universities (e.g., developing critical thinkers) cannot be distilled and reduced to variables that could be plugged into such a funding model.[24]

Finally, funding for higher education is not solely a domestic political issue, as countries such as China, explicitly aiming to supplant the United States as the largest economy of the world, are making massive investments in their higher education systems.[25] Although the traditional modes of pedagogy in East Asia, which typically have centered on rote memorization and teacher-centered pedagogies, are most likely holding back the creative habits of mind that are needed to fuel the "innovative spirit" evident in Western companies like Apple or US universities like the Massachusetts Institute of Technology, it is an open question as to where the center of intellectual activity and industrial innovation will be in 2050.[26]

Engage in an educator talent retention strategy

While state and local governments in the United States don't seem to support their public educators the way that countries like Japan and Finland do, it is not too late to change direction. One of the first steps should be to engage in an educator talent retention strategy, which would entail conducting an analysis of comparative pay for postsecondary educators in a given region. Then, based on the results, institutions must provide competitive pay and benefits packages to their instructional staff (both tenure-track and contingent faculty) as well as funding for merit bonuses. Just like in a private company, if administrators desire top-quality talent, they must be willing to pay for it.

Other components of a talent retention strategy include the cessation of policies that are driving talented educators away from states like Wisconsin, such as unnecessary "reforms" to tenure policies that ultimately create a competitive disadvantage. Finally, if they are sincere about wanting a top-notch educational infrastructure that can prepare a skilled workforce while also planting the seeds for the industries of the future, policy makers should cease publicly disparaging the education profession.

Foster strategic cross-field partnerships to support the entire skills infrastructure

Cross-field partnerships are essential to effectively support some of the key components of the skills infrastructure, such as student career counseling, the creation of multiple school-to-work pathways, and the development of curricula that integrates authentic, real-world problems and situations. While some partnership efforts may arise spontaneously between the postsecondary and business sectors, it is more likely that these collaborations would develop with the prompting of state and federal governments. Such prompts could include the creation of regional industry clusters, the development of state-level conferences to brainstorm collaborative efforts, and funding to support these and other partnership activities. In addition, such partnership efforts must pay careful attention to issues of autonomy, particularly for postsecondary educators whose professional autonomy has been eroded in recent years. Until and unless the autonomy of highly trained professionals is respected and preserved, productive collaborative work will be an uphill battle.

Recommendations for Policy Makers, Educators, and the General Public Around the World

Finally, we make a single recommendation to all readers and actors who play a role in education or the labor market, pertaining to the ideas that are embraced, repeated, and reified to the point of deeply influencing how we think and act.

Reject the skills gap narrative

We conclude our analysis with a simple appeal to those invested in a robust economy, renowned institutions of higher education, and a vibrant democracy: discard the skills gap narrative, particularly as it has been promoted and practiced in the state of Wisconsin. The one-dimensional version of education that this narrative represents is not only counter-productive to its purported goals, but myopic in its insistence that students can be prepared for only one part of their endlessly variable futures. Instead, we look to the past for inspiration, to the examples of Charles Van Hise and Thomas Jefferson, for instance, who heralded colleges and universities able to spark economic growth, inspire young minds, and, above all, cultivate a culture of critical inquiry and public service.

The coming decades will present remarkable and as of yet unforeseen challenges to the generation of children who are in prekindergarten and elementary school at the time of this writing. For those adults currently in positions of power and influence, failing to ensure that an educational system is in place by 2025 that will cultivate twenty-first-century competencies in all students is a failure of catastrophic proportions. Will our children and grandchildren look back to this era with pride, much like we look back on the Wisconsin Idea of the early twentieth century? Or will they look upon us with regret, disappointed that we did not have the courage, foresight, and creativity to set in motion the makings of a public higher education system that would be the envy of the world? Our educational institutions should give them the ability to recognize the difference.

APPENDIX

Methodology

This book is based on an in-depth qualitative case study, a research method that involves an intense analysis on a single, bounded phenomenon from a variety of perspectives in order to provide a rich and detailed account of that phenomenon.[1] In this instance, the case encompasses postsecondary institutions and private businesses in two fields—biotechnology and advanced manufacturing—in the state of Wisconsin. Using field theory as a guiding theoretical framework, we engaged in an inductive analysis of multiple datasets to identify how higher educational dynamics associated with the skills gap unfolded in specific contexts in Wisconsin.

STUDY SITES AND SAMPLING STRATEGIES

We focused on six regions in Wisconsin that roughly align with the state's economic development regions. Within each of these regions we identified cities with a high concentration of manufacturing and biotechnology companies as well as local colleges or universities whose graduates could work in those companies. These industries were selected because they represent both the old and the new economies of the state and region, and because both can be included in the broad category of high-demand, STEM-related industries, which have been a particular focus in recent years. The regions and key cities included the Northern region (Superior), the Eastern region (Green Bay, Appleton, Oshkosh, and Neenah), the Southeastern region (Milwaukee), the Southern region (Madison and Janesville), the Western region (La Crosse), and the Central region (Wausau, Marshfield, and Stevens Point).

Within each city we developed sampling frames for both educators and employers using publicly available documents like online Chamber of Commerce listings, industry-specific membership guides, and college or university websites. Criteria for incorporating employers in the sampling frame included company size (i.e., two or more individuals), industry niche (i.e., not pharmaceutical companies or clothing and food manufacturers), and hiring activity (i.e., currently or recently hiring new staff). We selected in each city two- and four-year educational programs whose students could conceivably work in the target industries, including engineering or manufacturing-related programs and biology-related or biotechnology programs. Individuals included in the sampling frames were limited to human resource staff or company executives, instructors, administrators directly involved with curricular decisions, and career counselors. Potential respondents were contacted requesting their voluntary participation in the study. We contacted a total of 456 companies and educators, and 121 individuals ultimately self-selected into the study (a 26.5 percent response rate). Seventy-five employers from 52 companies and 70 educators from 17 postsecondary institutions were included (see table A.1).

DATA COLLECTION

Our team collected all interview and observation data between 2013 and 2015. Prior to our fieldwork, we underwent intensive training with the research protocols, and also secured approval for human subjects research at UW-Madison.

Semistructured Interviews

The interview protocols included a free-list exercise and several open-ended questions. The free-list technique allows for the exploration of unique cultural domains by asking for terms or phrases that individuals associate with a particular concept or issue.[2] In this study each respondent was asked to tell us, using single words or short phrases that immediately came to mind, the skills that were necessary for success in either

TABLE A.1   Description of full sample

	Interview *n*
Total	145
Sex	
Male	8
Female	60
Region	
Southern	44
Central	27
Eastern	26
Southeastern	19
Northern	18
Western	11
Employers	
All employers	75
Manufacturing	64
Biotechnology	11
Educators	
All educators	70
Two-year	34
Two-year manufacturing	18
Two-year biotechnology	8
Two-year career advisors	8
Four-year	36
Four-year biotechnology	17
Four-year manufacturing	11
Four-year career advisors	8

the manufacturing or the biotechnology industry. We then asked a series of open-ended questions that allowed interviewees to elaborate on the most important skills they mentioned in the free-list exercise, how these skills were cultivated in the classroom or company, and the quality of communication and engagement with local industry or postsecondary institutions. Interviews were conducted either in person or over the telephone, typically took place with individual respondents, and were audio-recorded. Interviews took approximately forty-five minutes and were transcribed for later analysis.

DATA ANALYSIS

We applied three methods during our analysis of this data: (1) calculating the salience of free-list terms, (2) inductively identifying themes from interview transcripts, and (3) using root cause and causal network analysis techniques for a systems analysis of education-workplace relations.

Salience Analysis of Freelist Data

We analyzed the free-list data using Anthropac software, with the primary output measure being the salience for each term.[3] Salience is a measure that reflects the average percentile rank of a term across all respondent lists while weighting terms based on the order in which they were reported.[4] Salience is a commonly used metric in cognitive anthropology because it implies that a term or short phrase is psychologically relevant.[5]

Data for thirty respondents were not included in the analysis because they declined to be audio-recorded or provided information in unusable form. Then, because respondents listed terms that could be considered closely related but were in fact differently phrased (e.g., "work ethic," "hard worker," "dependable worker"), we needed a process of standardizing the terms.[6] For this step, two analysts reviewed the raw data and developed a list of ninety-four standardized terms. Each respondent's free-list data were then updated to use these terms and analyzed with Anthropac.

Thematic Analysis of Interview Transcripts

After all transcribed interviews were entered into NVivo qualitative software for analysis, we created a coding scheme to segment the data into more manageable units, which involved an inductive, open-coding process where ideas from the text were used to develop new codes.[7] One researcher applied the preliminary code list to 10 percent of the transcripts, and another analyst independently reviewed these transcripts, applied the code list, and compared her results to those of the other analyst. After multiple team discussions regarding the code list, a final code list was developed that consisted of nine categories and twenty-seven codes. Examples of codes included "valued cultural capital" and "teaching methods." The final code list was then applied to all of the transcribed interviews, with regular group meetings to calibrate coding and address questions emerging from the ongoing process.

We next performed an inductive thematic analysis for the text coded with each of these twenty-seven codes. This step involved another open-coding process whereby analysts reviewed the raw data within each category, making margin notes about important details related to the topic (e.g., valued cultural capital) or about themes that were mentioned repeatedly.[8] These margin notes were then converted to specific codes. Upon encountering a code in later text fragments, we would then compare each successive instance of a code to previous instances of that code to confirm or alter the definition of that code (i.e., the constant comparative method).[9] One analyst took the lead for analyzing text fragments for each of the research questions, with another analyst reviewing 10 percent of the raw data to independently derive codes. The primary analyst reviewed both analysts' initial code list, made updates and revisions during group discussions and meetings, and then analyzed the remainder of the data to produce a final list of codes. Once completed, the final list of codes was carefully reviewed by all analysts to ensure agreement across the team. Then, analysts revisited the raw data and assigned codes to each text fragment. This process was used to address the questions regarding the cultivation of cultural capital and cross-field relations.

Finally, we engaged in a comprehensive analysis of the data by looking for patterns and relationships between and among individual themes in order to provide a detailed account of the systemic relations that encompass the fields of higher education and industry. A key aspect of this analysis was identifying relationships between elements (e.g., classroom teaching and skills cultivation), which were based on evidence from our data as well as other documents and studies. This approach drew on the technique of causal network analysis and root cause analysis, both of which involve identifying relations among and graphically depicting elements in a complex system.[10]

LIMITATIONS TO THE STUDY

Some limitations to the study should be considered when interpreting the data reported in this book. First, the free-list question did not specify the occupational category with which "success" should be judged (e.g., entry-level or professional), which means that different respondents could have been thinking of different types of jobs when answering the question. Further, because the free-list technique requires standardizing unique respondent terms, variation between individual terms that may be important is lost. Second, the self-selected nature of the sample reduces the generalizability of the results to the larger population of educators and employers in Wisconsin and/or in the selected fields. Third, these data do not include the feedback of those who have a unique perspective on the issues addressed in this book—students and employees. Finally, it is important to note that in this book we used many respondents' real names and places of work with their express permission. In these cases we provided the sections of the book where they and their employer or company were discussed for final approval.

NOTES

INTRODUCTION

1. Adam Davidson, "Skills Don't Pay the Bills," *New York Times*, November 20, 2012, http://www.nytimes.com/2012/11/25/magazine/skills-dont-pay-t he-bills.html; Scott Cohn, "The Skills Gap in the US Killing Millions of Jobs," *CNBC*, June 24, 2015, http://finance.yahoo.com/news/skills-gap-us-killing-millions-204222974.html.

2. For a brief overview of the primary arguments fueling the skills gap narrative, see chapter 2 of this book and Tim Sullivan, "The Road Ahead: Restoring Wisconsin's Workforce Development" (report prepared for Governor Scott Walker, 2012), http://www.wmep.org/wp-content/uploads/2015/02/sullivanreport.pdf.

3. Marc Levine, "The Skills Gap and Unemployment in Wisconsin: Separating Fact from Fiction" (working paper, Center for Economic Development, University of Wisconsin–Milwaukee, 2013).

4. And, of course, it goes without saying that no matter what methodology or research paradigm is chosen, a researcher brings to the table his or her own unique perspectives, biases, and predilections borne from their own experiences and training.

5. Many terms are used to reference the combination of skills that people consider valuable for academic, workplace, and life success. These include *twenty-first-century skills* or *competencies, employability skills, noncognitive skills*, and others. While we were hesitant to add yet more jargon to a field already overwhelmed with it, the terminology in use did not capture the entirety of our thinking. We chose to use *habits of mind* as a qualifier to *twenty-first century* to emphasize that these competencies are both cognitive (in terms of being mental, in-the-head structures) as well as cultural (in terms of how they are acquired and developed). Our attraction to the term originated from a combination of exposure to cultural models theory from cognitive anthropology, situated cognition theory from the learning sciences, the aforementioned works on twenty-first-century skills, and the thinking of Gregory Bateson in his seminal book *Steps to an Ecology of Mind: Collected Essays in Anthropology, Psychiatry, Evolution, and Epistemology* (Chicago: University of Chicago Press, 1972). It is also important to note that other educational researchers and writers have described the important skills and competencies students should acquire via their education as *habits of mind*.

6. Michael S. Roth, *Beyond the University: Why Liberal Education Matters* (New Haven, Yale University Press, 2014).

7. John Seely Brown, Allan Collins, and Paul Duguid, "Situated Cognition and the Culture of Learning," *Educational Researcher* 18, no. 1 (1989): 32–42.

8. Perhaps the best data source that captures teaching methods used in post-secondary classrooms is the HERI Faculty Survey, a biannual survey administered by the UCLA Higher Education Research Institute, http://www.heri.ucla.edu. See also: President's Council of Advisors on Science and Technology, "Engage to Excel: Producing One Million Additional College Graduates with Degrees in Science, Technology, Engineering, and Mathematics," 2012, https://www.whitehouse.gov/sites/default/files/microsites/ostp/pcast-engage-to-excel-final_feb.pdf.

9. Kari Knutson, "'Career Kickstart' Kicking Off Next Year at Ogg Residence Hall," *UW-Madison News*, December 11, 2014.

10. http://host.madison.com/wsj/business/uw-extension-s-pending-fiscal-cuts-have-farmers-and-county/article_cac77f0b-199f-5db8-88f9-2b1eb2eb372a.html

11. For readers familiar with earlier work traversing similar territory, such as Richard Murnane and Frank Levy's 1996 book *Teaching the New Basic Skills*, or Anthony P. Carnevale et al.'s 1990 book *Workplace Basics*, we build upon these prior works and add to the conversation a discussion of skills and jobs within the broader context of politics, culture, and the economy in a single state at a particularly interesting point in time—Wisconsin during the contentious period of 2011–2015. In addition, our work focuses more deliberately on instructional design, or how educators can plan and teach their courses in ways that cultivate desirable skills.

CHAPTER 1

1. Adam Rodewald, "Walker Says He'll Take Responsibility, Reform State," *Oshkosh Northwestern*, October 27, 2010, http://media.journalinteractive.com/documents/Oshkosh_Northwestern1.pdf.

2. Jason Stein, "State's 2-year Budget Deficit Grows to $3.6 Billion," *Wisconsin Journal Sentinel*, February 7, 2011, http://www.jsonline.com/news/statepolitics/115501969.html.

3. Amy Hetzner and Erin Richards, "Budget Cuts $834 Million from Schools," *Wisconsin Journal Sentinel*, March 1, 2011, http://www.jsonline.com/news/statepolitics/117192683.html. Also see "Wis. Gov. Signs Budget Cutting Education $1.85B," *CBS News*, June 26, 2011, http://www.cbsnews.com/news/wis-gov-signs-budget-cutting-education-185b/.

4. Julie Underwood and Julie F. Mead, "A Smart ALEC Threatens Public Education," *Education Week*, February 29, 2012, http://www.edweek.org/ew/articles/2012/03/01/kappan_underwood.html; "About ALEC," American Legislative Exchange Council, http://www.alec.org/about/.

5. "New Poll: Wisconsinites Split on Walker's Budget Proposal," *Wisconsin Watchdog*, February 24, 2011, http://watchdog.org/1015/wirep-new-poll-wisconsinites-split-on-walkers-budget-proposal/.

6. Peter Schmidt, "Wisconsin GOP Seeks E-mails of a Madison Professor Who Criticized the Governor," *Chronicle of Higher Education*, March 25, 2011, http://chronicle.com/article/Wisconsin-GOP-Seeks-E-Mails-of/126911/; see also William Cronon, "NYT Editorial and Other Coverage of Cronon Open Records Case," *Scholar as Citizen Blog*, March 26, 2011, http://scholar citizen.williamcronon.net/2011/03/26/ coverage-cronon-open-records/.

7. William Cronon, "Who's Really Behind Recent Republican Legislation in Wisconsin and Elsewhere?" *Scholar as Citizen Blog*, March 15, 2011, http://scholarcitizen.williamcronon.net/2011/03/15/alec/.

8. "A Shabby Crusade in Wisconsin," *New York Times*, March 25, 2011, http://www.nytimes.com/2011/03/28/opinion/28mon3.html?ref=opinion.

9. "Wis. Gov. Signs Budget Cutting Education $1.85B," *CBS News*, June 26, 2011, http://www.cbsnews.com/news/wis-gov-signs-budget-cutting-education-185b/; "2011–12 Biennial Report," Wisconsin Technical College System, October 2013, http://www.doa.state.wi.us/documents/DEBF/Budget/Bie nnial%20Budget/Biennial%20Reports/2011-13/292%20-%202011-13%20 WTCS%20Biennial%20Report%20FINAL.pdf. See also "Provisions Affecting Technical Colleges," Wisconsin Technical College District Boards Association, June 28, 2011, http://districtboards.org/advocacy/budgetsummary provisions062811.pdf.

10. Scott Walker, "Walker: We Changed Broken Education System," *Des Moines Register*, June 9, 2015, http://www.desmoinesregister.com/story/opinion/columnists/caucus/2015/06/10/walker-changed-broken-education-system /28778201/.

11. Tim Sullivan, "The Road Ahead: Restoring Wisconsin's Workforce Development" (report prepared for Governor Scott Walker, 2012), http://www.wmep .org/wp-content/uploads/2015/02/sullivanreport.pdf.

12. Dr. Noland was a man of many talents who contributed greatly to the Zoology Department at UW-Madison. See Kiera Wiatrak, "The Person Behind the Building, Lowell Evan Noland," March 24, 2010, http://news.wisc .edu/17872.

13. These are taken directly from a document entitled "The Wisconsin Experience and the Essential Learning Outcomes." These are based on a combination of resources that include national surveys and interviews done by national associations that involve employers, faculty, staff, and alumni. *The Wisconsin Experience and the Essential Learning Outcomes*, Division of Student Life, Office of the Provost for Teaching and Learning, http://www.learning .wisc.edu/welo2010.pdf.

14. Charles Richard Van Hise, "Inaugural Address of President Charles Richard Van Hise," *Science* 20, no. 502 (1904): 204.

15. Merle Curti et al., *The University of Wisconsin: A History* (Madison: University of Wisconsin Press, 1949).

16. For comprehensive accounts of Wiscosin's history, see Richard Nelson Current, *Wisconsin: A History* (Urbana-Champaign: University of Illinois Press, 2001) and Robert Carrington Nesbit, *Wisconsin: A History* (Madison: University of Wisconsin Press, 2004).

17. Jack Stark, *The Wisconsin Idea: The University's Service to the State* (Madison, WI: Legislative Reference Bureau, 1995).

18. Ibid., 137.

19. Charles Van Hise, "Higher Education in the South and West," *The American Educational Review* 31 (1910): 607.

20. Colin B. Burke, *American Collegiate Populations: A Test of the Traditional View* (New York: New York University Press, 1982).

21. Claudia Goldin and Lawrence F. Katz, "The Shaping of Higher Education: The Formative Years in the United States, 1890 to 1940," *The Journal of Economic Perspectives* 13, no. 1 (1999).

22. Ibid., 38–39.

23. Roger L. Geiger, *Research and Relevant Knowledge: American Research Universities Since World War II* (New York: Oxford University Press, 1993).

24. Goldin and Katz, "The Shaping of Higher Education"; Reynolds, "The Education of Engineers in America."

25. See, for instance, Lana G. Snider, "The History and Development of the Two-Year Colleges in Wisconsin: The University of Wisconsin Colleges and the Wisconsin Technical College System," *Community College Journal of Research & Practice,* 23, no. 1 (1999): 107–128.

26. See, for instance, the contemporary mission statements of the University of Wisconsin–Madison (http://www.wisc.edu/about/mission/) and the Wisconsin Technical College System (http://www.wistechcolleges.org/about).

27. Thomas D. Snyder, Sally A. Dillow, and Charlene M. Hoffman, *Digest of Education Statistics 2007* (Washington, DC: National Center for Education Statistics, Institute of Education Sciences, US Department of Education, 2008), table 180.

28. Madison College 2014 Graduate Employment Report, "Associate Degree Program," Madison College, 2014, http://madisoncollege.edu/program-info/biotechnology-laboratory-technician.

29. For a good explication of the roots of the "college for all" ethos, see Dana Goldstein, "Should All Kids Go to College?" *The Nation,* June 15, 2011, http://www.thenation.com/article/should-all-kids-go-college/. This says nothing about the emphasis on students obtaining a four-year postsecondary credential, which is often based on misleading assumptions that James E. Rosenbaum, Jennifer L. Stephan, and Janet E. Rosenbaum identify in "Beyond One-Size-Fits-All College Dreams: Alternative Pathways to Desirable Careers," *American Educator* 34, no. 3 (2010): 2–13. They assert that

the emphasis on four-year college attainment is higher earnings and better jobs, among others. Additionally, people who may be accepting of a two-year degree often feel this way in regard to *others*, not themselves or their children. Note: Rosenbaum's argument has been controversial and also vigorously questioned by other researchers. See, for instance, Thurston Domina, AnneMarie Conley, and George Farkas, "The Link Between Educational Expectations and Effort in the College-for-All Era," *Sociology of Education* 84, no. 2, (2011): 93–112.

30. Anthony P. Carnevale, Nicole Smith, and Jeff Strohl, *Recovery: Projections of Jobs and Educational Requirements Through 2020* (Washington, DC: Georgetown University Center on Education and the Workforce, 2013).

31. Anthony P. Carnevale, Stephen J. Rose, and Ban Cheah, *The College Payoff: Education, Occupations, Lifetime Earnings* (Washington, DC: Georgetown University Center on Education and the Workforce, 2014). For example, a registered nurse with an associate's degree earns approximately $2.2 million over her lifetime, whereas an elementary or middle school teacher with a bachelor's degree will earn $1.7 million.

32. W. Norton Grubb and Marvin Lazerson, "The Education Gospel: The Economic Power of Schooling" (Cambridge, MA: Harvard University Press, 2004).

33. Evan Schofer and John W. Meyer, "The Worldwide Expansion of Higher Education in the Twentieth Century," *American Sociological Review* 70, no. 6 (2005): 898–920.

34. See, for example, Francis Oakley, *Community of Learning: The American College and the Liberal Arts Tradition* (New York: Oxford University Press, 1992).

35. "Mission Statement," University of Wisconsin–Madison, http://www.wisc.edu/about/mission/.

36. Robert A. Rhoads et al., *China's Rising Research Universities: A New Era of Global Ambition* (Baltimore: Johns Hopkins University Press, 2015).

37. W. Norton Grubb, "Vocationalism and the Differentiation of Tertiary Education: Lessons from US Community Colleges," *Journal of Further and Higher Education* 30, no. 1 (2006): 27–42.

38. Marissa Haegele, "Humanities, Social Science Courses Experience Enrollment Decrease While STEM Courses Rise," *The Badger Herald*, February 17, 2016, https://badgerherald.com/news/2016/02/17/humanities-social-science-courses-experience-enrollment-decrease-while-stem-courses-rise/.

39. Michael Roth, "A World Without Liberal Learning," *Inside Higher Ed*, June 3, 2014, https://www.insidehighered.com/views/2014/06/03/essay-idea-all-higher-education-should-focus-careers-or-practical-skills.

40. The data for the lab technician position is based on the aforementioned report from Madison College on the wages of alumni from the Biotechnology program. Wages for research associates were obtained from the salary

comparison website PayScale, http://www.payscale.com. The average hourly wage for a biological science laboratory technician on PayScale was $16 an hour, which is comparable to the Madison College data.

CHAPTER 2

1. Erin Richards, "MMAC Pushes Plan to Close Education Gap in Milwaukee," *Wisconsin Journal Sentinel,* November 7, 2011, http://www.jsonline.com/news/education/mmac-pushes-plan-to-close-education-gap-in-milwaukee-v42usqa-133415153.html.
2. James R. Morgan, "WMC Column: Solving the Workforce Paradox," Wisconsin Manufacturers and Commerce, May 8, 2012, https://www.wmc.org/news/wmc-column-solving-thR-workforce-paradox/.
3. In 2011 Bucyrus International was acquired by Caterpillar Inc.
4. John Schmid, "Finding Skilled Workers a Struggle for Bucyrus," *Wisconsin Journal Sentinel,* June 11, 2011, http://www.jsonline.com/business/123694664.html.
5. Larry Gross, "Blaming MATC Is Off the Mark," *Wisconsin-Journal Sentinel,* June 16, 2011, http://www.jsonline.com/news/opinion/124039274.html.
6. Bruce Murphy, "The Myth of the Welders Shortage," *Urban Milwaukee,* July 11, 2013, http://urbanmilwaukee.com/2013/07/11/murphys-law-the-myth-of-the-welders-shortage/.
7. Tim Sullivan, "The Road Ahead: Restoring Wisconsin's Workforce Development" (report prepared for Governor Scott Walker, 2012), 7, http://www.wmep.org/wp-content/uploads/2015/02/sullivanreport.pdf.
8. Discussions in "The Road Ahead" about workplace training center on government-funded programs and how they should be centralized to increase efficiency.
9. "Governor Walker announces Tim Sullivan to Serve as Special Consultant for Business and Workforce Development," Office of the Governor, February 16, 2012, http://walker.wi.gov/newsroom/press-release.
10. Competitive Wisconsin, Inc., "Be Bold 2: Growing Wisconsin's Talent Pool" (report prepared by ManpowerGroup and Right Management, 2012), 4, http://www.competitivewi.com/wp-content/uploads/2012/10/BeBold2_Study_October2012.pdf.
11. Competitive Wisconsin is currently working on a third report, tentatively titled "Be Bold 3: Accelerate Wisconsin," that promises to make just as large of a splash.
12. http://www.competitivewi.com/2013/02/competitive-wisconsin-praises-governors-commitment-to-workforce-development/
13. Ibid.
14. Stephen L. Mangum, "Impending Skill Shortages: Where Is the Crisis?" *Challenge* 33, no. 5 (1990): 46–53.
15. Christopher J. Goodman and Steven M. Mance, "Employment Loss and the

2007–09 Recession: An Overview," *Monthly Labor Review* (April 2011).

16. Peter Rebhahn, "Welders Wanted: Employers with Jobs Struggle to Fill Them," *Juneau County StarTimes*, January 29, 2014, http://www.wiscnews .com/news/local/article_32550070-f924-5dd1-a602-c93b5997e5f8.html.

17. The White House Office of the Press Secretary released a transcript of President Obama's State of the Union address given on January 28, 2014. Read it in full here: https://www.whitehouse.gov/the-press-office/2014/01/28/ president-barack-obamas-state-union-address.

18. "Addressing the Skills Gap," Office of the Governor, March 28, 2013, http:// walker.wi.gov/media/weekly-radio-address/addressing-skills-gap.

19. These distinctions are laid out by Peter H. Cappelli, "Skill Gaps, Skill Shortages, and Skill Mismatches: Evidence and Arguments for the United States," *ILR Review* 68, no. 2 (2015).

20. While the term *skills gap* is often used in the popular media, it is not widely accepted in academic circles or scholarly literature in economics, even if proponents point to wider structural unemployment and labor demand issues that have arguably propounded the issue.

21. ManpowerGroup, "2015 Talent Shortage Survey," http://www.manpower group.com/wps/wcm/connect/manpowergroup-en/home/thought-leadership/ research-insights/talent-shortage-2015.

22. "WMC Economic Outlook Survey: Worker Shortage Getting Worse; Holding Back Economy," Wisconsin Manufacturing and Commerce, June 15, 2015, https://www.wmc.org/news/press-releases/wmc-economic-outlook-survey-worker-shortage-getting-worse-holding-back-economy/.

23. Jim Morgan, "You Can't Legislate Career Choices, Can You?" WMC News Columns, January 2013, https://www.wmc.org/programs/workforcedevelop ment/news-column-solving-the-workforce-paradox/

24. Anthony P. Carnevale, Nicole Smith, and Jeff Strohl, *Recovery: Projections of Jobs and Education Requirements Through 2020* (Washington, DC: Georgetown University Center on Education and the Workforce, 2013).

25. Anthony P. Carnevale and Nicole Smith, *The Midwest Challenge: Matching Jobs with Education in the Post-Recession Economy* (Washington, DC: Georgetown University Center on Education and the Workforce, 2014). Note that the figure of 65 percent reported in chapter 1 to this point referred to the entire country.

26. JP Morgan Chase and Co., *Growing Skills for a Growing Chicago: Strengthening the Middle-Skill Workforce in the City That Works* (JP Morgan Chase and Co.), https://www.jpmorganchase.com/corporate/Corporate-Responsibility/ document/54841-jpmc-gap-chicago-aw3-v2-accessible.pdf.

27. MIT Living Wage Calculator, http://livingwage.mit.edu.

28. Sullivan, "The Road Ahead."

29. Erin Richards, "MMAC Pushes Plan."

30. More information about the Future Wisconsin Project, along with a video

from the inaugural summit in Milwaukee, can be found at https://www .wmc.org/programs/the-future-wisconsin-project/.

31. Patricia Cohen, "A Rising Call to Promote STEM Education and Cut Liberal Arts Funding," *New York Times*, February 22, 2016, http://www.nytimes.co m/2016/02/22/business/a-rising-call-to-promote-stem-education-and-cut-liberal-arts-funding.html.

32. Sullivan, "The Road Ahead."

33. "Aligning Education and Workforce Goals to Foster Economic Development" (proceedings from Cities for Success: A BHEF Leadership Summit, Louisville, Kentucky, October 28–29, 2010), 4, http://www.bhef.com/sites /g/files/g829556/f/201306/Cities_For_Success_Proceedings.pdf.

34. Ibid.

35. "Governor Walker Signs 'Wisconsin Fast Forward' Legislation at Jay Manufacturing Oshkosh, Inc.," Office of the Governor, March 13, 2013, http:// www.wisgov.state.wi.us/around-the-state/governor-walker-signs-wisconsin-fast-forward-legislation-jay-manufacturing-oshkosh.

36. 2013 Wisconsin Act 9, Wisconsin Legislature, March 13, 2013.

37. Samira Salem, Laura Dresser, and Michele Mackey, *Wisconsin Fast Forward: How Skills Training Is Working and Extending the Opportunity to Low-Wage Workers* (Madison: University of Wisconsin–Madison Center on Wisconsin Strategy, 2015), http://www.cows.org/_data/files/Wisconsin_Fast_Forward _v8_FINAL.pdf.

38. Brian E. Clark, "Jansen: DWD's New Office of Skills Development to Work with Private Sector on Worker Training," WisBusiness.com, June 20, 2013, http://www.wisbusiness.com/index.iml?Article=299778; Scott Jansen, "2013 Wisconsin Act 9 Wisconsin Fast Forward" (presentation at the Department of Workforce Development, Madison, Wisconsin, May 17, 2013), http://www.wi-cwi.org/council/2013/jansen_act9_wff_051713.pdf.

39. Andy Clark, "Whatever Next? Predictive Brains, Situated Agents, and the Future of Cognitive Science," *Behavioral and Brain Sciences* 38, no. 3 (2013).

40. See reports at "Wisconsin Fast Forward 2013 Quarter 4 Release Summary," Department of Workforce Development, http://wisconsinfastforward.com/ pdf/awards_summary_rd_01.pdf.

41. In early 2015, Wisconsin's labor force of 3.1 million people was concentrated in trade, transportation, and utilities (2.8M), followed by manufacturing (472,600) and education and health services (434,400); sectors with the highest projected growth from 2012 to 2022 include construction (18.4 percent growth), professional and business services (14.5 percent), education and health services (11.1 percent), and financial activities (9.8 percent). From the Wisconsin Department of Workforce Development Office of Economic Advisors: Industry Employment Projections and Occupation Projections 2012–2022.

42. Grants: average post-training wage (round 1: $17.19/hour; round 2: $12.17/

hour). MIT Living Wage Green Bay MSA: two adults (one working) and two kids: $21.95; poverty wage $11.00.

43. "Blueprint for Prosperity," Wisconsin Fast Forward, Department of Workforce Development, http://wisconsinfastforward.com/prosperity/.

44. Christopher Colclough, "Structuralism Versus Neoliberalism: An Introduction," in *States and Markets? Neoliberalism and the Development Policy Debate*, eds. Christopher Colclough and James Manor (Oxford, UK: Clarendon Press, 1991): 1–25. Also see David Harvey, *A Brief History of Neoliberalism* (Oxford, UK: Oxford University Press, 2005). Also see Daniel B. Saunders, "Neoliberal Ideology and Public Higher Education in the United States," *Journal for Critical Education Policy Studies* 8, no. 1 (2010): 41–77.

45. Dan Berrett, "The Day the Purpose of College Changed," *Chronicle of Higher Education*, January 26, 2015, http://chronicle.com/article/The-Day-the-Purpose-of-College/151359/.

46. Sheila Slaughter and Larry L. Leslie, *Academic Capitalism: Politics, Policies, and the Entrepreneurial University* (Baltimore: The Johns Hopkins University Press, 1997), 125. See also Sheila Slaughter and Gary Rhoades, *Academic Capitalism and the New Economy: Markets, State, and Higher Education* (Baltimore: John Hopkins University Press, 2004).

47. "WPRI: Free Market Paths to Better Lives," Wisconsin Policy Research Institute, Inc., http://www.wpri.org/WPRI.htm.

48. Charles Sorensen and Michael Flaherty, "Beyond the Ivory Tower: How to Get the UW System More Involved in Ground-Level Economic Development" (Wisconsin Policy Research Institute report, 2015): 2, http://www.wpri.org/WPRI-Files/Special-Reports/Reports-Documents/UWsystemsorensenmay2015vol28no2.pdf.

49. Ibid.

50. Zac Anderson, "Rick Scott Wants to Shift University Funding Away from Some Degrees," *Hearld Tribune*, October 10, 2011, http://politics.heraldtribune.com/2011/10/10/rick-scott-wants-to-shift-university-funding-away-from-some-majors/.

51. "Who Said What and What It Meant: The 4th GOP Debate, Annotated," *Washington Post*, November 10, 2015, https://www.washingtonpost.com/news/the-fix/wp/2015/11/10/well-be-annotating-the-gop-debate-here/.

52. Michael Barbaro, "Chris Christie's Punch Lines vs. Marco Rubio's Polish on Iowa Campaign Trail," *New York Times*, December 31, 2015, http://www.nytimes.com/2016/01/01/us/politics/chris-christie-marco-rubio-iowa-campaign.html.

53. Mitsuru Obe, "Japan Rethinks Higher Education in Skills Push," *Wall Street Journal*, August 2, 2015, http://www.wsj.com/articles/japan-rethinks-higher-education-in-skills-push-1438571119.

54. Alex Dean, "Japan's Humanities Chop Sends Shivers Down Academic Spines," *The Guardian*, September 26, 2015, http://www.theguardian.com/

higher-education-network/2015/sep/25/japans-humanities-chop-sends-shivers-down-academic-spines.

CHAPTER 3

1. Carl Gustav Jung, "A Review of the Complex Theory," in *The Collected Works of C. G. Jung*, vol. 8, eds., trs. Gerhard Adler and R. F. C. Hull (New York: Bollingen Foundation, 1960), 96.
2. This observation gives the earlier comment about "years off the farm" an interesting twist, as it is possible that the types of skills obtained from an agricultural upbringing may be correlated with the era in which one grew up.
3. Menards is a midwestern chain of stores featuring home repair products, much like the national chain Home Depot.
4. See Peter Cappelli, "Is the 'Skills Gap' Really About Attitudes?" *California Management Review* 37, no. 4 (1995): 108–124.
5. Gordon Lafer, *The Job Training Charade* (Ithaca, NY: Cornell University Press, 2002), 19.
6. James Bessen, "Employers Aren't Just Whining—The 'Skills Gap' Is Real," *Harvard Business Review*, August 25, 2014, https://hbr.org/2014/08/employers-arent-just-whining-the-skills-gap-is-real/.
7. Paul Krugman, "Jobs and Skills and Zombies," *New York Times*, March 30, 2014, http://www.nytimes.com/2014/03/31/opinion/krugman-jobs-and-skills-and-zombies.html.
8. Ibid.
9. Marc Levine, "The Skills Gap and Unemployment in Wisconsin: Separating Fact from Fiction" (working paper, Center for Economic Development, University of Wisconsin–Milwaukee, 2013).
10. Ibid.
11. Levine, "The Skills Gap and Unemployment in Wisconsin." Another 2013 report (cited earlier), this one by four UW-Madison master's students in their final semester of Robert La Follette School of Public Affairs, used many of the same methods to analyze labor market data across the United States and in Wisconsin in particular to gauge the existence of a skills gap. They concluded, first, that there was "no conclusive evidence that there is an economy-wide skills gap" and, second, that while there was indeed a shortage of labor in Wisconsin for certain job openings, this shortage represented "openings that do not require post-secondary formal education . . . and a relatively small shortage of doctoral and professional degree holders." Those advocating the existence of a skills gap quickly responded to Levine's report, with WMC's Jim Morgan claiming that the analysis was "so far off the mark that many of the manufacturers I spoke with were almost speechless." Reminding the *Wisconsin Business Journal* that he had spoken directly to over three hundred manufacturing executives over the year, he further quipped, "If the determination of what is actually going on in the marketplace is between

a theoretical review of academic studies and data sources, or the reality of hundreds and hundreds of Wisconsin manufacturers who are trying to hire, we will trust the manufacturers." See Jeff Engel, "WMC: UWM Prof Should've Talked to Manufacturers for Skills Gap Study," *Milwaukee Business Journal*, March 1, 2013, http://www.bizjournals.com/milwaukee/blog/2013/03/wmc-uwm-prof-shouldve-talked-to.html.

12. Matthew T. Hora, *Preparing Students for Success in the 21st-Century Economy: Challenges with Aligning Educational Policy and Curricula with Employer Expectations* (Madison: Wisconsin Center for Education Research working paper no. 2013-08, 2013).

13. Peter Cappelli, *Why Good People Can't Get Jobs: The Skills Gap and What Companies Can Do About It* (Philadelphia: Wharton Digital Press, 2012).

14. Peter Cappelli, "Why Companies Aren't Getting the Employees They Need," *The Wall Street Journal*, October 24, 2011.

15. Cappelli, 2012.

16. ManpowerGroup, "2015 Talent Shortage Survey," http://www.manpowergroup.com/wps/wcm/connect/manpowergroup-en/home/thought-leadership/research-insights/talent-shortage-2015.

17. Anthony P. Carnevale, Nicole Smith, and Jeff Strohl, *Recovery: Projections of Jobs and Educational Requirements Through 2020* (Washington, DC: Georgetown University Center on Education and the Workforce, 2013).

18. Another important point on this issue is made by Peter Cappelli in "Skill Gaps, Skill Shortages and Skill Mismatches: Evidence for the US" (working paper no. 20382, National Bureau of Economic Research, August 2014): "One factor in the relative lack of academic research on these topics no doubt has been the lack of information and data about skills per se. The standard classification of job requirements into 'knowledge, skills, and abilities' reminds us that education, which has served as a proxy for skills in most discussions, maps onto only part of the 'knowledge' category, leaving the other attributes of job requirements out of the picture. Many important reasons exist for being concerned about education, but seeing it as the equivalent of skill is certainly a mistake." Along similar lines, recognizing the complexity inherent in many jobs, in the 1990s the US Department of Labor developed the O*NET occupational classification system, which categorizes jobs according to personal requirements (e.g., skills and knowledge required for a job), personal characteristics (e.g., abilities and interests required for a job), and experience requirements. Thus, it is no longer tenable to simply equate "skills" with the name of an occupation as the Competitive Wisconsin reports have done.

19. Anthony P. Carnevale, Tamara Jayasundera, and Andrew R. Hanson, *Career and Technical Education: Five Ways That Pay Along the Way to the B.A.* (Washington, DC: Georgetown University Center on Education and the Workforce, 2012).

20. Jon Marcus, "Community College Grads Out-Earn Bachelor's Degree Holders," *CNNMoney*, February 26, 2013, http://money.cnn.com/2013/02/26/pf/college/community-college-earnings/.

21. Wisconsin Department of Workforce Development, *Worknet*, http://worknet.wisconsin.gov/worknet/default.aspx.

22. Anthony P. Carnevale, Tamara Jayasundera, and Artem Gulish, *Good Jobs Are Back: College Graduates Are First in Line* (Washington, DC: Georgetown University Center on Education and the Workforce, 2015), https://cew.georgetown.edu/cew-reports/goodjobsareback/.

23. Chuck Quirmbach, "Walker Blames Lack of Trained Workers for Flagging Job Growth," *Wisconsin Public Radio*, December 18, 2015, http://www.wpr.org/walker-blames-lack-trained-workers-flagging-job-growth.

24. For seminal critiques, see Lauren B. Resnick, "The 1987 Presidential Address: Learning in School and Out," *Educational Researcher* 16, no. 9 (1987): 13–54; and John D. Bransford, Ann L. Brown, and Rodney R. Cocking, eds., *How People Learn: Brain, Mind, Experience, and School* (Washington DC: National Academy Press, 1999).

25. Pat Schneider, "Increased Demand Packing UW-Madison Computer Science Classes," *Capital Times*, October 1, 2015, http://host.madison.com/ct/news/local/education/university/increased-demand-packing-uw-madison-computer-science-classes/article_b5237410-517d-5bc3-9350-de8274ef2df7.html.

26. Karen Herzog and Kathleen Gallagher, "As Demand for Data Skills Grows, Big Gift Bolsters UW Computer Sciences," *Wisconsin Journal Sentinel*, November 27, 2015, http://www.jsonline.com/news/education/as-demand-for-data-skills-grows-big-gift-bolsters-uw-computer-sciences-b99620344z1-356457911.html.

27. Kathy Cramer, *The Politics of Resentment* (Chicago: University of Chicago Press, 2016).

28. Peter H. Cappelli, "Skill Gaps, Skill Shortages, and Skill Mismatches Evidence and Arguments for the United States," *ILR Review* 68, no. 2 (2015).

29. Without employer investments in training and professional development, it is also hard to envision apprenticeships taking off in the US in the near future, as the private sector generally contributes a substantial amount of time and money to apprentices in countries like Germany.

30. Amy L. Kristof, "Person-Organization Fit: An Integrative Review of Its Conceptualizations, Measurement, and Implications," *Personnel Psychology* 49, no. 1 (1996): 7.

31. Derek S. Chapman et al., "Applicant Attraction to Organizations and Job Choice: A Meta-Analytic Review of the Correlates of Recruiting Outcomes," *Journal of Applied Psychology* 90, no. 5 (2005): 928–944; John E. Sheridan, "Organizational Culture and Employee Retention," *Academy of Management Journal* 35, no. 5 (1992): 1036–1056.

32. To the best of our knowledge, one other scholar has explicitly explored the cultural aspects of hiring. See Lauren A. Rivera, "Hiring as Cultural Matching: The Case of Elite Professional Service Firms," *American Sociological Review* 77, no. 6 (2012): 999–1022.

33. ManpowerGroup, "2015 Talent Shortage Survey."

34. Marianne Bertrand and Sendhil Mullainathan, "Implicit Discrimination," *The American Economic Review* 95, no. 2 (2005): 94–98.

35. This is obviously an extremely complicated and well-researched set of issues that cannot be explored in depth in this book. Recent works that have informed these sentiments include Amanda E. Lewis and John B. Diamond, *Despite the Best Intentions: How Racial Inequality Thrives in Good Schools* (New York: Oxford University Press, 2015); and Gloria Ladson-Billings, "From the Achievement Gap to the Education Debt: Understanding Achievement in US Schools," *Educational Researcher* 35, no. 7 (2006): 3–12.

36. Daphna Oyserman, Larry Gant, and Joel Ager, "A Socially Contextualized Model of African American Identity: Possible Selves and School Persistence," *Journal of Personality and Social Psychology* 69, no. 6 (1995): 1216.

37. Andre Perry, "Black and Brown Boys Don't Need to Learn Grit; They Need Schools to Stop Being Racist," The Root, May 2, 2016, http://www.theroot.com/articles/culture/2016/05/black_and_brown_boys_don_t_need_to_learn_grit_they_need_schools_to_stop.html.

CHAPTER 4

1. Clifford Geertz, *The Interpretation of Cultures* (New York: Basic Books, 1973), 5.

2. For a review of Boas's works, see Franz Boas, *A Franz Boas Reader: The Shaping of American Anthropology, 1883–1911* (Chicago: University of Chicago Press, 1989). Also, two additional positions that Boas advocated included that anthropology should strive to be a "science," where the study of culture should originate from a position of objectivity and methodological clarity, and that cultural phenomena cannot be divorced from the contexts in which they develop. This emphasis on the contextuality of culture did not necessarily keep Boas from seeking universals in his research, but he strongly emphasized that cultural analysis needs to be grounded in rich and detailed observation of culture in specific settings.

3. Edward Burnett Tylor, *Primitive Culture* (New York: Bretano's, 1924), 1.

4. Geertz, *The Interpretation of Cultures*, 5.

5. Ibid, 58

6. Gregory Bateson, *Steps to an Ecology of Mind: Collected Essays in Anthropology, Psychiatry, Evolution, and Epistemology* (Chicago: University of Chicago Press, 1972).

7. See James Clifford and George E. Marcus, *Writing Culture: The Poetics and Politics of Ethnography* (Berkeley: University of California Press, 1986) for

a text that heralded the introduction of postmodern criticism and thought into anthropology, which has strongly shaped the field in the ensuing years.

8. William H. Bergquist, *The Four Cultures of the Academy* (San Francisco: Jossey-Bass, 1992).

9. John Van Maanen and Stephen R. Barley, "Cultural Organization: Fragments of a Theory," in *Organizational Culture*, eds. Peter J. Frost et al. (Thousand Oaks, CA: Sage, 1985).

10. Linda Smircich, "Concepts of Culture and Organizational Analysis," *Administrative Science Quarterly* 28, no. 3 (1983): 339–358.

11. Melville J. Herskovits, *Cultural Anthropology* (New York: Knopf, 1956).

12. Alfred L. Kroeber, *Configurations of Culture Growth* (Berkeley: University of California Press, 1944).

13. Roy G. D'Andrade, "Cultural Meaning Systems," in *Culture Theory: Essays on Mind, Self, and Emotion*, eds. Richard A. Shweder and Robert LeVine (Cambridge, UK: Cambridge University Press, 1984), 88–119.

14. Paul DiMaggio, "Culture and Cognition," *Annual Review of Sociology* (1997): 277.

15. Roy G. D'Andrade, *The Development of Cognitive Anthropology* (Cambridge, UK: Cambridge University Press, 1995); Claudia Strauss and Naomi Quinn, *A Cognitive Theory of Cultural Meaning* (Cambridge, UK: Cambridge University Press, 1997); Norbert Ross, *Culture and Cognition: Implications for Theory and Method* (Thousand Oaks, CA: Sage, 2004). The idea of cultural models is not dissimilar to the psychological constructs of scripts (e.g., Schank and Abelson's restaurant script) and frames that operate according to principles of cognition, while also being shared among a group of people.

16. Pierre Bourdieu, *Practical Reason: On the Theory of Action* (Palo Alto, CA: Stanford University Press, 1998).

17. Neil Fligstein and Doug McAdam, *A Theory of Fields* (New York: Oxford University Press, 2012).

18. Pierre Bourdieu, "The Forms of Capital (1986)," in *Handbook of Theory and Research for the Sociology of Education*, eds. Alain Coulon and John Richardson (New York: Greenwood, 1989), 241–258.

19. Pierre Bourdieu, "The Forms of Capital (1986)," in *Cultural Theory: An Anthology*, eds. Imre Szeman and Timothy Kaposy (Hoboken, NJ: Wiley-Blackwell, 2011), 81–93.

20. Pierre Bourdieu, *Outline of a Theory of Practice* (Cambridge, UK: Cambridge University Press, 1977), 95.

21. Omar Lizardo, "The Cognitive Origins of Bourdieu's Habitus," *Journal for the Theory of Social Behavior* 34, no. 4 (2004): 381.

22. "Cirrus Design's Alan and Dale Klapmeier: 'Dumb Enough to Start and Smart Enough to Finish'," *Airport Journals*, http://airportjournals.com/cirrus-designs-alan-and-dale-klapmeier-dumb-enough-to-start-and-smart-enough-to-finish/.

23. Bob Kelleher, "Cirrus Aircraft Company Timeline," *Minnesota Public Radio*, February 28, 2011, http://www.mprnews.org/story/2011/02/28/cirrus-time line; Mark Phelps, "Cirrus Trims Production to Three-Day Work Week," *Flying Magazine*, October 29, 2008, http://www.flyingmag.com/news/cirrus-trims-production-three-day-work-week.

24. Kelleher, "Cirrus."

25. In explaining his decision to scrap a long-standing public agency, Walker explained that the WEDC will "help the state climb out of recession by shedding bureaucratic rules and drawing on private sector expertise." For details, see Andy Sullivan, "As Scott Walker Mulls White House Bid, a Spotlight on His Jobs Agency," *Reuters*, February 15, 2015, http://mobile.reuters.com/article/idUSKBN0LJ0R320150215.

26. http://www.witc.edu/newscontent/2012/Workforce-Partnership-Grantcontent.htm

CHAPTER 5

1. Alvin Toffler, *Future Shock* (New York: Bantam, 1990), 414.

2. Lucy McCalmont, "Walker Urges Professors to Work Harder," *Politico*, January 29, 2015, http://www.politico.com/story/2015/01/scott-walker-higher-education-university-professors-114716.

3. Karen Herzog, "Walker Proposes Changing Wisconsin Idea- Then Backs Away," *Wisconsin Journal Sentinel*, February 4, 2015, http://www.jsonline.com/news/education/scott-walkers-uw-mission-rewrite-could-end-the-wis consin-idea-b99439020z1-290797681.html.

4. Ibid.

5. In fact, the paper stated, "His original claim was not only inaccurate, but ridiculous. Pants on Fire." Tom Kertscher, "Despite Deliberate Actions, Scott Walker Calls Change to University Mission a 'Drafting Error'," PolitiFact.com, February 6, 2015, http://www.politifact.com/wisconsin/statements/2015/feb/06/scott-walker/despite-deliberate-actions-scott-walker-calls-chan/.

6. Pat Schneider, "Q&A: David Vanness Became a Spokesperson for UW Faculty Opposing Scott Walker's Budget," *Capital Times*, August 9, 2015, http://host.madison.com/ct/news/local/writers/pat_schneider/q-a-david-vanness-became-a-spokesperson-for-uw-faculty/article_025b0c24-828f-52f 1-8844-1e05225a29b9.html.

7. See the appendix for more details about the methods used in our study. See also, Susan C. Weller and A. Kimball Romney, *Systematic Data Collection*, vol. 10 (Thousand Oaks, CA: Sage, 1988).

8. James Heckman and Tim Kautz, "Hard Evidence on Soft Skills," *Labour Economics* 19, no. 4 (2012): 451–464.

9. Anthony P. Carnevale, Leila J. Gainer, and Ann S. Meltzer, *Workplace Basics: The Essential Skills Employers Want* (San Francisco: Jossey-Bass, 1990).

10. The phrase "rise of the robots" is from the book of the same title by Martin

Ford (New York: Basic Books, 2015).

11. David H. Autor, Frank Levy, and Richard J. Murnane, "The Skill Content of Recent Technological Change: An Empirical Exploration," *Quarterly Journal of Economics* 118, no. 4 (2003): 1279–1333.

12. For a review of their research, see Tim Kautz et al., "Fostering and Measuring Skills: Improving Cognitive and Non-Cognitive Skills to Promote Lifetime Success" (working paper no. 20749, National Bureau of Economic Research, 2014).

13. James J. Heckman and Yona Rubinstein, "The Importance of Noncognitive Skills: Lessons from the GED Testing Program," *The American Economic Review* 91, no. 2 (2001): 145–149.

14. Psychologists have long made a distinction between fluid (i.e., pattern-matching and problem-solving aptitudes that are independent of content knowledge) and crystallized intelligence (see Richard E. Nisbett et al., "Intelligence: New Findings and Theoretical Developments," *American Psychologist* 67, no. 2 (2012): 130.

15. James Heckman and Tim Kautz, 2012.

16. James W. Pellegrino and Margaret L. Hilton, eds., *Education for Life and Work: Developing Transferable Knowledge and Skills in the 21st Century* (Washington, DC: National Academies Press, 2012).

17. In the NRC report the authors note that they preferred the term *competencies* to *skills* because they viewed skills and knowledge as intertwined and thus inseparable.

18. Indeed, the influence of the report was evident in a session at the 2015 meeting of the American Educational Research Association in Chicago, where representatives from national departments of education and education researchers from China, Singapore, India, Peru, and Mexico all spoke of the need for their countries to figure out how to embed the findings of the NRC report into their national education systems. What was hindering many of these efforts, however, was a seemingly simple issue: how to get teachers in the classroom to teach these competencies effectively. In some cases, like Peru, there simply wasn't enough money to provide teachers with professional development, whereas in others, like Singapore, the traditional modes of teaching by lecture were making the transition to a more hands-on approach challenging.

19. George Anders, "That 'Useless' Liberal Arts Degree Has Become Tech's Hottest Ticket," *Forbes*, July 29, 2015, http://www.forbes.com/sites/george anders/2015/07/29/liberal-arts-degree-tech/#2f9425eb5a75; Beckie Supiano, "Employers Want Broadly Educated New Hires, Survey Finds," *Chronicle of Higher Education*, April 10, 2013, http://chronicle.com/article/ Employers-Want-Broadly/138453/; Mark Koba, "Why Businesses Prefer a Liberal Arts Education," *CNBC*, April 15, 2013, http://www.cnbc.com/id /100642178.

20. Koba, "Why Businesses Prefer a Liberal Arts Education."

21. Anders, "That 'Useless' Liberal Arts Degree."

22. Martha C. Nussbaum, *Not for Profit: Why Democracy Needs the Humanities* (Princeton, NJ: Princeton University Press, 2010).

23. W. Norton Grubb and Marvin Lazerson, "The Education Gospel: The Economic Power of Schooling" (Cambridge, MA: Harvard University Press, 2004).

24. These ideas are beautifully explored in Jean Lave and Etienne Wenger, *Situated Learning: Legitimate Peripheral Participation* (Cambridge, UK: Cambridge University Press, 1991).

25. Interestingly, this is a question that was being asked by many learning scientists who were recognizing that out-of-school learning was an unknown proposition in terms of the field's understanding of how people develop new competencies. Learning scientist Lauren Resnick's 1987 presidential address to the American Educational Research Association explores this territory in depth, linking the limitations of formal K–12 schooling and workplace training programs in their reliance on rote memorization and direct instruction without spending time on teaching deeper understandings that could be transferred to novel situations. See Lauren B. Resnick, "The 1987 Presidential Address: Learning in School and Out," *Educational Researcher* 16, no. 9 (1987): 13–54.

26. See also Jean Lave, *Apprenticeship in Critical Ethnographic Practice* (Chicago: University of Chicago Press, 2011).

27. See Ann L. Brown and Joseph C. Campione, *Guided Discovery in a Community of Learners* (Cambridge, MA: MIT Press, 1994); John Seeley Brown, Allan Collins, and Paul Duguid, "Situated Cognition and the Culture of Learning," *Educational Researcher* 18, no. 1 (1989): 32–42.

28. Patrick B. Anderson, "More Cuts in Store for UW–La Crosse," *La Cross Tribune*, October 19, 2011, http://lacrossetribune.com/news/local/more-cuts -in-store-for-uw-la-crosse/article_fe66c04c-fa0b-11e0-9049-001cc4c03286 .html; "Budget Cuts Could Affect New Science Building on UW–La Crosse Campus," WKBT News8000.com, July 16, 2015, http://www.news8000 .com/schools/budget-cuts-could-affect-new-science-building-on-uwla-crosse -campus/34213270.

CHAPTER 6

1. James W. Pellegrino and Margaret L. Hilton, *Education for Life and Work: Developing Transferable Knowledge and Skills in the 21st Century* (Washington, DC: National Research Council, 2012): 78.

2. Anthony P. Carnevale, Nicole Smith, and Jeff Strohl, *Recovery: Job Growth and Education Requirements Through 2020* (Georgetown University; Center on Education and the Workforce, 2013).

3. See "Accreditation," ABET, http://www.abet.org/accreditation/. While ABET

proposed new standards in 2015 in which a number of their noncognitive skill requirements were removed, the ability to "communicate effectively with a range of audiences through various media" remained. See Colleen Flaherty, "Watered-Down Gen Ed for Engineers?" *Inside Higher Ed,* June 26, 2015, https://www.insidehighered.com/news/2015/06/26/faculty-mem bers-criticize-proposed-changes-gen-ed-accreditation-standards-engineers.

4. Carnevale, Smith, and Strohl, *Recovery.* In fact, active listening was the most in-demand skill, with 48 percent of jobs requiring high levels of this competency.

5. Carolyn R. Miller, "Genre as Social Action," *Quarterly Journal of Speech* 70, no. 2 (1984): 151–167.

6. Gary Troia, "Evidence-Based Practices for Writing Instruction" (Document No. IC-5, Collaboration for Effective Educator, Development, Accountability, and Reform Center, University of Florida, 2014); Thomas A. Angelo and Patricia K. Cross, *Classroom Assessment Techniques: A Handbook for College Teachers* (San Francisco: Jossey-Bass, 1993). Robert L. Bangert-Drowns, Marlene M. Hurley, and Barbara Wilkinson, "The Effects of School-Based Writing-to-Learn Interventions on Academic Achievement: A Meta-Analysis," *Review of Educational Research* 74, no. 1 (2004): 29–58. Timothy O'Connell and Janet Dyment, "Reflections on Using Journals in Higher Education: A Focus Group Discussion with Faculty," *Assessment and Evaluation in Higher Education* 31, no. 6 (2006): 671–691.

7. For a rundown of the Cornell method, see https://www.usu.edu/asc/studys mart/pdf/note_taking_cornell.pdf; Arthur N. Applebee, "Writing and Reasoning," *Review of Educational Research* 54, no. 4 (1984): 577–596; Peter R. Denner, "Comparison of the Effects of Episodic Organizers and Traditional Note Taking on Story Recall" (final report, Faculty Research Committee of Idaho State University, 1986); Kathy J. Knipper and Timothy J. Duggan, "Writing to Learn Across the Curriculum: Tools for Comprehension in Content Area Classes," *The Reading Teacher* 59, no. 5 (2006): 462–470; Léonard P. Rivard, "A Review of Writing to Learn in Science: Implications for Practice and Research," *Journal of Research in Science Teaching* 31, no. 9 (1994): 969–983.

8. Research literature in a number of fields, including education, business communication, and applied psychology, presents strategies for teaching such skills. See, for example, Todd J. Maurer et al., "Interviewee Coaching, Preparation Strategies, and Response Strategies in Relation to Performance in Situational Employment Interviews: An Extension of Maurer, Solamon, and Troxtel (1998)," *Journal of Applied Psychology* 86, no. 4 (2001): 709; Mark R. Mathews and Stephen B. Fawcett, "Building the Capacities of Job Candidates Through Behavioral Instruction," *Journal of Community Psychology* 12, no. 2 (1984): 123–129; Joan C. Roderick and Herbert M. Jelley, "An Innovative Method for Teaching Resume Design," *Bulletin of the*

Association for Business Communication 55, no. 2 (1992): 1–4.

9. B. P. Abbott et al., "Observation of Gravitational Waves from a Binary Black Hole Merger," *Physical Review Letters* 116, no. 6 (2016): 061102.

10. Lisa Gueldenzoph Snyder, "The Use of Pre-Group Instruction to Improve Student Collaboration," *Journal of Applied Research for Business Instruction* 8, no. 1 (2010). This is a refereed publication of Delta Pi Epsilon, Inc., and it won the Outstanding Instructional Practices Paper Award at the Delta Pi Epsilon National Conference in 2008.

11. Larry K. Michaelsen, "Getting Started with Team-Based Learning," in Larry K. Michaelsen, Arletta Bauman Knight, and L. Dee Fink, eds., *Team-Based Learning: A Transformative Use of Small Groups* (Westport, CT: Praeger Publishers, 2002), 27–51.

12. Donald R. Bacon, Kim A. Stewart, and William S. Silver, "Lessons from the Best and Worst Student Team Experiences: How a Teacher Can Make the Difference," *Journal of Management Education* 23, no. 5 (1999): 467–488.

13. Robert W. Lingard, "Teaching and Assessing Teamwork Skills in Engineering and Computer Science," *Journal of Systemics, Cybernetics and Informatics* 8, no. 1 (2010): 34–37.

14. A common definition of *self-regulated learning* is offered by one of the leading scholars in the field of self-regulation, educational psychologist Barry Zimmerman, who observes that it is not, strictly speaking, an innate capacity or mental skill; instead, it is "the self-directive process by which learners transform their mental abilities into academic skills." See Barry J. Zimmerman, "Becoming a Self-Regulated Learner: An Overview," *Theory into Practice* 41, no. 2 (2002): 65.

15. Research on work ethic is rich, varied, and historic. For a brief overview, and a glimpse at contemporary thinking on the topic, see Michael J. Miller, David J. Woehr, and Natasha Hudspeth, "The Meaning and Measurement of Work Ethic: Construction and Initial Validation of a Multidimensional Inventory," *Journal of Vocational Behavior* 60, no. 3 (2002): 451–489.

16. Anthony P. Carnevale, *Workplace Basics: The Essential Skills Employers Want*, ASTD Best Practices Series: Training for a Changing Work Force (San Francisco: Jossey-Bass Inc., 1990).

17. While we are not claiming that instruction in self-regulated learning will teach someone a solid work ethic, it can cultivate certain habits and aptitudes that are commonly associated with a work ethic, such as self-monitoring, self-correction, and persistence.

18. Linda B. Nilson, *Creating Self-Regulated Learners: Strategies to Strengthen Students' Self-Awareness and Learning Skills* (Sterling, VA: Stylus, 2013), 4.

19. Ibid.

20. As he would hold up and turn off his cell phone in front of his students the first day, Wright also assured them that he, too, would abide by the rules. "I'm turning my cell phone off right now," he reported telling his classes.

"Here's my promise to you: I'm not going to answer my phone while I'm in class with you. If Barack Obama calls me, he's going to have to leave a message."

21. Very similar observations were made in a piece for the *Chronicle of Higher Education* about how educators could cultivate work ethic–related values in the classroom: Charlotte Kent, "To Solve the Skills Gap in Hiring, Create Expectations in the Classroom," *Chronicle of Higher Education*, February 7, 2016, http://chronicle.com/article/To-Solve-the-Skills-Gap-in/235206.

22. Diane F. Halpern, "Teaching Critical Thinking for Transfer Across Domains: Dispositions, Skills, Structure Training, and Metacognitive Monitoring," *American Psychologist* 53, no. 4 (1998): 449–455.

23. Michael Roth, "Young Minds in Critical Condition," *New York Times*, May 10, 2014, http://opinionator.blogs.nytimes.com/2014/05/10/young-minds-in-critical-condition/.

24. Ali Simsek, interview with David H. Jonassen: "Looking at the Field of Educational Technology from Radical and Multiple Perspectives," *Contemporary Educational Technology* 3, no. 1 (2012): 76–80.

25. David Jonassen, Johannes Strobel, and Chwee Beng Lee, "Everyday Problem Solving in Engineering: Lessons for Engineering Educators." *Journal of Engineering Education-Washington* 95, no. 2 (2006): 139.

26. John Butterworth and Geoff Thwaites, *Thinking Skills: Critical Thinking and Problem Solving*, 2nd edition (Cambridge, UK: Cambridge University Press, 2013), 13.

27. Grant P. Wiggins and Jay McTighe, *Understanding by Design* (Alexandria, VA: Association for Supervision and Curriculum Development, 2005).

28. Ibid.

29. Richard Arum and Josipa Roksa, *Academically Adrift: Limited Learning on College Campuses* (Chicago: University of Chicago Press, 2011).

30. Ibid., 34.

31. Derek Bok, "A Test Colleges Don't Need," *Washington Post*, March 5, 2006, http://www.washingtonpost.com/wp-dyn/content/article/2006/03/03/AR2006030301759.html.

32. Steve Olson and Donna Gerardi Riordan, "Engage to Excel: Producing One Million Additional College Graduates with Degrees in Science, Technology, Engineering, and Mathematics. Report to the President" (President's Council of Advisors on Science and Technology, Executive Office of the President, 2012).

33. Eric Mazur, "Farewell, Lecture?" *Science* 323, no. 5910 (2009): 50–51.

34. It is important to note that we roundly reject the notion that teaching can be accurately summarized in terms of a binary opposition, with lecturing on the one hand and active learning on the other. Unfortunately, such a characterization is often made. Instead, teaching techniques are best thought of as a continuum, with most instructors using combinations of both depending on

the lesson, topic, and students. See Matthew T. Hora, "Toward a Descriptive Science of Teaching: How the TDOP Illuminates the Multidimensional Nature of Active Learning in Postsecondary Classrooms," *Science Education* 99, no. 5 (2015): 783–818; Matthew T. Hora, "Limitations in Experimental Design Mean That the Jury Is Still Out on Lecturing ," *Proceedings of the National Academy of Sciences* 111, no. 30 (2014): 3024.

35. Michelene Chi and Ruth Wylie, "The ICAP Framework: Linking Cognitive Engagement to Active Learning Outcomes," *Educational Psychologist* 49, no. 4 (2014): 219–243.

36. This is the case throughout the UW System, whereas the technical college system in Wisconsin requires that aspiring instructors take several courses in learning theory, teaching methods, and so on.

37. See Matthew T. Hora, "Navigating the Problem Space of Academic Work," *AERA Open* 2, no. 1 (2016).

38. Chandra Turpen and Noah D. Finkelstein, "Not All Interactive Engagement Is the Same: Variations in Physics Professors' Implementation of Peer Instruction," *Physical Review Special Topics-Physics Education Research* 5, no. 2 (2009).

39. Carl E. Wieman, "Large-Scale Comparison of Science Teaching Methods Sends Clear Message," *Proceedings of the National Academy of Sciences* 111, no. 23 (2014): 8319–8320. For an examination of the role of identity in instructional reform, see Sara E. Brownell and Kimberly D. Tanner, "Barriers to Faculty Pedagogical Change: Lack of Training, Time, Incentives, and . . . Tensions with Professional Identity?." *CBE-Life Sciences Education* 11, no. 4 (2012): 339–346.

40. Parker J. Palmer, *The Courage to Teach: Exploring the Inner Landscape of a Teacher's Life* (Hoboken, NJ: John Wiley & Sons, 2010), 10.

41. Pierre Bourdieu and Jean-Claude Passeron, *Reproduction in Education, Culture and Society* (Thousand Oaks, CA: SAGE, 1977).

42. Our thinking here is also influenced by the ideas of sociologist Basil Bernstein, whose notions of pedagogic classification and framing speak to similar issue. See Basil Bernstein, *The Structuring of Pedagogic Discourse* (New York: Routledge, 2004).

43. Brownell and Tanner, "Barriers."

44. Robert B. Barr and John Tagg, "From Teaching to Learning—A New Paradigm for Undergraduate Education," *Change: The Magazine of Higher Learning* 27, no. 6 (1995): 12–26.

CHAPTER 7

1. H. William Dettmer, *Goldratt's Theory of Constraints: A Systems Approach to Continuous Improvement* (Milwaukee: American Society for Quality Press, 1997), 4.

2. While the focus of this book is on formal postsecondary education, the

remainder of our discussion also applies to those educators working in other settings, including workplace training and online/distance education.

3. The seminal paper on complex systems in weather was Edward N. Lorenz, "Deterministic Nonperiodic Flow," *Journal of the Atmospheric Sciences* 20, no. 2 (1963): 130–141, though it is important to point out that ideas about complexity and systems dynamics predated the 1960s. This paper and the subsequent popularization of the butterfly effect, however, brought the idea to the attention of the general public and other disciplines.

4. Barry Richmond, "Systems Thinking: Critical Thinking Skills for the 1990s and Beyond," *System Dynamics Review* 9, no. 2 (1993): 113–133.

5. Horst Rittel and Melvin Webber, "Dilemmas in a General Theory of Planning," *Policy Sciences* 4, no. 2 (1973): 155–169.

6. For discussions about food deserts see: Julie Beaulac, Elizabeth Kristjansson, and Steven Cummins, "A Systematic Review of Food Deserts, 1966–2007," *Prev Chronic Dis* 6, no. 3 (2009): A105. Originally, researchers thought that simply located supermarkets in these areas lacking them would solve the problem; instead, food behaviors are shaped by a far more complex combination of factors.

7. See Ana V. Diez Roux, "Complex Systems Thinking and Current Impasses in Health Disparities Research," *American Journal of Public Health* 101, no. 9 (2011): 1627–1634.

8. For examples, see J. Sterman, *Business Dynamics: Systems Thinking and Modeling for a Complex World* (Boston: McGraw Hill, 2000); Michael W. Macy and Robert Willer, From Factors to Actors: Computational Sociology and Agent-Based Modeling," *Annual Review of Sociology* 28 (2002): 143–166.

9. James P. Spillane, Brian J. Reiser, and Todd Reimer, "Policy Implementation and Cognition: Reframing and Refocusing Implementation Research," *Review of Educational Research* 72, no. 3 (2002): 387–431; Cynthia E. Coburn and Erica O. Turner, "Research on Data Use: A Framework and Analysis," *Measurement: Interdisciplinary Research & Perspective* 9, no. 4 (2011): 173–206.

10. For the scapegoating argument, considerable evidence for this point has been provided in this book. An additional example is that in December 2015 Governor Walker was asked about the reasons for Wisconsin's sluggish job growth, and he stated that it was due to the lack of skilled workers being produced by the educational system. See http://www.wpr.org/walker-blames-lack-trained-workers-flagging-job-growth.

11. See Robert Axelrod and Michael D. Cohen, *Harnessing Complexity: Organizational Implications of a Scientific Frontier* (New York: Basic Books, 2000), 9. For an application of systems thinking in educational contexts, see James P. Spillane, Richard Halverson, and John B. Diamond, "Investigating School Leadership Practice: A Distributed Perspective," *Educational Researcher* 30, no. 3 (2001): 23–28.

12. Source material from which we developed the techniques to conduct this analysis includes: H. William Dettmer, *The Logical Thinking Process: A Systems Approach to Complex Problem Solving* (Milwaukee: American Society for Quality Press, 2007); Matthew B. Miles, A. Michael Huberman, and Johnny Saldaña, *Qualitative Data Analysis: A Methods Sourcebook* (Thousand Oaks, CA: SAGE Publications, 2013).

13. Charles S. Benson, "New Vocationalism in the United States: Potential Problems and Outlook," *Economics of Education Review* 16, no. 3 (1997): 201–212.

14. Anthony P. Carnevale, Jeff Strohl, and Artem Gulish, *College Is Just the Beginning: Employers' Role in the $1.1 Trillion Postsecondary Education and Training System* (Washington, DC: Georgetown University Center on Education and the Workforce, 2015).

15. ManpowerGroup, *2015 Talent Shortage Survey* (Milwaukee, WI: Manpower Group, 2015).

CHAPTER 8

1. Lee S. Shulman, *The Wisdom of Practice: Essays on Teaching, Learning, and Learning to Teach*, ed. Suzanne M. Wilson (San Francisco: Jossey-Bass, 2004), 151.

2. Ruth Chung Wei et al., *Professional Learning in the Learning Profession: A Status Report on Teacher Development in the United States and Abroad* (Dallas: National Staff Development Council, 2009).

3. Ibid.

4. Ibid.

5. "A Summary of the Wisconsin Budget for K–12 Education," *Wisconsin Budget Project*, June 2, 2015, http://www.wisconsinbudgetproject.org/an-updated-summary-of-the-proposed-wisconsin-budget-for-k-12-education-sthash.fLn Vgcs9.dpuf.

6. Amy Hetzner and Erin Richards, "Budget Fight an Unexpected Civics Lesson for Teachers," *Wisconsin Journal Sentinel*, April 17, 2011, http://www.jsonline .com/news/education/120042569.html.

7. Ibid.

8. Trip Gariel, "Teachers Wonder, Why the Scorn?" *New York Times*, March 2, 2011, http://www.nytimes.com/2011/03/03/education/03teacher.html? emc=etal.

9. Patrick Marley and Karen Herzog, "UW System Predicts Layoffs, No Campus Closings Under Budget Cuts," *Wisconsin Journal Sentinel*, January 27, 2015, http://www.jsonline.com/news/statepolitics/walker-proposes-300-million-cut-more-autonomy-for-uw-b99433799z1-289929831.html.

10. Pat Schneider, "Tenure, Campus Governance New Focus of Scott Walker Budget Bill Scrutiny," *Capital Times*, February 7, 2015, http://host.madison .com/ct/news/local/writers/pat_schneider/tenure-campus-governance-new-

focus-of-scott-walker-budget-bill/article_f1cb7284-1bcc-52a9-a356-926157
4372f3.html.

11. Monica Davey, "Stakes High, Scott Walker Signs Wisconsin Budget," *New York Times*, July 12, 2015, http://www.nytimes.com/2015/07/13/us/politics/stakes-high-scott-walker-signs-wisconsin-budget.html?_r=0.

12. John Gurda, "Gov. Scott Walker's Wisconsin Idea: Cut Taxes, Cut Services," *Wisconsin Journal Sentinel*, February 27, 2015, http://www.jsonline.com/news/opinion/gov-scott-walkers-wisconsin-idea-cut-taxes-cut-services-b99450518z1-294394431.html.

13. Todd Milewsk, "'Denigration' Wears on the Morale of Faculty, UW Professor Grant Petty Says," *Capital Times*, February 1, 2015, http://host.madison.com/ct/news/local/city-life/denigration-wears-on-the-morale-of-faculty-uw-madison-professor/article_07c3278c-aa37-11e4-ac62-eb022214d05f.html.

14. John Hall, "Letter to the Assembly on the Importance of the UW System," *Milwaukee Journal Sentinel*, February 10, 2015, http://www.jsonline.com/news/opinion/letter-to-the-assembly-on-the-importance-of-the-uw-system-b99442749z1-291436501.html.

15. Mike Longaecker, "UW-RF Students Return to Budget-Slashed Campus," *New Richmond News*, September 3, 2015, http://www.newrichmondnews.com/news/education/3831285-uw-rf-students-return-budget-slashed-campus

16. Pat Schneider, "UW Regent Jose Vasquez Resists Pressure to Change Tenure; Blames State for Fiscal Crisis," *The Capital Times*, March 10, 2016, http://host.madison.com/ct/news/local/education/university/uw-regent-jose-vasquez-resists-pressure-to-change-tenure-blames/article_799f6852-226c-58e3-9073-0de69a07ba69.html.

17. In fact, a ban on stem cell research was proposed in Wisconsin but did not make it to a full vote of the state legislature.

18. American Association of University Professors, "Tenure Weakened in Wisconsin," March 10, 2016, http://www.aaup.org/news/tenure-weakened-wisconsin.

19. Parker J. Palmer, *The Courage to Teach: Exploring the Inner Landscape of a Teacher's Life* (San Francisco: Jossey-Bass, 1998), 3.

20. The cuts to UW System campuses are being compiled by the Wisconsin Center for the Advancement of Postsecondary Education (WISCAPE). The data reported here are based on their reports up until October 2015: https://www.wiscape.wisc.edu/wiscape/home/blog. See also Karen Herzog, "From Larger Classes to Fewer Campus Jobs, UW Outlines Cuts," *Milwaukee Journal Sentinel*, April 12, 2016, http://www.jsonline.com/news/education/from-larger-classes-to-fewer-campus-jobs-uw-outlines-budget-cuts-b99704918z1-375373711.html.

21. See Karen Herzog, "UW-Madison Spends Nearly $9 Million to Retain Faculty Stars," *Milwaukee Journal Sentinel*, March 8, 2016, http://www.jsonline

.com/news/education/uw-spends-nearly-9-million-in-effort-to-retain-faculty-stars-b99682882z1-371376511.html; Polo Rocha, "Amid Tenure Debate, UW System Campuses Say Faculty Departures Rise, Wisbusiness.com, March 9, 2016, http://wisbusiness.com/index.iml?Article=366623.

22. Aaron Mudd, "Higher Education Officials Disappointed with Bevin's Budget," *Bowling Green Daily News*, January 18, 2016, http://www.bgdailynews.com/news/higher-education-officials-disappointed-with-bevin-s-budget/article_3f1c7d91-b865-5f9e-abb1-2710c343eb07.html?utm_medium=social&utm_source=twitter&utm_campaign=user-share.

23. Karen Herzog, "UW Regents OK New Tenure Policy After Tense Session," *Milwaukee Journal Sentinel*, March 10, 2016, http://www.jsonline.com/news/education/uw-regents-ok-new-tenure-policy-after-tense-session-b99685309z1-371733961.html.

24. John K. Wilson, "Wisconsin Survey Spring 2015: Highlights and Analysis," Wisconsin Public Radio, April 21, 2015.

25. National Science and Technology Council, "Federal Science, Technology, Engineering, and Mathematics (STEM) Education: 5-Year Strategic Plan," Executive Office of the President of the United States, 2013.

26. Edwin Hutchins, *Cognition in the Wild* (Cambridge, MA: MIT Press, 1995).

27. Some of the papers describing this research program include: Matthew T. Hora, "Exploring Faculty Beliefs About Student Learning and Their Role in Instructional Decision-Making," *The Review of Higher Education* 38, no. 1 (2014): 37–70; Joseph J. Ferrare and Matthew T. Hora, "Cultural Models of Teaching and Learning in Math and Science. Exploring the Intersections of Culture, Cognition, and Pedagogical Situations," *The Journal of Higher Education* 85, no. 6 (2014): 792–825.

28. James G. Greeno, "The Situativity of Knowing, Learning, and Research," *American Psychologist* 53, no. 1 (1998): 5. See also Matthew T. Hora, "Organizational Factors and Instructional Decision-Making: A Cognitive Perspective," *Review of Higher Education* 35, no. 2 (2012): 207–235; Matthew T. Hora and Anne-Barrie Hunter. "Exploring the Dynamics of Organizational Learning: Identifying the Decision Chains Science and Math Faculty Use to Plan and Teach Undergraduate Courses," *International Journal of STEM Education* 1, no. 1 (2014): 1–21.

29. For a review of some of the medical anthropology literature, see Cecil G. Helman, *Culture, Health and Illness* (Boca Raton, FL: CRC Press, 2007).

30. Aleszu Bajak, "Lectures Aren't Just Boring, They're Ineffective, Too, Study Finds," *Science*, May 12, 2014.

31. Daniel L. Schwartz and John D. Bransford, "A Time for Telling," *Cognition and Instruction* 16, no. 4 (1998): 475–5223.

32. Bajak, "Lectures Aren't Just Boring."

33. For an extended discussion of methodological and conceptual issues pertaining to the "lecture" versus "active learning" dichotomy, see Matthew

T. Hora, "Toward a Descriptive Science of Teaching: How the TDOP Illuminates the Multidimensional Nature of Active Learning in Postsecondary Classrooms," *Science Education* 99, no. 5 (2015): 783–818.

34. Some resources for instructional reform at the postsecondary level include Project Kaleidoscope of the Association of American Colleges and Universities (https://www.aacu.org/pkal); the Professional and Organizational Development Network (http://podnetwork.org/), which is the national association for faculty development; and the national Network of STEM Education Centers (http://serc.carleton.edu/StemEdCenters/index.html).

35. For more information see Daniel L. Reinholz et al., "Towards a Model of Systemic Change in University STEM Education," *ARXIV* (2014); and Joel C. Corbo et al., "A Framework for Transforming Departmental Culture to Support Educational Innovation," *ARXIV* (2014).

36. Lee Shulman, "Knowledge and Teaching: Foundations of the New Reform," *Harvard Educational Review* 57, no. 1 (1987): 1–23.

37. Grant P. Wiggins and Jay McTighe, *Understanding By Design* (Alexandria, VA: Association for Supervision and Curriculum Development, 2005).

38. See "Accreditation," ABET, http://www.abet.org/accreditation/. At the time of this writing, however, ABET was in the process of revising criteria for student outcomes and curricular requirements.

39. Colleen Flaherty, "Watered-Down Gen Ed for Engineers?" *Inside Higher Ed*, June 26, 2015, https://www.insidehighered.com/news/2015/06/26/faculty-members-criticize-proposed-changes-gen-ed-accreditation-standards-engineers.

40. "Preparing Future STEM Faculty for Diverse Classrooms at the University of Wisconsin–Madison," Association of American College and Universities, https://www.aacu.org/campus-model/preparing-future-stem-faculty-diverse-classrooms-university-wisconsin%E2%80%93madison. For more on the DELTA program, see http://delta.wisc.edu/index.html#.VuH8AZMrIdV.

41. Vanessa Smith Morest, "Accountability, Accreditation, and Continuous Improvement: Building a Culture of Evidence," *New Directions for Institutional Research* 2009, no. 143 (2009): 17–27.

42. "The Trouble with Tenure" (report, Wisconsin Policy Research Institute, February 2016), http://www.wpri.org/WPRI-Files/Special-Reports/Reports-Documents/WPRIwhitepaper_TENURE_FINALrevised.pdf.

43. Rich Halverson and R. Benjamin Shapiro, "Technologies for Education and Technologies for Learners: How Information Technologies Are (and Should Be) Changing Schools" (working paper 6, Wisconsin Center for Educational Research, University of Wisconsin–Madison, 2012).

44. Robert M. Wachter, "How Measurement Fails Doctors and Teachers," *New York Times*, January 16, 2016, http://www.nytimes.com/2016/01/17/opinion/sunday/how-measurement-fails-doctors-and-teachers.html.

CHAPTER 9

1. Katrina Schwartz, "Remixing Melville: Moby Dick Meets the Digital Generation," *Mind Shift*, March 8, 2013, http://ww2.kqed.org/mindshift /2013/03/08/remixing-melville-moby-dick-meets-the-digital-generation/.

2. While we don't address the issue of whether college students should be considered adults in this book, we point out that the notion of "emerging adulthood"—the idea that the ages between eighteen and twenty-five represent a physiologically and culturally unique phase of life—is gaining traction. Thus, principles of adult education, which typically have been applied only to workplace training or continuing education contexts, may also be applicable for traditional college students. See Jeffrey J. Arnett, "Emerging Adulthood: A Theory of Development from the Late Teens Through the Twenties," *American Psychologist* 55, no. 5 (2000): 469.

3. Matt Reed, "When Student Preferences Don't Align," *Inside Higher Ed*, February 14, 2016, https://www.insidehighered.com/blogs/confessions-commu nity-college-dean/when-student-preferences-don%E2%80%99t-align.

4. For reviews of the millennial generation on these topics, see Neil Howe and William Strauss, *Millennials Go to College* (Great Falls, VA: LifeCourse Associates, 2007); Pew Research Center, "The Rising Cost of *Not* Going to College," http://www.pewsocialtrends.org/2014/02/11/the-rising-cost-of-not-going-to-college/; Pew Research Center, "Millennials in Adulthood: Detached from Institutions, Networked with Friends," http://www.pewsocial trends.org/files/2014/03/2014-03-07_generations-report-version-for-web .pdf; Richard Fry, "More Millennials Living with Family Despite Improved Job Market," *Pew Research Center*, July 29, 2015, http://www.pewsocialtrends .org/files/2015/07/2015-07-29_young-adult-living_FINAL.pdf.

5. Andrea Hershatter and Molly Epstein, "Millennials and the World of Work: An Organization and Management Perspective," *Journal of Business and Psychology* 25, no. 2 (2010): 211–223.

6. Deborah A. Abowitz, "Does Money Buy Happiness? A Look at Gen Y College Student Beliefs," *Free Inquiry in Creative Sociology* 33, no. 2 (2005): 119–130.

7. Hershatter and Epstein, "Millennials and the World of Work," 219.

8. Quentin Hardy, "Gearing Up for the Cloud, AT&T Tells Its Workers: Adapt, or Else," *New York Times*, February 13, 2016, http://www.nytimes.com/ 2016/02/14/technology/gearing-up-for-the-cloud-att-tells-its-workers-adapt-or-else.html.

9. Kevin Eagan et al., *The American Freshman: National Norms Fall 2014* (Los Angeles: Higher Education Research Institute, UCLA, 2014). See page 38 for responses to the question and quote, http://www.heri.ucla.edu/monographs/ TheAmericanFreshman2014.pdf.

10. https://www.insidehighered.com/news/2014/04/07/study-finds-increased-stem-enrollment-recession

11. John Dunlosky et al., "Improving Students' Learning with Effective Learning Techniques Promising Directions from Cognitive and Educational Psychology," *Psychological Science in the Public Interest* 14, no. 1 (2013), 4-58.

12. This claim is based on a series of focus groups held at three large universities from a previous study, where we found that most students were cue seekers and attended class mostly to get tips about upcoming exams—not necessarily to learn the material. See C. M. L. Miller and M. Parlett, *Up to the Mark: A Study of the Examination Game* (London: Society for Research into Higher Education, 1974). This work is just an example of a long tradition of excellent research on student learning conducted in the UK and Australia since the 1970s. For example, see research by John Biggs, Noel Entwistle, and Paul Ramsden on the topics of student learning styles and approaches, and their implications for effective instruction and assessment.

13. Virginia R. Jones, "Essentials for Engaged 21st-Century Students," *Techniques: Connecting Education and Careers (J3)* 87, no. 7 (2012): 16–19; Susan A. Dumais, "The Academic Attitudes of American Teenagers, 1990–2002: Cohort and Gender Effects on Math Achievement," *Social Science Research* 38, no. 4 (2009): 767–780.

14. Sylvia Ruiz et al., "Findings from the 2009 Administration of the Your First College Year (YFCY): National Aggregates," *Higher Education Research Institute* (2010), http://www.heri.ucla.edu/PDFs/pubs/Reports/YFCY2009 Final_January.pdf; Ray Franke et al., "Findings from the 2009 Administration of the College Senior Survey (CSS): National Aggregates," *Higher Education Research Institute* (2010), http://www.heri.ucla.edu/PDFs/pubs/Reports/2009_CSS_Report.pdf.

15. Arlene Nicholas, "Preferred Learning Methods of the Millennial Generation" (Salve Regina University, Faculty and Staff–Articles & Papers, paper 18, 2008).

16. Lynn Silipigni Connaway et al., "Sense-Making and Synchronicity: Information-Seeking Behaviors of Millennials and Baby Boomers," *Libri* 58, no. 2 (2008): 123–135.

17. Bernard R. McCoy, "Digital Distractions in the Classroom Phase II: Student Classroom Use of Digital Devices for Non-Class Related Purposes," *Journal of Media Education* 7, no. 1 (2016): 5–32.

18. Henry Jenkins et al., "Confronting the Challenges of Participatory Culture: Media Education for the 21st Century" (The John D. and Catherine T. MacArthur Foundation Reports on Digital Media and Learning, 2006): 9.

19. http://guts.studentorg.wisc.edu/programs/ss.html

20. "Your First College Year Survey 2012" (research brief, Higher Education Research Institute at UCLA, 2013), http://www.heri.ucla.edu/briefs/YFCY2012-Brief.pdf.

21. George D. Kuh, "Student Engagement in the First Year of College," in *Challenging and Supporting the First-Year Student: A Handbook for Improving the*

First Year of College, eds. M. Lee Upcraft, John N. Gardner, and Betsy O. Barefoot (San Francisco: Jossey-Bass, 2005), 86–107.

22. Career Advisory Board, DeVry University, "Effectively Counseling Graduating Students" (report, National Association of Colleges and Employers, 2012), http://careeradvisoryboard.org/public/uploads/2012/09/Effectively-Counseling-Graduating-Students_Report-FINAL.pdf.

23. Critics may rightly wonder why it took so long for the college and university to institute such a course.

24. http://news.ls.wisc.edu/student-life/new-ls-careers-course-sparks-reflective-exploration/

25. http://news.ls.wisc.edu/announcements/chancellor-blank-highlights-progress-need-for-investment/

26. https://cew.georgetown.edu/cew-reports/valueofcollegemajors/#explore-data

27. Debra Humphreys and Patrick Kelly, *How Liberal Arts and Sciences Majors Fare in Employment* (Washington, DC: Association of American Colleges and Universities, 2014).

28. For an example of scholarship examining career pathways from a more nuanced perspective, see Gavin Moodi et al., "Towards a New Approach to Mid-Level Qualifications" (research report, National Centre for Vocational Education Research [NCVER], Adelaide, Australia, 2015).

29. http://www.bizjournals.com/milwaukee/blog/2013/03/wmc-uwm-prof-shouldve-talked-to.html

30. Tom Zicmer, "Surveys: UW-Madison Liberal Arts Grads Landing Jobs," University of Wisconsin–Madison, October 7, 2015, http://news.wisc.edu/surveys-show-uw-madison-liberal-arts-graduates-landing-jobs/.

31. http://www.americanbar.org/news/abanews/aba-news-archives/2015/04/american_bar_associa0.html

32. One of the pieces that WMC's Jim Morgan wrote was titled "You Can't Legislate Career Choices, Can You?" and mentioned that China was considering cutting majors that could not guarantee a 60 percent employment rate: https://www.wmc.org/programs/workforcedevelopment/news-column-solving-the-workforce-paradox/.

33. Younger baby boomers held an average of 11.7 jobs from ages eighteen to forty-eight; http://www.bls.gov/news.release/pdf/nlsoy.pdf.

34. Reed, "When Student Preferences Don't Align."

35. Timothy A. Judge et al., "The Job Satisfaction–Job Performance Relationship: A Qualitative and Quantitative Review," *Psychological Bulletin* 127, no. 3 (2001): 376.

36. Wisconsin Department of Workforce Development, http://worknet.wisconsin.gov/worknet/joblist_mostopen.aspx?menuselection=js. The living wage for a family of four (one working adult) in Wisconsin is $22.50 according to the MIT Living Wage calculator.

37. Marc V. Levine, "Is Wisconsin Becoming a Low-Wage Economy?

Employment Growth in Low, Middle, and High Wage Occupations: 2000–2013" (data brief, Center for Economic Development, University of Wisconsin–Milwaukee, 2014).

38. W. Norton Grubb and Marvin Lazerson, *The Education Gospel: The Economic Power of Schooling* (Cambridge, MA: Harvard University Press, 2004), 236.

39. http://ticas.org/sites/default/files/pub_files/classof2014.pdf

40. Marc Levine, "The Skills Gap and Unemployment in Wisconsin: Separating Fact from Fiction" (working paper, Center for Economic Development, University of Wisconsin–Milwaukee, 2013).

41. Hardy, "Gearing Up for the Cloud."

CHAPTER 10

1. Brian Eno, "Singing: The Key to a Long Life," *National Public Radio*, April 1, 2009, http://www.npr.org/templates/story/story.php?storyId=97320958.

2. Geert Duysters, Gerard Kok, and Maaike Vaandrager, "Crafting Successful Strategic Technology Partnerships," *R&D Management* 29, no. 4 (1999): 343–351; Elisa S. Weiss, Rebecca Miller Anderson, and Roz D. Lasker. "Making the Most of Collaboration: Exploring the Relationship Between Partnership Synergy and Partnership Functioning," *Health Education & Behavior* 29, no. 6 (2002): 683–698.

3. Kris D. Gutiérrez, Patricia Baquedano-López, and Carlos Tejeda, "Rethinking Diversity: Hybridity and Hybrid Language Practices in the Third Space," *Mind, Culture, and Activity* 6, no. 4 (1999): 286–303.

4. Neil Fligstein and Doug McAdam, *A Theory of Fields* (Oxford, UK: Oxford University Press, 2012).

5. Clyde Kluckhohn and Dorothea Cross Leighton, *The Navajo* (Cambridge, MA: Harvard University Press, 1951), 1.

6. Jason Stein, Patrick Marley, and Lee Bergquist, "Assembly Passes Union Measure after Bitter Debate," *Milwaukee Journal Sentinel*, March 10, 2011, http://www.jsonline.com/news/statepolitics/117735163.html.

7. "Chancellor Blank Statement on Tenure," UW-Madison and the State Budget, June 3, 2015, https://budget.wisc.edu/budget-news/chancellor-blank-statement-on-tenure/.

8. Hank Reichman, "AAUP/AFT-Wisconsin Statement on Proposed Regent Policies," *Acadme Blog*, February 3, 2016, https://academeblog.org/2016/02/03/aaupaft-wisconsin-statement-on-proposed-regent-policies/.

9. Jack Stark, *The Wisconsin Idea: The University's Service to the State* (Madison, WI: Legislative Reference Bureau, 1995), 101.

10. Walter Powell, "Neither Market nor Hierarchy," *The Sociology of Organizations: Classic, Contemporary, and Critical Readings* 315 (2003): 104–117.

11. Ann Marie Thomson, James L. Perry, and Theodore K. Miller, "Conceptualizing and Measuring Collaboration," *Journal of Public Administration Research and Theory* 19, no. 1 (2009): 23–56.

12. These observations are drawn from the excellent 2015 book by Peter J. Stokes titled *Higher Education and Employability: New Models for Integrating Study and Work* (Cambridge, MA: Harvard Education Press, 2015).
13. Duysters, Kok, and Vaandrager, "Crafting Successful Strategic Technology Partnerships."
14. Matthew T. Hora and Susan Bolyard Millar, *A Guide to Building Education Partnerships: Navigating Diverse Cultural Contexts to Turn Challenge into Promise* (Sterling, VA: Stylus Publishing, LLC, 2011).
15. In their guide for forging education-workplace partnerships, BHEF does take it a step further, recommending: development of a joint statement about vision and strategic goals, designating key leadership, identifying program-level goals and metrics, and evaluation plan. This is certainly a step in the right direction—as many partnerships fail to develop a shared vision, talk about leadership, and especially think about evaluation. See "Aligning Education and Workforce Goals to Foster Economic Development" (proceedings from Cities for Success: A BHEF Leadership Summit, Louisville, Kentucky, October 28–29, 2010), http://www.bhef.com/sites/g/files/g829556/f/201306/Cities_For_Success_Proceedings.pdf.
16. Barbara Gray, *Collaborating: Finding Common Ground for Multiparty Problems* (San Francisco: Jossey-Bass, 1989), 5.
17. Excellent resources for ideas about education-workplace partnerships include Stokes, *Higher Education and Employability*, and "Aligning Education and Workforce Goals."

CONCLUSION

1. Jack Stark, "The Wisconsin Idea: The University's Service to the State" (Legislative Reference Bureau, Madison, Wisconsin, 1995), 101. (Quote from a speech in Madison on October 8, 1952.)
2. Jeff Engel, "WMC: UWM Prof Should've Talked to Manufacturers for Skills Gap Study," *Milwaukee Business Journal*, March 1, 2013, http://www.bizjournals.com/milwaukee/blog/2013/03/wmc-uwm-prof-shouldve-talked-to.html. In addition, several of the videos available at WMC's website (https://www.wmc.org/programs/the-future-wisconsin-project) for their Future Wisconsin Project provide details of their take on the skills gap.
3. For more information about the UW–La Crosse undergraduate research program, see https://www.uwlax.edu/URC.
4. Glenn Pew, "Kestrel Running Rough," *Avwebflash: World's Premier Independent Aviation News Service*, volume 20, 13a, http://www.avweb.com/eletter/archives/101/2640-full.html.
5. *Tribune* Wire Reports, "Scott Walker's Wisconsin Jobs Agency Gave Out $124 Million Without Review," *Chicago Tribune*, June 19, 2015, http://www.chicagotribune.com/news/local/breaking/ct-scott-walker-jobs-agency-20150619-story.html.

6. Maria Lockwood, "WITC Suspends Composite Program," *Superior Telegram*, January 22, 2016, http://www.superiortelegram.com/news/schools /3929943-witc-suspends-composites-program.

7. Jamie P. Merisotis, "It's the Learning, Stupid" (lecture at Claremont Graduate University, Claremont, California, 2009), http://www.luminafoundation .org/about_us/president/speeches/2009-10-14.html. This source and quote was found in Michael Roth's book, *Beyond the University: Why Liberal Education Matters* (New Haven, CT: Yale University Press, 2014).

8. Ibid., 190.

9. Ibid.

10. Frank Bruni, "Higher Education, Liberal Arts and Shakespeare," *New York Times*, February 11, 2015, http://www.nytimes.com/2015/02/11/opinion/fr ank-bruni-higher-education-liberal-arts-and-shakespeare.html.

11. Charles Richard Van Hise, "Inaugural Address of President Charles Richard Van Hise," *Science* 20, no. 502 (1904): 204.

12. Jonah Lehrer, "Steve Jobs: Technology Alone Is Not Enough," *New Yorker*, October 7, 2011, http://www.newyorker.com/news/news-desk/steve-jobs-te chnology-alone-is-not-enough

13. Loretta Jackson-Hayes, "We Don't Need More STEM Majors. We Need More STEM Majors with Liberal Arts Training," *Washington Post*, February 18, 2015, https://www.washingtonpost.com/posteverything/wp/2015/02/18/w e-dont-need-more-stem-majors-we-need-more-stem-majors-with-liberal-art s-training/?tid=ss_tw.

14. Johann N. Neem, "The Arts and Sciences, or STEM?," *WISCAPE Blog*, February 23, 2016, https://www.wiscape.wisc.edu/wiscape/home/blog/wiscape -blog/2016/02/23/the-arts-and-sciences-or-stem.

15. David Lazer et al., "The Parable of Google Flu: Traps in Big Data Analysis," *Science* 343 (2014): 1203–1205.

16. Alex Peysakhovich and Seth Stephens-Davidowitz, "How Not to Drown in Numbers," *New York Times*, May 2, 2015, http://www.nytimes.com /2015/05/03/opinion/sunday/how-not-to-drown-in-numbers.html.

17. Kira Hamman, "Why STEM Should Care about the Humanities," *Chronicle of Higher Education*, April 12, 2013, http://chronicle.com/blogs/conversati on/2013/04/12/why-stem-should-care-about-the-humanities/?cid=at&utm _source=at&utm_medium=en.

18. John W. Hall, "Letter to the Assembly on the Importance of the UW System," *Milwaukee Journal Sentinel*, February 10, 2015, http://www.jsonline.c om/news/opinion/letter-to-the-assembly-on-the-importance-of-the-uw-syst em-b99442749z1-291436501.html.

19. Damian Carrington, "Sea-Level Rise 'Could Last Twice as Long as Human History,'" *The Guardian*, February 8, 2016, http://www.theguardian.com/ environment/2016/feb/08/sea-level-rise-could-last-twice-as-long-as-human- history.

20. Fareed Zakaria, "Why America's Obsession with STEM Education Is Dangerous," *Washington Post*, March 26, 2015, https://www.washingtonpost.co m/opinions/why-stem-wont-make-us-successful/2015/03/26/5f4604f2-d2a 5-11e4-ab77-9646eea6a4c7_story.html.
21. Neem, "Arts and Sciences."
22. The *Times* Editorial Board, "What's Next for Berkeley and UC?," *LA Times*, February 23, 2016, http://www.latimes.com/opinion/editorials/la-ed-future -uc-20160223-story.html.
23. Thomas G. Mortenson, "State Funding: A Race to the Bottom," *American Council on Education* (Winter 2012), http://www.acenet.edu/the-presidency /columns-and-features/Pages/state-funding-a-race-to-the-bottom.aspx.
24. Nicholas W. Hillman, David A. Tandberg, and Jacob PK Gross, "Performance Funding in Higher Education: Do Financial Incentives Impact College Completions?" *Journal of Higher Education* 85, no. 6 (2014): 826–857.
25. Robert A. Rhoads, Xiaoguang Shi, and Yongcai Chang, *China's Rising Research Universities: A New Era of Global Ambition* (Baltimore: Johns Hopkins University Press, 2014).
26. Mark S. Ferrara, *Palace of Ashes: China and the Decline of American Higher Education* (Baltimore: Johns Hopkins University Press, 2015).

APPENDIX

1. Robert K. Yin, *Case Study Research: Design and Methods* (Thousand Oaks, CA: Sage, 2013).
2. Susan C. Weller and A. Kimball Romney, *Systematic Data Collection*, vol. 10 (Thousand Oaks, CA: Sage, 1988).
3. Stephen P. Borgatti, *Anthropac 4* (Natick, MA: Analytic Technologies, 1996).
4. J. Jerome Smith and Stephen P. Borgatti, "Salience Counts—And So Does Accuracy: Correcting and Updating a Measure for Free-List-Item Salience," *Journal of Linguistic Anthropology* 7 (1997): 208–209.
5. J. Jerome Smith, "Using ANTHOPAC 3.5 and a Spreadsheet to Compute a Free-List Salience Index," *Field Methods* 5, no. 3 (1993): 1–3.
6. Marsha Quinlan, "Considerations for Collecting Freelists in the Field: Examples from Ethobotany," *Field Methods* 17, no. 3 (2005): 219–234.
7. Michelene TH Chi, "Quantifying Qualitative Analyses of Verbal Data: A Practical Guide," *Journal of the Learning Sciences* 6, no. 3 (1997): 271–315.
8. Gery W. Ryan and H. Russell Bernard, "Techniques to Identify Themes," *Field Methods* 15, no. 1 (2003): 85–109.
9. Barney Glaser and Anselm Strauss, *The Discovery of Grounded Theory* (London: Weidenfeld and Nicholson, 1967).
10. Matthew B. Miles, A. Michael Huberman, and Johnny Saldana, *Qualitative Data Analysis: A Methods Sourcebook* (Thousand Oaks, CA: Sage, 2013); H. William Dettmer, *The Logical Thinking Process: A Systems Approach to Complex Problem Solving* (Milwaukee: ASQ Press, 2007).

ACKNOWLEDGMENTS

From Matthew T. Hora

Writing a book is an exhausting, inspirational, and sometimes painful experience, and it wouldn't have been possible without a rich personal and professional support system. To my coauthors and coconspirators in the field, Ross and Amanda, I thank you for your patience, hard work, diligence, and creativity through these times, and over the years we've been working together. This book is truly the product of a team effort in terms of words on the page, thoughts being hammered out in meetings, and insights about design and analysis. I also would like to thank my colleagues in the Department of Liberal Arts and Applied Studies for being so supportive as I undertook this project, mentors at the University of Wisconsin Madison and the University of Maryland–College Park for their training in the social sciences, and the hundreds of respondents who participated in this study. In particular, effusive thanks go out to the individual educators who are featured in this book—your daily work spent preparing the next generation is truly an inspiration. I also must thank my parents, without whom my education would not have been possible. Finally, for the endless encouragement, support, and well-placed questions, I thank my wife, Kelly, and for moments of respite and questions like "Are you done with that book yet?" I also thank my two boys, Robin and Weston, whose future in an uncertain world is never too far from my mind.

From Ross J. Benbow

First, I thank Matt and Amanda for giving me the chance to work with and learn from them through the last few years as we undertook this project. Thank you both for your incredibly hard work and guidance. I thank my parents, John and Margaret Benbow, for their continued support and the head start they gave me with the written word. I also would like to express my sincere gratitude and love to Abby Byrne and Aria Benbow for their encouragement, understanding, and interminable patience.

From Amanda K. Oleson

This book was made possible by the hard work of my fellow authors, whose work ethics and brilliance know no bounds. We set out on this adventure years ago, and now the tree is bearing fruit! A special thanks to my family: my parents, Randy and Jeanette Oleson, and my big brother, Dustin Oleson, for supporting me in all of my pursuits. The years of character development you invested in me not only gave me perspective while writing this book, but the inspiration to push on and push through. Gunnar Jeppson, you are my soulmate. Thank you for keeping the ship afloat as I toiled away at my laptop for many a day and night. Your care kept me going throughout.

This study is supported by the National Science Foundation (DGE #1348648). Any opinions, findings, and conclusions or recommendations expressed in this material are those of the author(s) and do not necessarily reflect the views of the National Science Foundation.

ABOUT THE AUTHORS

Matthew T. Hora is an assistant professor of Adult and Higher Education in the Department of Liberal Arts and Applied Studies at the University of Wisconsin–Madison, and a research scientist at the Wisconsin Center for Education Research. After several years of experience in organic agriculture and food systems research, Matthew received his master's degree in applied anthropology from the University of Maryland–College Park. He then worked as a program evaluator of public health initiatives and STEM education initiatives before earning a PhD in the learning sciences from the Department of Educational Psychology at UW-Madison in 2012.

Matthew's research interests are situated in the fields of applied anthropology, the learning sciences, and education policy analysis. In his current work he addresses three questions: What is the purpose and role of higher education in the early twenty-first century? How can we best design learning environments (organizations, classrooms, and digital spaces) that facilitate the acquisition of disciplinary content and transferable skills? How do cultural, political, historical, and economic factors shape how national higher education systems approach their roles in workforce development and advancing the public good?

Matthew lives in Madison, Wisconsin, with his family.

Ross J. Benbow is an associate researcher with the Wisconsin Center for Education Research at UW-Madison. With a background in political science, international development, and comparative analysis, Ross earned his PhD from the Department of Educational Policy Studies at UW-Madison in 2011 after conducting a yearlong ethnographic study of higher education reform in the United Republic of Tanzania. He has more recently worked as a writer and analyst focusing on the relationships between public policy, teaching and learning, and individual meaning making in domestic and international educational contexts, with a particular interest in patterns of inequity in colleges and universities.

Ross lives in Madison, Wisconsin, with his partner and daughter.

Amanda K. Oleson, Wisconsin born and bred, is an education scholar particularly interested in research and policies related to PK–20/workforce pathways. She spent several years as an assistant researcher at the Wisconsin Center for Education Research in the Center on Education and Work after graduating with her master's degree in Educational Policy Studies from UW-Madison, where she also earned her bachelor's degree in psychology and English. Amanda previously worked on research studies related to higher education reform and data-driven decision making. She is now a qualitative analyst at the Madison Metropolitan School District in Madison, Wisconsin.

A nascent connoisseur of coffee and an old bookshop enthusiast, Amanda enjoys the adventures that accompany reading, writing, and (lifelong) learning.

INDEX